SHOW US AS WE ARE

SHOW US AS WE ARE

Place, Nation and Identity in Jamaican Film

Rachel Moseley-Wood

The University of the West Indies Press
Jamaica • Barbados • Trinidad and Tobago

The University of the West Indies Press
7A Gibraltar Hall Road, Mona
Kingston 7, Jamaica
www.uwipress.com

© 2019 by Rachel Moseley-Wood
All rights reserved. Published 2019

A catalogue record of this book is available from the
National Library of Jamaica.

ISBN: 978-976-640-717-9 (paper)
      978-976-640-718-6 (Kindle)
      978-976-640-719-3 (ePub)

Cover photograph: A behind-the-scenes look at the proof-of-concept shoot for Gabrielle Blackwood's film *Kendal*. Photograph by Editson Brown, 2019.
Book and cover design by Robert Harris
Set in Scala 10.5/15 x 24

The University of the West Indies Press has no responsibility for the persistence or accuracy of URLs for external or third-party Internet websites referred to in this publication and does not guarantee that any content on such websites is, or will remain, accurate or appropriate.

Printed in the United States of America

CONTENTS

Acknowledgements / **vii**

Abbreviations / **xi**

Introduction: Show Us as We Are / **1**

1. Imagined Bonds in the New Nation: The 1962 Independence Films / **20**

2. "Badda Dan Dead": Resistance and Intertextuality in *The Harder They Come* / **46**

3. The Trickster as Cocksman: The Hotel as Contact Zone in *Smile Orange* / **66**

4. Reggae and *Rockers*: Privileging the Local, Disrupting Paradigms of the External Gaze / **83**

5. Love and Sex in Babylon: Nation and Desire in *Children of Babylon* and *One Love* / **104**

6. Negotiating Patriarchy: The Erotic Performance of *Dancehall Queen* / **130**

7. Real/Reel Life in Jungle: Alienated Spaces in *Third World Cop* and *Ghett'a Life* / **148**

8. Dreaming History and the Nightmare World of Jamaican Politics in *Better Mus' Come* / **172**

Epilogue: Expanding Narratives of Identity in Jamaican Film / **193**

Notes / **203**

Selected Bibliography / **227**

Index / **239**

ACKNOWLEDGEMENTS

THE STUDY OF CARIBBEAN FILM, AND JAMAICAN FILM in particular, has certainly come a long way since I first delved into the subject, more than two decades ago, when I decided to read for a PhD at the University of the West Indies, Mona. I was accepted by the Department of Literatures in English, where senior lecturer David Williams kindly and generously agreed to be my co-supervisor, along with Professor Aggrey Brown (now deceased), who was then director of the Caribbean Institute of Mass Communications. The arrangement of two supervisors straddling different departments and disciplines may have been a little unusual at the time, but as there was no specialist in film studies it was deemed necessary to draw on the expertise of both departments. Indeed, the Department of Literatures in English now offers a bachelor of arts in film studies, but when I applied to do the doctorate there was not a single film course on offer. When I was doing my PhD, which examined representations of gender in Caribbean romance fiction and Jamaican film, I felt less like a pioneer and more like I was doing something that few people were interested in or regarded as deserving of scholarly attention. That is certainly no longer the case. I thank David and Aggrey for their invaluable help and guidance. I always felt that at least they were vitally interested in my work.

Numerous persons helped me along the path to completion of this project. I thank Professor Emeritus Carl Campbell, Esther Figueroa, Candace Ward, Michelle Serieux and Jean Antoine-Dunne, who took the time to read extracts and chapters and offer useful comments. It was Jean's idea that I begin this story of Jamaican film with the work of the Jamaica Film Unit, but I thank her most of all for her critical response to my work at conferences over the years and for conveying that what I had to say was both interesting and worthwhile. Candace's friendship, encouragement and support have been invaluable; she extended two invitations to Florida State

University in Tallahassee to present my work, with the generous hospitality of her family thrown in as an extra.

Filmmakers and others involved in the film industry in Jamaica have been extremely generous in taking time out of busy schedules to meet and talk, and to answer what I expect must have been a long list of tiresome questions: Gabrielle Blackwood, Chris Browne, Barbara Blake-Hanna, Paul Bucknor, Amba Chevannes, Rick Elgood, Esther Figueroa, Douglas Graham, Perry Henzell, Kiddus I, David Morrison, Trevor Rhone, Renee Robinson, Storm Saulter, Michelle Serieux, Brian St Juste and Mary Wells all gave of their time and knowledge. Franklyn "Chappie" St Juste deserves special mention here. He is a walking encyclopaedia of Caribbean cinema and a veteran cinematographer. Chappie not only sat down for an interview, he was always happy to answer questions whenever I called or emailed.

Encouragement and support have come from many quarters. In the early stages of the project, I was working at times without affiliation to an institution and encountered all the challenges that "independent" status entails, including lack of access to resources and the absence of a critical community. I received valuable feedback on early drafts of chapters and loans of books from a circle of supportive friends: Paulette Bell-Kerr, Lisa Brown, Barbara Collash, Haidee Heron, Rachael Mair-Boxhill, Tanya Shirley and, as we were fond of saying, the lone male member of the group, Harold McDermott. Former and current colleagues at the University of the West Indies have also encouraged me, including Nadi Edwards, who downloaded so many film studies e-books for me that I still haven't been able to read them all. Miss Mary Gray believed in my ability to complete this book long before I did. Carolyn Cooper, Anthea Morrison and Claudette Williams frequently urged me to complete this book and, along with Swithin Wilmot, were instrumental at various points along the path, in the development and progress of my academic career.

It has always been a great benefit to be able to discuss the films I study with my students, who know much more than I do about Jamaican Creole and Jamaican culture. Their insight and perceptive comments on these films have been invaluable. At the National Library of Jamaica, Bernadette Worrell-Johnson was patient and helpful in assisting with my many queries, while Yulande Lindsay assisted with access to the Jamaica Film Unit films.

I am fortunate to be part of a warm and loving extended family who helped keep my spirits up over the many years of this demanding project. In particular, the Bradshaws and the Driscoll-Bradshaws have been known to comb the streets of London looking for books and DVDs that I needed, and they have always generously provided a home away from home whenever conferences or research took me to the United Kingdom. On such visits, my son Ashley was good company and an excellent guide. He also assisted with searches in the UK National Archives and in libraries. At home, Nicholas, my younger son, is a calming presence and, when he is not in the mood for an argument, full of sound counsel. Allan Wood's support has been generous and constant. He is my go-to person for obscure information on Westerns, but more important, he is always there for me, through good times and bad.

Without the support and assistance of all these people, and more, this book would not have been possible.

ABBREVIATIONS

CFU   Colonial Film Unit
JDF   Jamaica Defence Force
JFU   Jamaica Film Unit
JLP   Jamaica Labour Party
PNP   People's National Party

INTRODUCTION
Show Us as We Are

"We want to be shown just as we are. We do not wish to be pictured differently."
—*Daily Gleaner*, 1 February 1913, 3

IN JANUARY 1913, A SERIES OF letters appeared in Jamaica's leading newspaper, the *Daily Gleaner*, responding to a report that the British and Colonial Kinematograph Company Limited was on the island shooting footage for a film that was to be part of the *Lieutenant Daring* action adventure series.[1] Local sensibilities were offended by the description of a scene in the proposed film which depicted "natives" attacking a missionary's house, kidnapping him and demanding ransom for his return. This minor controversy, a small local quarrel, is now all but forgotten, but it is here that I want to begin. The brief but robust debate that resulted from the report resonates with the issues I explore in this book, namely, the immense investment in place as a constitutive element of identity and the function of cinema as a powerful mediating apparatus in disseminating meaning in this arena; the unstable, mobile nature of the identity of place and the resulting competing claims for authenticity; and the struggle over cinematic representation within the context of a people's desire to define self rather than be defined by an exoticizing external gaze.

One of the first letters to appear in response to the report was written by an English clergyman resident in Jamaica, the Reverend Ernest Price, who stated that "the impression created on many who see this film will be that the people of this island are half-savage; that 'missionaries' here live in danger of their lives, and that Myrtle Bank Hotel is the last outpost of civilization in this land".[2] A few days later, another letter of protest by Price was published as well as one written by D.C. Beckford, who insisted that audiences tended to equate what they saw on the screen with the real world and would accept the moving pictures as "bona fide scenes of what actually occurred".³ The following day, two more letters appeared. One writer protested that "there are millions of people in London who do not know the conditions existing in Jamaica and so will readily believe what they see reproduced by a Kinematograph as conditions obtaining here"; the other asked, "Will the promoters take the precaution of informing their audience that it is a 'fake' picture, and that missionaries are not in reality subject to such treatment out here?"⁴

In response to the initial newspaper report of his company's activities, J. O'Neal Farrell, of the British and Colonial Kinematograph Company, went in person to the *Gleaner* offices to "give assurances that no possible injury would result to Jamaica as the result of the work with the camera, of his comrades and himself". Farrell explained:

> There is certainly no intention on our part to show up the people of Jamaica as being uncivilized savages who would attack a missionary's house and demand ransom money. We will show our dramas but we do not tell people where the plots were laid and the pictures taken and there is no fear of our doing the island any injury in this connection. On the contrary, Jamaica should benefit through our visits as we have taken pictures depicting scenes in banana cultivation and other things of interest the tourist travelling around will see.⁵

Farrell further insisted on the ability of the British filmmakers to exercise good judgement in representing the island on the screen: "We know how far we can go in this business and we do not over-step the mark. We have taken pictures in Ireland, Wales, Scotland, Newfoundland, New Brunswick, all over Canada and other parts of the Empire and believe me we are quite competent to fulfil our mission without doing anything that is likely to give offence to the people of the lands where the pictures are taken."⁶

An editorial on the issue reported that the government did not intend to allow the exhibition of the offending pictures,⁷ and went on to acknowledge that the footage showing scenes of life in Jamaica, Jamaican industries and so on would do the colony "an immense amount of good in the way of advertisement". In regard to the pictures of natives attacking missionaries, however, the writer was emphatic: "What we object to is misrepresentation and libel. We want to be shown just as we are. We do not wish to be pictured differently. If we may make a suggestion to this company, it is that they should show Jamaica as a colony without a colour problem. That would be the truth."[8]

The *Lieutenant Daring* controversy speaks volumes about Jamaicans' early relationship to cinema. Occurring in the pages of the *Daily Gleaner* more than a hundred years ago, the letters and editorial establish a long tradition of critical response to the cinematic representation of the island and its people and register an uneasiness in local quarters with the way Jamaica might be depicted on the screen. The incident records an early attempt to appropriate "moving pictures" of Jamaica for circulation in a global network of images in ways that reflected the colonial relationship and also indicates that Jamaicans had a fairly sophisticated appreciation of the power of such images to convey meaning and influence audiences' perceptions. The writer of the editorial is not at all appeased by the cinematograph company's assurance that Jamaica would not be specifically referred to in the film and thus would be immune from negative associations. Nor does he draw any comfort from the company's smug insistence on its competence to speak on behalf of Jamaicans and judge what is appropriate in terms of the representation of the country's identity as a place. Rather, in the editorial writer's privileging of the local perspective and in his demand for Jamaicans' right to be shown just as they are, there emerges a nascent nationalism, undeniably marked by an anxiety about reception by those beyond the island's shores but, nonetheless, insistent on a difference in perspective, sensibility and interest that demarcates colony from metropole.

In the exchange in the newspaper, meanings attached to place coalesced around two opposing positions that spoke to internal and external perspectives, colonial and local objectives and concerns. It is also apparent, however, that both perspectives supported hegemonic intentions: both threatened to appropriate, fix and capture place; both threatened to silence dissenting voices. In its apparent representation of the colony as a site of savagery where the lives of white missionaries were under threat, the cinematograph company supported a view of Jamaica that was alien to those who wrote letters of protest to the paper. Equally erroneous, however, is the editorial writer's confident assertion of a homogeneous perspective. His insistence that "we want to be shown just as we are. We do not wish to be pictured differently" raises critical questions: who comprises the collective "we" and who, therefore, participates in defining what it is that "*we* are"? One can safely assume that black Jamaicans would not have unanimously accepted as truth the assertion that Jamaica was a colony without a colour problem. Indeed, this would be revealed as false two decades later when black Jamaican workers' agitation for better pay and improved working and living conditions resulted in major social unrest. Notable for the absence of the voices of the black masses, therefore, the *Lieutenant Daring* controversy not only raises the issue of the cinematic appropriation of images of Jamaica by external interests, it also anticipates the discursive tensions that would emerge in the latter part of the twentieth century, when Jamaicans started to make their own films.

THE EMERGENCE OF LOCAL FILM PRODUCTION

An indigenous film practice emerged in Jamaica in the 1950s with the production of state-sponsored educational documentaries, docudramas and newsreels. Early in the 1970s, ten years after political independence from Britain, a second wave of production began when independently produced narrative films began to emerge. These two discrete modes of film production signalled important shifts in the struggle over representation. The paradigm of the opposition between an external and an internal perspective remained in operation as local films continued to reflect the concerns voiced in the *Lieutenant Daring* debate and contest what Mbye Cham has described as the misuse of the Caribbean as "exotic background to Euro-American romantic narratives and spectacles".[9] One of the inevitable outcomes of the assertion of an internal perspective, however, has been the expression of diverse subject positions that challenge the unifying and homogenizing myths and narratives of nationalism. Far from supporting the idea that "the people [are] one"[10] (that seemingly inclusive, homogeneous "we" so confidently affirmed in the *Daily Gleaner* editorial in 1913), local films, whether inadvertently (in the case of the state-produced documentaries) or more explicitly (in narrative features), define Jamaica as a nation marked by difference, by deep socioeconomic and cultural divides that inevitably produce widely variant perspectives.

This struggle over representation, the ongoing process of defining the identity or identities of place as it is expressed in local film, is the primary concern of this book. I am interested in the varied ways in which local films contest colonial and externally imposed conceptions of place and identity and, more specifically, in the tensions that surface in opposing claims for authenticity. I explore what Jamaican films tell us about what it means to be a "placeling" – to use Edward Casey's term[11] – in Jamaica at specific points in space–time. This is the postcolonial project of reclaiming place as it is expressed in local cinema. I attempt, then, to trace the ruptures and continuities with the past as local filmmakers "take control of [their] own cinematic image, speak in [their] own voice",[12] and forge a relationship with cinema that reflects the lived experiences of Jamaicans and which inevitably resounds with the tensions of opposing perspectives vying for dominance within the space of the postcolonial nation.[13]

The book is organized as a series of largely discrete discussions of specific films. I begin with the two "independence documentaries", *Towards Independence* (1962) and *A Nation Is Born* (1962) – both released in the year Jamaica attained independence – and continue with what could be loosely described as the major local films up to 2011: *The Harder They Come* (1972), *Smile Orange* (1976), *Rockers* (1978), *Children of Babylon* (1980), *Dancehall Queen* (1997), *Third World Cop* (1999), *One Love* (2003), *Better Mus' Come* (2010) and *Ghett'a Life* (2011). Readers should not expect an exhaustive study of what is still a relatively small but steadily growing body of local films. Rather, I have selected for discussion eleven films that express a pointed and explicit concern with defining place, frequently in ways that suggest, in varying degrees, alternative perspectives to colonial or mainstream cinemas that have tended to manufacture images of Jamaica "radically at odds with the reality of the people".[14] Out of this discussion, the faint outlines of a narrative of the emergence of a Jamaican cinema materializes, but I hasten to point out that it is not my objective to provide a full and historical account of the development of a national cinema. My concern with nation is thematic: I am interested in how the selected films engage with the concept of place as it is expressed in the abstract construct of the nation and how the preoccupations, anxieties, and concerns of the national body are reflected in the film text and how they help to shape it.

DEFINING JAMAICAN FILMS

The book is, however, concerned with Jamaican films and so the troublesome task of defining this category must be dealt with. Jean Antoine-Dunne has remarked that "filmmaking, perhaps more than any other art form, complicates the question of national or regional affiliation".[15] In my own engagement with what Antoine-Dunne refers to as the vexed question of the national category,[16] I have drawn on a range of criteria, including the commonly used markers of nationality and the origin of financing. All of the films I refer to as "Jamaican" or "local" meet Diaram Ramjeesingh's criteria that a Jamaican film is one which "is *produced* or *directed* by a Jamaican national, or if *at least* 50% of the funding needed to produce the film is sourced locally".[17] But as filmmaking is a collective effort and increasingly transnational in its funding, attempting to define a film solely on the basis of this criteria can be problematic. Paul Willemen notes that the "economic facts of cinematic life dictate that an industrially viable cinema shall be multinational".[18] In small, marginal locations such as Jamaica, these "economic facts" include the very real need to seek markets, funding and investment abroad because, as Stephen Crofts points out, most Third World economies are rarely capable of providing the continuous infrastructural support which is needed to nurture indigenous cinemas.[19] Indeed, Ramjeesingh observes that the Jamaican Motion Picture Industry (Encouragement) Act, in place since 1948 and amended in 1991, "is silent on one perennial challenge that typically confronts domestic filmmakers, particularly in developing countries", that is, "the availability and accessibility of funds at low interest rates for film projects".[20] While there has been increasing interest and discussion about developing and supporting a stable local industry, as well as a growing recognition of the contribution such an industry can make towards national economic growth, state support for production in Jamaica remains minimal. The failure to implement policy that would specifically seek to bolster local production is reflected in Ramjeesingh's list of Jamaican films that shows only thirty-nine feature films produced between 1972 and 2012: on average, less than one film per year in a forty-year period.

Such statistics also indicate that models which propose defining a national cinema on an economic basis as the history of an industry, or "a business seeking a secure foothold in the market place",[21] might be usefully employed elsewhere, but are hardly appropriate for Jamaica, where production takes place in the context of a monopoly on exhibition theatres (all the cinemas in the island are currently operated by a single company), an absence of state support and, because of the long-standing recessionary economy, a scarcity of private investment or funding. The cumulative result of these factors is a sphere of activity that is less like an industry and more accurately defined by irregular and occasional feature production.

What then constitutes a Jamaican film? With the exception of *Towards Independence*, the eleven films I discuss in this book were shot entirely in Jamaica,[22] and the Jamaican setting is critical to the narrative: not merely generic backdrop, it is specifically identified, thematically and aesthetically important. These films, to rephrase Mette Hjort's discussion of Danish films, use recognizably Jamaican locations, Jamaican language, Jamaican actors and props that reflect the material culture of Jamaicans. They thus signal a certain Jamaican quality and specificity.[23] I am certain that the filmmakers whose work I discuss in this book harbour ambitions to penetrate external markets, but their films speak primarily and quite pointedly to a Jamaican audience. Thus, in defining Jamaican film, I also call into play Paul Willemen's idea that the issue of national cinema is primarily a question of address, rather than the filmmaker's citizenship or even the production finance company's country of origin.[24] In the films I identify as Jamaican and subject to extended analysis and discussion, the frequent use of Jamaican Creole and the assumption of a certain familiarity of the viewer with things Jamaican suggest that the films are primarily directed at a Jamaican audience.

PLACE AND IDENTITY

In my exploration of place in these films, I draw on concepts that define place as a dynamic, mobile construct. Place is, as Edward Casey affirms, not merely a physical entity made up of things contained within it – "a mere patch of ground, a bare stretch of earth, a sedentary set of stones" – rather, it is in continuous production; it is more like an event: "places not only *are* they *happen*".²⁵ From this perspective, place "while still possessed of a distinctly spatial quality, becomes imbued with a temporal dimension".²⁶ This idea resonates with Doreen Massey's concept of place as being formed by networks of social relations. Massey extrapolates from Lefebvre's axiom that "(Social) space is a (social) product",²⁷ and argues that space can be understood as being constituted of social relations which "are never still; they are inherently dynamic".²⁸ Place, then, is formed of "the particular set of social relations which interact at a particular location".²⁹ Or, as Simon During explains, place is "space broken down into localities and regions as experienced, valued and conceived of by individuals and groups".³⁰ Massey points out that the "identities of places are inevitably unfixed"³¹ because of the changing and dynamic nature of the social relations which produce them and that, furthermore, this "lack of fixity has always been so. The past was no more static than is the present."³² Place, then, can be understood as consisting of several dimensions: it is both spatial and temporal, it has physical, material as well as social qualities, and it is also constituted by the way people perceive, experience and conceptualize it.³³

The sense of place or, to be more precise, the sense of the identity of place, as unfixed, multiple and unstable both resonates with the postcolonial project of reclaiming place as well as complicates it. Ashcroft, Griffiths and Tiffin point out that the "gap which opens between the experience of 'place' and the language available to describe it forms a classic and all-pervasive feature of post-colonial texts".³⁴ Reclaiming place within the postcolonial context then necessarily entails "the development or recovery of an effective identifying relationship between self and place"³⁵ that may involve recuperating what Glissant refers to as the history that lies beneath the surface of the landscape,³⁶ and which, in the Caribbean, has been suppressed in Eurocentric accounts of place. It may also involve, however, "imagining a new relation to place beyond colonial violence".³⁷ Yet in the move to forge new relationships with place we must be mindful that, as Massey observes, space is "a complex web of relations of domination and subordination, of solidarity and cooperation".³⁸ Thus, Ashcroft et al.'s definition of place in the postcolonial context as "a complex interaction of language, history and environment"³⁹ might be more specifically qualified by adding the word "power" to the list of variables as a further elaboration of "history". An example of the interrelation between power and history emerges in Chris Tiffin and Alan Lawson's reminder that "names and codes of naming are obvious, basic ways of curving the account to indicate who matters and who is subordinate".[40]

It is precisely because place is such a critical constitutive element of identity as well as a decidedly mobile concept that is subject to change and transformation, that the meanings or identities attached to place are frequently expressed within highly charged and politicized exchanges. Thus, the relationship between place and identity may emerge in a context when identity is challenged or threatened.[41] What prompted the passionate responses of the letter-writers in the *Daily Gleaner* was an anxiety about the displacement of their concept of the identity of Jamaica as a place. Bazin's sense of the immediacy of the photographic image, the tendency of the viewer to respond as if the "photographic image is the object itself",[42] informs the Jamaican letter-writers' concerns about the film's reception abroad. Their sense of a slippage between reality (that is, *their* definition of place) and its proposed representation in moving pictures produces a moment of anxiety as they confront two incontrovertible facts. The first is that the new photographic technology, rather than reproducing "the object itself", creates an image that results from the manipulation of its authors. This is the realization that the film is a product of mediation and that meaning in the film depends, as John David Rhodes and Elena Gorfinkel state, less on "the world it photographs and more on its operations as a text".[43] And yet, paradoxically, underlying their protests and anxiety is a naive belief that the new medium *can* reproduce reality; that it can, indeed, show us as we are. The second fact the letter-writers confront has to do with the comprehension that the new technology of moving pictures, in the hands of a company with international reach and influence, had the power to displace their reality in the global imaginary and define Jamaica differently for an audience far removed from the island's shores.

"TWO JAMAICAS"

In their attempts to grapple with "the reality" of the Jamaican people, the films discussed in this book speak to experiences that are not readily acknowledged by tourism-oriented "Euro-American image factories"[44] which reduce the Caribbean to a site for the hedonistic pursuit of sun, sea, sand and sex: clichés, as Jane Bryce observes, that are now "so intrinsic to the popular concept of 'Caribbean' that they can be left unspoken".[45] Nor, indeed, do the experiences these films reproduce always coincide with formations of national identity generated through the agencies and institutions which function as vehicles for nationalism. Instead, in their complex evocation of place, the films discussed in this book, in particular, the narrative films, define Jamaica as a site marked by the accretion of history. That acknowledgement of history frequently takes the form of identification with the marginalized, expressing a desire on the part of the filmmakers to bring attention to the plight of the poor: those whose lives and experiences are often concealed from public view and whose voices are seldom heard in the clamour of public discourse. In some instances, the films do provide some limited insight into the lives of the middle class and elites and the spaces they occupy, but this often functions primarily to create a sense of the contrast that exists in Jamaica between widespread poverty and conspicuous displays of wealth.

This contrast is both disturbing and apparent. Commenting on the "incongruity of the 'Two Jamaicas'", Brian Meeks notes that the increasing disparity between rich and poor is "already one of the most notoriously wide in the region". Meeks points out that the "lifestyles of the wealthy . . . with their Mercedes Benzs, BMWs and shopping junkets to Miami, rival anything to be found in the USA", but contrast sharply with ways of life in ghetto communities, such as in the "desperate Riverton City, where thousands of people live literally on the city dump and many survive by a daily schedule of picking through the refuse for spoilt food and saleable junk".[46] In the context of patterns of socioeconomic disparity that have created a geography of bounded communities, spatial alienation and social separation, the Jamaican films' privileging of the perspectives of the marginalized and the places they occupy can be understood as engaging in social commentary that seeks to expose the failure of the nation state to realize the promises of independence. By repeatedly reminding audiences of this "gap between promise and fulfilment",[47] Jamaican films participate in an ongoing dialogue about what it means to be Jamaican in ways that expand our understanding of the consequences of postcolonial political arrangements that have denied the benefits of full citizenship to certain groups and individuals.

In some respects, this focus on the poor evokes parallels between Jamaican film and the West Indian novel. In an essay written as the introduction to his classic Bildungsroman of West Indian colonial experience, *In The Castle of My Skin*, George Lamming comments on the preoccupation of the Caribbean novelist with the poor and explains this as an attempt to restore humanity to a class of people that plantation slave society sought to reduce to mere components of an economic system. It also reflects, he states, the recognition that "this world of men and women from down below" represents "the richest collective reservoir of experience on which the creative imagination could draw".[48] Lamming states:

> This world . . . is not simply poor. This world is black, and it has a long history at once vital and complex. It is vital because it constitutes the base of labour on which the entire Caribbean society has rested; and it is complex because Plantation Slave Society (the point at which the modern Caribbean began) conspired to smash its ancestral African culture and to bring about a total alienation of man the source of labour from man the human person.[49]

The attempt Lamming identifies in the West Indian novel to heal the "fractured consciousness" and "psychological injury"[50] that resulted from this rupture with the past is evident in the work of Jamaican filmmakers. While considered problematic in some quarters, their insistent focus on the lives of the poor (and in particular, the urban poor), the use of inner-city spaces as setting, and the reproduction of violence and crime as defining features of Jamaican life and experience can also be understood as an attempt to claim, as part of the fabric of national culture, the perspectives and experiences of those who have been socially and culturally stigmatized and systematically excluded from access to the state's resources. Like the novelist, these filmmakers also attempt to restore humanity to denigrated individuals; not the peasant or the folk, but the black urban dweller who, bearing the brunt of what Meeks describes as "a long and drawn out economic trauma",[51] experiences intense forms of social alienation and cultural stigmatization.

Stuart Hall writes that the vocation of a modern Caribbean cinema is to allow us "to see and recognize different parts and histories of ourselves".[52] With a cast of characters that includes gunmen, badmen, dons, gigolos, ghetto dwellers, babymothers, Rastafarians, dancehall queens, rebels, reggae and dancehall musicians, tricksters and "sufferers", Jamaican narrative films are peopled by figures from which so-called polite society seeks to distance itself, but which undeniably exist as important, if often denigrated, elements of the national culture and identity. In essence, these are Lamming's men and women from down below.

The emphasis in the narrative films that emerged after independence, on socioeconomic disparities, essentially contradicts notions of the nation as a community marked by homogeneity rather than diversity, and also exposes the vaunted ideal of a deep horizontal camaraderie as a myth: all citizens are *not* equal. Indeed, these films are vitally engaged with the concept of place as it is expressed in the abstract construct of the nation. There is a persistent concern – explicit, self-conscious and affirmative (as one would expect) in the independence documentaries and less overt but undeniably present in the narrative films – with the notion of defining the nation. The independence films thus create a useful and expected contrast with the later films. Made by the state, the independence documentaries reproduce an ideal representation of the nation and attempt to do the work of nationalism, which Paul Willemen defines as binding people to reductive, politically functional identities.[53] In the decades following independence, the narrative films chart the fragmentation and disintegration of those concepts of identity, interrogate an assumed national unity and draw on modes of popular culture to express diverse cultural values.

In their intention to challenge nationalism's myths and claim legitimacy for subjects and identities which remained marginalized after independence, the narrative films mount an unavoidable incursion on official representations of national identity and work to define nation in ways which acknowledge and embrace difference. They contest, whether explicitly or implicitly, the idea underpinning the *Daily Gleaner* editorial, and echoed in the independence films, of a singular, coherent Jamaican (or national) perspective and identity. The post-independence narrative films speak not merely to a broadening of the definition of what constitutes "us" (that is, the

Jamaican people and nation); more fundamentally, they underscore the idea that the work of defining "us" is always incomplete and always in progress.

AESTHETICS AND THE CLAIM FOR AUTHENTICITY

Members of the elite and the middle class, those with greater access to traditional media and other vehicles of public discourse, at times react vociferously to the tendency in Jamaican cinema to approach social commentary by focussing on the marginalized and by highlighting instances of societal dysfunction.[54] Such criticism, often expressed in letters to the editor or in the op-ed columns of newspapers (as occurred in response to the *Lieutenant Daring* film), raise important and related questions about aesthetics and authenticity. While the early West Indian writer also had to confront aesthetic issues of crafting an appropriate language with which to convey the identity and experiences of the West Indian, the commercial and industrial nature of film production lends a greater urgency and immediacy to such considerations in the film sector. As occurs in most small localities, the need to generate profits to ensure survival and continued production is critical and can exert pressure on filmmakers to conform to local (and international) demand for films which maintain the familiar codes of commercial cinema. This is a recurring tension that is expressed in the films discussed: the impetus to explore new and alternative aesthetics in an attempt to speak in a more authentic voice to local experience is held in balance with the need to remain within familiar aesthetic territory and, possibly, sensational subject areas. The pressure on local filmmakers to gain points in the marketplace was brought home to me in a conversation with Douglas Graham, executive chairman of Palace Amusement, Jamaica's sole cinema chain and film distributor. Lauding Disney's commercially successful formulas, Graham said that he had encouraged the young director Storm Saulter to create an upbeat, happy ending for his film *Better Mus' Come*. Had he done so, Graham stated, the film would have been more successful. When I pointed out that the movie was very successful and had run for many weeks in his cinemas, Graham responded that if the protagonist had been reunited with his love interest rather than killed at the end of the film, it would have run for twice as long.[55] Happily, Saulter did not follow Graham's advice.

What then might be the most appropriate narrative forms and approaches for telling stories about poor black urban communities affected by crime and violence so that an intended social commentary does not create opportunities for the reproduction of harmful stereotypes about blackness, masculinity, poverty and violence? Some of the strategies used by Jamaican filmmakers as they negotiate competing demands and attempt, with varying degrees of success, to create textured, complex stories of lives in marginal spaces include the use of local cultural elements, particularly popular music and dance, but also folk elements; alternative aesthetics such as self-reflexivity; the engagement with history; and the use of mise en scène that contrasts the "two Jamaicas".

Even as Jamaican filmmakers attempt to give voice to the marginalized, however, significant gaps remain in the experiences and issues addressed in Jamaican cinema. Female directors and writers are underrepresented in feature film production, which probably explains why male protagonists continue to dominate and women's experiences remain largely unaddressed in Jamaican narrative film.[56] Further, we are yet to see a local feature film that openly explores non-hegemonic sexual identities and challenges a deeply entrenched homophobia in Jamaican society. Such aspects of identity, if fully engaged, threaten to further explode the myth of homogeneity. In addition, the failure, as yet, to fully explore contradictions and existential issues in the lives of the middle class and the elite also neglects significant aspects of Jamaican life and has not allowed for the full examination of important nexuses of power and social networks that perpetuate hegemonic attitudes and social structures. At a 2012 forum on film at the University of the West Indies, Mona, activist documentary filmmaker Esther Figueroa provocatively declared, tongue-in-cheek, that she would be interested to see what tales of dysfunction would emerge if residents of downtown were given the opportunity to make films about the rich and the middle class. Figueroa's comment emphasizes the tendency of Jamaican filmmakers (many of whom are educated and middle class) to focus on the poor instead of the communities to which they belong and how this focus can perpetuate, rather than alleviate, certain imbalances of power in the society.

Manthia Diawara makes a powerful argument proposing that race, like gender, is an important variable that enters the process of spectator identification.⁵⁷ Given the frequent use of the Caribbean as a location for American commercial films, one might also consider the possible dynamics that might operate in the relationship between postcolonial spectators and the cinematic text when they confront what, for them, is a slippage of representation. Thus, in *The Middle Passage*, V.S. Naipaul relates an incident in a Trinidad cinema where, because of their particular identification with the place where the film was set, local patrons become what Diawara would describe as resisting spectators: "'Where do you come from?' Lauren Bacall is asked in *To Have and Have Not*. 'Port of Spain, Trinidad,' she replies, and the audience shouts delightedly, 'You lie! You lie!'"⁵⁸ Experiencing such moments of rupture in the process of identification with foreign-made films set in the Caribbean may well intensify demands for authenticity when the postcolonial spectator watches locally made productions. However, because the number of features produced in Jamaica remains quite small, each new release, normally greeted with much fanfare, public excitement and expectation, tends to bear the full weight of such demands. Each film is thus quite unreasonably expected – by both local and diasporic Jamaican audiences, the main consumers of Jamaican films – to achieve the impossible task of representing Jamaica in ways that satisfy what may be quite diverse, even opposing, concepts of what constitutes "authentic" representations of "home". This is one of the consequences of limited production. As Isaac Julien and Kobena Mercer point out in reference to black British film, where access and opportunities are rationed so that films tend to get made only one at a time, "each film text is burdened with an inordinate pressure to be 'representative' and to act, like a delegate does, as a statement that 'speaks'" for the community as a whole.⁵⁹

STRUCTURE OF THE BOOK

The problematic task of affirming authenticity is addressed throughout this book and emerges in the first chapter, which examines the representation of Jamaica in the two "independence documentaries", the newsreels *Towards Independence* (1962) and *A Nation Is Born* (1962). The chapter explores the inevitable ideological tensions that emerge in these films' explicit and self-conscious attempts to define the new nation for its new citizens by drawing on old colonial paradigms and values. By contextualizing the representation of place in these two state-produced documentaries against the background of the formation of the Jamaica Film Unit (JFU) and its contribution to an indigenous film practice in Jamaica, the chapter also identifies the emergence of this new mode of production as an important aspect of the decolonization process as well as the move to nurture a national culture.

The Harder They Come (1972), one of the most provocative and complex representations of place and identity in Jamaican cinema, is the subject of chapter 2. Ivan, the country bwai (boy) come-to-town, embarks on a quest for identity and visibility in a place defined by a series of contrasts: wealth and poverty, promise and denial, dream and reality, tradition and modernity. In the discussion of this iconic tale of the badman, *The Harder They Come* is treated as a hypertext – that is, a text that engages with and draws on another text, in this instance the accounts of Rhygin, the notorious gunman of 1948. I use this historical context to explore "badmanism" as a cultural narrative that has allowed poor Jamaicans to infuse their marginality with agency and meaning. I propose that Ivan's exploits as gunman can be seen as a strategy through which he constructs an identity that demands respect and honour in a post-independence society in which the poor black masses still struggle to claim the benefits of full citizenship.

In chapter 3, I discuss another enduring expression of male identity, the playboy trickster, in Trevor Rhone's film, *Smile Orange* (1976). This film shifts the discussion of place beyond the city to the rural environment and, more precisely, Jamaica's north coast, which is the centre of the country's tourist industry. In this satire, Rhone deflates the problematic but durable image of the Caribbean island as paradise by constructing the north coast hotel as a place informed by the racial, social and economic politics of the plantation. Like the gunman/badman, the trickster assumes a role in order to aid survival, but within the context of the hotel/plantation this role both enriches and debases the protagonist. As Ringo uses role play and deception to outwit the hotel's manager, and as he plays gigolo to the female guests, his body becomes the site of both accommodation and resistance to historical forces.

Chapter 4 moves the focus back to the inner city with a discussion of *Rockers* (1978). Directed and produced by non-Jamaicans, this film disturbs common assumptions about the alienating external gaze and prompts us to think anew about the usefulness of defining film on the basis of the citizenship of the director or primary creatives. A focus on the Rastafari and its relationship to the production of reggae music as a rich cultural form as well as an expression of resistance is intrinsic to this film's atypical view of inner-city life. The familiar problems of the ghetto – social discrimination, harsh living conditions and the perpetual struggle for economic survival – are evident, but *Rockers* emphasizes the positive attributes of the community. Here there is no struggle for visibility in an uncaring society or the need for the alienated individual to redefine self. Instead, the male protagonist exists at the centre of a caring network of "brethren" who support each other in the struggle, rather than compete for scarce resources or dominance.

More than twenty years separate the release dates of the films *Children of Babylon* (1980) and *One Love* (2003), but they are paired for discussion in chapter 5 on the basis of their common concern with heterosexual bonding, not a popular focus in Jamaican cinema. Both films use rural locations as the setting for stories about interpersonal relationships, and the quest for a partner functions as a vehicle to explore concepts of nation. Set against the backdrop of the ideological clashes and conflict of the turbulent period of the late 1970s, in *Children of Babylon* the quest for national unity is undermined by the failure to resolve deep-seated conflict in a society that has been divided by a history of slavery and colonialism. *One Love* offers a far more optimistic vision of nation, but here, social and political differences are more superficially drawn and, therefore, easier to reconcile. In this film, true to the generic conventions of the utopian romance, love conquers all and the film concludes with the idealistic vision of a unified community.

In *Dancehall Queen* (1997), the film discussed in chapter 6, we see our first working-class female protagonist and one who, unlike several female characters in earlier films, succeeds in overcoming the challenges that confront her. The film reflects the shift from reggae to dancehall music, which by the 1990s was dominating Jamaican airwaves. However, unlike what occurs in *Rockers*, where music and musical performance constitute an integral part of community life, in *Dancehall Queen* the dancehall is associated with specific, discrete sites in the urban area. Characterized in the film by the revealing, erotic costuming of its female participants and their equally daring and erotic dance, the dancehall is a place to see and be seen, where women claim the freedom to assume expressive erotic identities. In the discussion of this film, I attempt to work through what I identify as a tension in the narrative. This is the reproduction of an objectifying male gaze to view the erotic dance of the female and the narrative's insistence that this performance is the source of the protagonist's empowerment and liberation from patriarchal thinking. This complex representation of the dancehall compels us to ponder what happens when an erotic cultural performance is mediated by the camera and becomes detached from its source and context of production.

In chapter 7, I return to the issue of authenticity, examined here in the context of the use of realist and popular genre conventions to tell stories about social dysfunction in poor black communities. While several of the other films incorporate self-reflexivity and other elements that suggest the referencing of alternative aesthetics, *Third World Cop* (1999) and *Ghett'a Life* (2011) operate mostly within the boundaries of mainstream realist and generic conventions. These two films, in which black men, gun violence and social dysfunction feature heavily, are popularly conceived as conveying authentic representations of ghetto life and perhaps even functioning for the middle class and elite as a means of imagining the nation, that is, imagining the lives of fellow citizens with whom they may have limited personal contact. The chapter interrogates the claim for these films' authentic representation of "ghetto life" and proposes that they confirm and support ideas about the poor that maintain the status quo.

The concern with history in Storm Saulter's *Better Mus' Come* (2010) suggests that it is an appropriate subject with which to close this discussion of Jamaican film. This concern with history is expressed in the film's focus on the critical period of the 1970s as well as in its referencing of *The Harder They Come*, the first narrative film discussed in this book. In his revisiting of the decade following independence, Saulter is concerned with the political schisms that emerged more forcefully in the latter part of the decade and which lead to brutal acts of violence. The chapter explores Saulter's vision of the 1970s and the cultural narrative of badmanism played out within the context of partisan political violence, as well as, more broadly, the film's concern with reconciling the bitter memory of one of the most divisive periods of modern Jamaican history.

Collectively, these films provide compelling and textured representations of place, nation and identity in Jamaica. It is my hope that this book will generate greater interest in Jamaican cinema and encourage more people to seek out Jamaican films, and that audiences will become more open to the complexity, nuance and the craft involved in making these films. Jamaican films are certainly good entertainment, but they also make a valuable contribution to the continuing conversation about what and who the Jamaican people are.

1
IMAGINED BONDS IN THE NEW NATION
The 1962 Independence Films

ONE OF THE HIGHLIGHTS OF JAMAICA'S inaugural independence celebrations was the opening of the new national stadium. This moment is captured in the JFU production *A Nation Is Born* (1962), a thirty-nine-minute documentary that records the week-long independence celebrations of August 1962. According to the film's narrator, about an hour before the start of the opening ceremony there was, as often happens in Jamaica in August, a torrential shower of rain. There are ample signs of this in the film: a significant part of the new stadium track is flooded and, if one looks closely at the scene of a large troupe of schoolchildren performing on the stadium field, it is evident they are dancing in a few inches of water. Watching this performance more than fifty years after it was recorded by the camera, I am distracted from the main thrust of the narrative by what, for me, is an incongruous image: children dancing barefoot in a flooded field before a crowd of some twenty thousand people on the occasion of the opening of what the film describes as the country's "most impressive monument of independence".

As I monitor my response to the images, I am reminded of Elena Gorfinkel and John David Rhodes's discussion of Siegfried Kracauer's comment that the image of a face or street in a film may affect the spectator in ways that lead to the opening up of "a dimension much wider than that of the plots which they sustain".[1] Gorfinkel and Rhodes note that "a spectator's concentration on what might be the 'wrong' or unimportant part of the image threatens (or promises) to usurp the stately or hurried progress of the narrative, and a world of meaning that the image does not mean to impart seems to pour down on us from the screen".[2]

In this instance, it is not a face nor, strictly speaking, a place which distracts me. It is, rather, the incongruity of a performance which prompts me to take note, as I watch the film, of the differential treatment accorded the young citizens of the new nation and the visiting dignitaries who are carefully brought to the foot of the stadium stands by motorcar in order to avoid getting their feet wet. One readily acknowledges that protocol demands such action on behalf of the special guests, which included Princess Margaret; and perhaps the children – as children will – enjoyed splashing about in the sodden field. As I watch, however, I wonder about their parents' reactions: were they proud of their children's stoicism in the face of hostile weather and poor drainage in the newly built stadium? Or were they dismayed at what might seem like the new state's scant concern for the health and well-being of the most vulnerable of its citizens?

That image of the children in the flooded field can be understood in various ways. For me, it provokes a train of thought that could hardly have been intended by the makers of the film. Indeed, I am struck throughout by a sense of dissonance between the kinds of meaning the narrative might produce in a twenty-first century spectator and what I imagine was the response the filmmakers intended and hoped for. Some degree of dissonance is to be expected. Bakhtin reminds us that the word does not relate to its object in a singular way: an utterance, having taken meaning and shape at a particular historical moment in a socially specific environment, becomes an active participant in social dialogue so that its meaning and shape are constantly subject to change.[3] More than fifty years on, I wonder about the silences and spaces in this narrative of independence, and ponder the tensions and contradictions, precariously contained in the frame, which provoke questions about nation, identity, the ambivalence attending the achievement of independence and the filmmakers' attempt to capture this pivotal moment in Jamaican history.

When it was determined that Jamaica would move towards political independence, in keeping with the practice established in other former British colonies, an "independence conference" was held in London to agree on the constitution and fix the date for the formal transfer of power. The JFU documented the February 1962 Jamaica independence conference in a twenty-four-minute newsreel feature called *Towards Independence* (1962).

Produced just before and just after independence, both *Towards Independence* and *A Nation Is Born* explicitly seek to do the work of nationalism by attempting to define the new nation, as well as create a sense of identity and belonging around the concept of nation. As Andrew Higson points out, however, this work that nationalistic films undertake of holding the people of a nation together as a community "is never completely achieved".[4] The two independence films and the ideological tensions created in these texts from the inevitable partial achievement of the objective of forging a national community are the focus of this chapter. What emerges is a singular contradiction: despite the films' intention to create a cohesive identity for the new emergent nation, subtextual elements reveal the dogged persistence of divisive features. Ambivalence persists in the films' repeated referencing and reinforcement of social and cultural hierarchies that echo the divisive colonial past.

A Nation Is Born and *Towards Independence* present both a convenient and appropriate point at which to begin this exploration of place, nation and identity in Jamaican film. The two narratives record and reflect on the final events of the journey to independence, defining the formal transfer of power as a signal feature in the formation of a Jamaican identity and a major paradigm shift in how Jamaicans defined and thought of themselves. Further, indigenous film practice in Jamaica has its roots in the decolonization process. Film functioned in the pre- and post-independence eras as an important means of self-expression for the emerging nation and as a sign of the new nation's mastery of modern technology, and thus of its entry into modernity. It was also an important medium used by the state to further development by encouraging, particularly in rural communities, the adoption of new agricultural and health practices as well as cultural values more closely identified with Western or modern life. The two independence films, therefore, can be located in both the early period of the emergence of indigenous film production as well as the period of emergent nationhood. The conjunction of these two processes is not accidental; indeed, as will be discussed, the local production of films, specifically documentaries, newsreels and docudramas, can be seen as a corollary of the movement towards full self-government.

Paul Willemen characterizes nationalism as "the range of institutionalised practices seeking to define and impose a particular, reductive, politically functional identity".⁵ The independence films, therefore, may be regarded as products of the apparatus of nationalism, for they are part of a deliberate attempt by the nation state to "bind people to identities".⁶ These films represent an expression of national identity, however, that evokes Benedict Anderson's insistence that "nationalism has to be understood by aligning it, not with self-consciously held political ideologies, but with the large cultural systems that preceded it, out of which – as well as against which – it came into being".⁷ The persistent referencing of colonial values and hierarchies in the independence films, even as they attempt to construct an identity for the emerging nation, thus also evokes Homi Bhabha's notion of a "particular ambivalence that haunts the idea of the nation, the language of those who write of it and the lives of those who live it".⁸ This ambivalence, manifested in these two films, assures us that national identity, as with other expressions of identity, is "constantly shifting, constantly in the process of becoming",⁹ although the films attempt to persuade us of the stability of the concept. Ambivalence resonates in the films in myriad ways, perhaps most visibly in the rituals of independence that reflect the cultural traditions of the colonial power, but also in the aesthetic choices of the filmmakers and in the ideological intentions of the two films. The latter is best understood by contextualizing the production of the independence films against the background of the establishment of the JFU, the government agency which made the films and which came into being in the pre-independence era.

Despite its signal importance to the history of film in Jamaica, insufficient attention has been paid to the JFU and the films it created. Scholarly references to the development of filmmaking in the anglophone Caribbean tend to begin with the advent of narrative films in the 1970s and 1980s.¹⁰ One notable exception is Terri Francis's essay "Sounding the Nation: Martin Rennalls and the Jamaica Film Unit", which highlights the work of Martin Rennalls, the influential first director of the JFU.¹¹ In general, however, the existence of an important phase of filmmaking in which short films, docudramas, documentaries, newsreels and filmstrips were produced as early as 1951 by film units in colonial Jamaica, Barbados, British Guiana, and Trinidad and Tobago, for both local consumption and export, has been largely unexplored. In Jamaica, the production of these early films dates the emergence of a sustained and organized indigenous film practice to the era preceding independence, rather than the postcolonial period.

The establishment of the JFU can be located within the framework of the global trend towards decolonization after the Second World War and was also closely tied to the process of nation formation and the agitation for self-government. After the granting of universal adult suffrage in 1944, Jamaica moved progressively towards full internal self-rule, culminating in political independence in 1962. The journey to independence saw the adoption of successive constitutions in the decade of the 1950s, which granted increasingly larger powers to local administrators. This included a period, 1958–1961, when Jamaica, as part of the Federation of the West Indies, had full internal self-rule, although the Crown retained the right to legislate on foreign affairs, defence and the maintenance of financial stability. Jamaica's movement towards self-government was reflected in the increasing use of the JFU, after 1957, to communicate the government's achievements, plans and intentions to an audience that seemed to be increasingly conceptualized not simply as citizens of a new nation or a rural population in need of uplift, but as potential supporters of a political party or administration. In this sense, the films of the JFU can be thought of as reflecting the movement towards modernity, characterized by the emergence of the nation state and an accompanying awareness, on the part of the local administration, of the efficacy of modern communications technology as a tool of persuasion within the context of the local partisan struggle for political power. In the JFU's mode of production up to 1962 and in the content, style and ideology of the films it produced in that period, lies the story of filmmakers struggling to craft an appropriate cinematic voice with which to express and define the identity of the emerging nation as they grappled with the implications and meaning of its existence.

Many of the early JFU productions are no longer extant, so that any generalizations must be made cautiously, but it would appear that prior to independence, the productions of the JFU were primarily documentaries and newsreels. In 1956 the output of the unit was summarized as twenty-one 16mm productions and seven 35mm productions, categorized as newsreel,

newsreel type, instructional, motivational, and one historical/instructional travelogue.[12] Terri Francis identifies four basic categories of production:

> instructional films that focus on a practical skill such as *Farmer Brown Learns Good Dairying*; history films that anthologize highlights from Jamaica's past, such as *Historic Jamaica* (1956); news films focused on a prominent visitor, such as *Churchill Visits Jamaica* (1953) and *Princess Margaret Visits Jamaica* (1955); and story films that used narrative to convey a specific message, such as *Let's Stop Them* (1953) and *It Can Happen To You* (1956).[13]

A 1959 catalogue compiled by the Government of Jamaica, Public Relations Department confirms that, for the most part, the unit's output largely conformed to the colonial authorities' intention that state-funded indigenous filmmaking in the colonies should be located within a developmental and educational framework. This focus is indicated by such titles as *Let's Stop Them*, a twenty-five-minute film discouraging predial larceny; *Coffee Co-operatives*; *4-H Achievement Day Newsreel*, about an annual 4-H Club event; *An Agricultural Show in Jamaica*; *You Can Help Your Children*, which encouraged greater self-help in rural communities; and *One Way Out*, about the treatment of leaf-spot disease in bananas.[14] *Historic Jamaica*, a colour film which is no longer extant, appears to be an exception to this general trend. According to the minutes of a meeting of the advisory committee, Martin Rennalls, then director of the JFU, explained that the film was intended to "interest foreign audiences, especially tourists, in Jamaica's historical attractions and so help in boosting the tourist trade".[15] Rennalls's statement suggests the JFU had an extensive distribution network but one wonders why the unit would have produced a film targeting tourists, when its mandate was to make films for Jamaicans and it was unable to fulfil all the requests for films from local agencies and government departments.

As a British colony, Jamaica was located within a network of imperial film production and distribution and received films and newsreels produced by the Colonial Film Unit (CFU) as well as private sector and business interests in Britain. The London-based CFU, originally conceived to produce propaganda films encouraging African support for the war effort, had shifted focus after the Second World War to the production of instructional and educational films to promote community development in the colonies. In Jamaica, these films and newsreels were screened in theatres in Kingston and other towns, as well as in schools and public venues in rural areas using cinema vans. Usually preceded by the playing of the British national anthem, the screenings were often blatant expressions of British propaganda that encouraged support for colonial rule. The films allowed Jamaicans glimpses of faraway places and provided news of events overseas, but, in the context of their use in rural communities as instruments of development, they may also have seemed irrelevant and disconnected from the lives and realities of spectators. Martin Rennalls, for instance, notes that the films screened in the rural district where he lived, Carron Hall, St Mary, were enthusiastically received, but he also points out that they "were considered inapplicable in many instances to local conditions".[16] Even when these films were about local subjects and their content was familiar, they often promoted colonial values and ideology. *Jamaican Harvest*, for example, a 1938 film produced by Gaumont-British Instructional Limited as an educational film for non-theatrical distribution in England, was one of the titles sent to Jamaica for local screening. The film is about the cultivation and export of Jamaican bananas but its focus is the production process rather than the people who participate in it. Indeed, the Jamaicans in the film function as nameless entities hardly differentiated one from the other and constructed as mere forces of production, the main purpose of which is to put bananas on breakfast tables in Britain.

The establishment of the JFU can be directly linked to the gradual decline of the CFU and its network of documentary film production and distribution. According to Rice, there was a shift in imperial film policy that was intricately connected to and reflected the movement towards decolonization that occurred after the Second World War. This shift was evident in the discussions that took place at the 1948 conference in London, "The Film in Colonial Development", which addressed the function, structure and future direction of the CFU. Participants at the conference readily acknowledged the need for the colonies to create and produce their own films and passionately advocated the means by which this could come about. Rice points out, however, that deliberations at the conference revealed both ambivalence and anxiety towards the decentralization of film production, and even the broader process of decolonization as well.[17] Such ambivalence is evident in the address by K.W. Blackburne, director of information services in the Colonial Office. Blackburne asserted at the conference that the "one main thing" the Colonial Office was working at was "trying to teach the people of the Colonies to run the show themselves", but he recommended a continued central role for the CFU: "Gradually, as the years go on, we plan to see the Colonial Film Unit gradually extinguished and replaced by local units leaving one guiding branch of the Colonial Film Unit in London which will act as the centre for all this film work going on over the Colonies."[18]

There are indications that the problems of funding the expensive activity of filmmaking may also have played a role in the move to decentralize film production. In response to some of the rather ambitious proposals for work to be undertaken by the CFU in support of film production in the colonies, Blackburne sounded a cautionary note, stating, "I think we have to be realistic about the financial difficulties we are up against in developing the film in the Colonies. We all know that film production is extremely expensive."[19] Indeed, by 1953, the financing of the CFU appeared to be so onerous that urgent appeals were made to colonial governments asking them to contribute to the upkeep of the unit. The Jamaican government, asked to pay two hundred pounds per year for a period of two years, was pressed to respond to the request as soon as possible.[20]

As a step towards achieving the goal of decentralization, the CFU did establish a small number of what were referred to as film training schools: in the Gold Coast in 1948; in Jamaica in 1950; and Cyprus in 1951. The term "school" gives the erroneous impression of permanence; in the case of Jamaica, what was set up was a twelve-month instructional programme that used equipment and instructors provided by the CFU. Housed at the then University College of the West Indies at Mona, the programme trained six men: three from Jamaica and one each from Trinidad and Tobago, Barbados, and British Guiana.[21] According to an article in *Colonial Cinema*, "the aim and object of the course was to train technicians to a standard that would enable them to produce educational and newsreel films and filmstrips of high quality".[22] The school was financed by a grant to the CFU under the Colonial Development and Welfare Act, while students' expenses were borne by their respective governments.[23] The tensions of decolonization also emerged in the establishment of the school and its pedagogical practices. Paternalism reverberates in a 1951 report published in *Colonial Cinema*, in which an unidentified writer commends the progress and enthusiasm of the participants, but sounds a rather patronizing and – considering the scarcity of funding for local productions – unnecessary call for caution and restraint. The writer states:

> It should be emphasized that the aim in production should be simplicity. Any inclinations, either of producer or of the Department for whom production is being undertaken, to aspire to the heights of a Hollywood production must be instantly checked. There is no glamour in documentary film production, no film premieres with radiant film stars, glittering cars, and publicity stunts. The reward will come if the production completed has aroused and maintained the interest of the audience and achieved its purpose by communicating the ideas intended.[24]

Reflecting on his experience in the programme, Martin Rennalls criticized certain aspects of the training methods. In his master's thesis, Rennalls wrote:

> No attempts were made ever to relate the methods of production to the customs and ways of life of the majority of the people of Jamaica or the other West Indian territories. There was no study into the cultural characteristics of the local audiences. The approaches, characteristics, and techniques of production were an adaptation of the Grierson style of documentary. The result was that the trainees learned the Grierson approach as the only approach and considered it as the hallmark of what good documentary productions ought to be.[25]

An iconic theorist and practitioner in early British documentary cinema, it is not surprising that John Grierson held such weight with the instructors, but Rennalls's statement reveals how aesthetic values that were not necessarily appropriate or relevant to the culture and realities of the West Indian filmmakers-in-training, informed the approach to instruction. The influence of the CFU instructors is evident in the film *Farmer Brown Learns Good Dairying*, which, as Rice points out, adheres to the "Mr Wise and Mr Foolish" narrative structure that was a favoured format in British colonial instructional film. This film was started by the Training School participants and completed by the JFU with assistance from the CFU. Commenting on the film, Rice points out that while it illustrates the move towards indigenous production, it also indicates that this was a gradual shift, as the making of the film was overseen and edited by the CFU and, importantly, the film also retains elements of colonial rhetoric and ideology.[26]

Indeed, while the establishment of the Jamaica Film Production Unit (as it was initially called) in 1951, after the closure of the training school, marked the beginning of a more independent phase of filmmaking, the Jamaican films continued to reflect the influence of the CFU both in terms of ideology and the production process.[27] The lack of necessary post-production equipment meant that the JFU was obliged to send its 16mm and 35mm prints to London for processing and for the dubbing of sound. In her account of the development of the JFU, Terri Francis identifies this as the unit's core problem in its first decade of operation, stating that the JFU participated in "a complex transatlantic post-production process, with prints transported between Kingston and London".[28] Rennalls described this as a time-consuming procedure and noted that "it also prevented the local unit from having full control over all the stages of production. But it was the best that could be done under the prevailing circumstances."[29] Typically, sound was added to the unit's films during the post-production editing phase in London, so that, as Francis notes, voice-over narration and commentary, and even the post-production dubbing of certain lines of dialogue, characterized the unit's films in its first decade of existence. As a result, she states, spectators did not hear the actual voices of the people on the screen in most instances.[30] This resulted in a distancing or alienating effect, Francis notes, but she points out that "despite the problems with sound, by focusing on images of Jamaican people and Jamaican locations, drawing scenarios from everyday life in Jamaica, Rennalls's films offered a counter to the colonialist erasure of the Jamaican subject which . . . would have been the model in other colonial film units".[31]

In terms of administration and the creation of policy, the JFU appears to have enjoyed a high level of independence from the CFU in London. Rennalls notes in his thesis that there was close contact between the two entities, with the CFU acting as the Jamaican unit's agent and advisor, and providing services such as the purchasing of raw stock and the processing of prints. But Rennalls's extended description of the local framework within which the Jamaican unit operated, indicates an autonomous local administrative structure. In keeping with the initial intention that the JFU should play a developmental and educational role, it was set up in 1951 as part of the Central Film Organization in the Education Department. Until 1956, the unit was governed by an advisory committee chaired by the director of education. Rennalls states that membership of the committee was drawn from all the agencies involved in the operation of the film services as well as other government departments and agencies involved in public education, such as the Department of Agriculture, the Jamaica Agricultural Society and the Voluntary Children Services.[32] The scant surviving minutes of the committee meetings also show that a representative from the British Council sat on the advisory committee and that, ahead of changes to be made in the administration of the JFU, in late 1956 the (government) public relations officer; the permanent secretaries of the ministries of education, labour, and trade and industry; and a representative from the Central Planning Unit were added to the committee.[33]

The process that Rennalls describes for the selection of subjects for films also suggests a large degree of local autonomy. Requests were sent by various bodies or government departments to the Central Film Organization, and then considered by the advisory committee, which could also make its own suggestions for productions. When a subject was selected, Rennalls states, the JFU normally accepted the responsibility for its financing,[34] although, not surprisingly, minutes from the advisory committee meetings indicate that the unit was unable to cope with the volume of requests made. While surviving documents do not provide information on what criteria were used to determine priority for production, both Rennalls's appointment as director of the production arm of the Central Film Organization and the broad-based composition of the advisory committee suggest a decision-making structure that was in contrast to what occurred in the African colonies up to independence, where Africans were involved in film production but operated within units that continued to be run and administered by Europeans resident in the colonies.[35]

Beginning in 1957, changes were introduced in the administration of the JFU that reflected a conceptual shift in the unit's perceived role and function in national life. These modifications occurred in tandem with changes in the local political administration and constitutional change as Jamaica moved along the path towards federation and, later, full independence. Norman Manley, leader of the People's National Party (PNP) which won the 1955 election, enjoyed increased power as chief minister, granted by the constitution of 1957. Under his administration, the Central Film Organization was transferred from the Ministry of Education (formerly the Education Department) to the Government Public Relations Office, which came under the direct administration of the chief minister. In his November 1956 submission to the executive council on the issue, Manley noted the need for the Public Relations Office to assume responsibility for disseminating information on all government activities.[36] This signalled the intention on the part of the political administration to expand the objectives of film production beyond the original focus on education and development.

In his thesis, Rennalls identifies two important outcomes of this change. One was the severing of what had previously been a close and direct relationship between the JFU and the government department which provided educational services. The other was "the shifting of the Unit's sphere of activity and attention to productions that were primarily for presenting the government's policies and activities".[37] This trend was further intensified in 1958 when, after the launching of the government's five-year development plan, the Central Film Organization was given the additional responsibility to communicate the government's "new policies to the people, to stimulate and motivate them, to cooperate, to make a record of activities and to report the programs of development throughout the country".[38] This new mandate for the JFU coincided with the inauguration of the Federation of the West Indies in 1958. These administrative changes signalled a new phase of operation in which the unit appeared to become incorporated into the more overtly political structures of the modern emerging state. The new responsibilities and functions imposed on the JFU appear to be more in line with the role of a modern-day government information service as it tends to operate in the anglophone Caribbean. Through such entities, Caribbean states communicate with their citizens not merely for purposes of development and the creation of a sense of civic responsibility, necessary for the cohesive functioning of a society, but also to promote the work of a specific administration in order to bolster public support for the political party that forms the government. These administrative changes, therefore, also indicated a sophisticated appreciation on the part of the political directorate of the ways that the visual medium could be formally used to create social meaning through image construction and myth-making. A new JFU production, *Government at Work*, thus sought to give government ministers greater visibility in the public eye. According to Rennalls, "the government maintained and demanded that in every production dealing with the work of a particular ministry, the relative Minister had to be brought into the film and visually portrayed".[39] Consequently, Rennalls observes that the new programmes introduced in the unit "could be regarded as informational reportage. It brought the Unit's activities closer to propaganda than ever before."[40]

Further changes would come after independence in 1962. When leader of the Jamaica Labour Party (JLP), Sir Alexander Bustamante, declared in 1961 that his party no longer supported Federation, a referendum was held on the issue that resulted in Jamaica withdrawing from that arrangement and embarking on the path towards full independence. In the election held prior to independence, the PNP was voted out of power and Bustamante became the country's first prime minister. In response to what was identified as a "serious communication problem, particularly in dealing with the rural areas",[41] the newly elected JLP government expanded and reorganized the Public Relations Office, including the Central Film Organization. Again, there were reassignments of departments and name changes that reflected new emphases in policies: the Public Relations Office was moved from the Prime Minister's Office to the Ministry of Development and Welfare and was rechristened the Jamaica Information Service, while the Central Film Organization became the film unit of the Jamaica Information Service. Francis proposes that the PNP government relocated the unit "from an educational context to a PR context",[42] while the new JLP administration "blurred the potential of film to be used as either an educational tool or as a vehicle of propaganda".[43] In essence, both administrations sought to exploit the communication potential of the JFU in support of narrow partisan interests.

Importantly, after independence the unit acquired equipment and processing facilities that allowed the complete processing and printing of 16mm and 35mm black and white films, thus achieving, according to Rennalls, a "major advance in the progress of the Unit towards complete independence and responsibility for the completion of the productions".[44] One of the most important changes at this time was the introduction of television into Jamaica in 1963. This resulted in JFU productions becoming principally directed at this new medium and restricted almost entirely to 16mm format, although Rennalls makes reference to the production of a series of full-length documentaries that were not intended for inclusion in television programmes.[45]

Towards Independence and *A Nation Is Born* reflect the trend described above, in their shift from a focus on community development to a more nationalist agenda. The two films provide vital information about the important political changes that were taking place at the time, but in their content and ideological inflection they also reveal the nation state's sophisticated use of film as a form of myth-making to create a common and cohesive concept and understanding of the new nation among the newly defined citizenry. Undoubtedly, earlier JFU films also attempted to do this. Films with agricultural and farming content, like *Farmer Brown Learns Good Dairying*, *One Way Out* and *Let's Stop Them*, all validate social values deemed necessary for development by the nation state. In the two independence films, however, specific social and cultural values are explicitly linked to the concept of national identity. Ella Shohat and Robert Stam state that in modern societies, films perform the creation of national self-consciousness: the shared belief of disparate individuals that they have common origins, status, location and aspirations. They affirm that, "just as nationalist literary fictions inscribe onto a multitude of events the notion of a linear, comprehensible destiny, so films arrange events and actions in a temporal narrative that moves towards fulfilment, and thus shape thinking about historical time and national history".[46] Indeed, the two independence films do the work of narrating the founding of the Jamaican nation and thus attempt to orient citizens towards certain ways of thinking about and conceptualizing this event, national identity and what it means to be a citizen of Jamaica.

In describing the independence films in this way, I do not mean to assert that there was necessarily any direct communication between the political directorate and the makers of the films as to how national identity should be defined and how it might even fit into a larger scheme of social control. Rather, I see these films as part of what Willemen describes as nationalism's "broad-ranging array of modes of address organised not just rhetorically, but also embodied in the very organisation and policies of institutions".[47] As such, direct instruction from the political directorate may not have been necessary in order to ensure that the films reflected a certain way of thinking about self and nation. As members of the collective themselves, the makers of the films, like the spectators for whom they were intended, were also subject to nationalism's mode of address and to the influence of the "cluster of assumptions it ensures are written into our social bodies from early childhood and repeated with ritualised regularity thenceforth".[48] In my discussion of the films, therefore, I focus on the ways in which national identity is defined and how these films reflect assumptions about dominance and power on a broad cultural and social scale. Willemen asserts that the ultimate goal of nationalism is to maintain the dominance of certain social groups or power blocs. The films' ambivalence and ideological inconsistencies, evident in the persistent referencing of colonial values and hierarchies, reflect an impulse – even as the new nation stood on the brink or in the immediate aftermath of political change – to maintain the old social order, in a sense, to keep the people "in their place". Independence meant a fundamental shift in political power; it did not mean, and was not represented in the JFU films as meaning, the abandonment of colonial social and cultural values and hierarchies.

It would not be unreasonable to presume that Rennalls's opinions and recommendations held considerable weight and influence on decisions regarding the JFU films' content, aesthetic choices and ideological intentions. Rennalls was one of the graduates of the Film Training School at Mona, one of the founding members of the JFU and the unit's first director, a position he held until 1970. Prior to entering the film training programme, he was known for his early efforts using film as a medium of instruction and community development for both schoolchildren and adults, and in particular for an impressive project in which he had mobilized members of a rural community to build an underground wattle and daub room to facilitate film screenings during daylight hours.[49] Francis identifies Rennalls as a dominant presence in the JFU and pays tribute to him as an influential figure in early Jamaican documentary production. Rennalls and Trevor Welsh (also one of the graduates of the Film Training School) are identified in the credits of *A Nation Is Born* as responsible for "Direction"; Albert Miller is credited as scriptwriter. *Towards Independence* has survived without any credits but is identified by the National Library of Jamaica, the official repository of the film, as a JFU production.[50] While I do not intend to argue that Rennalls set out to consciously and deliberately reinforce colonial hierarchies in the film as a means of social control, it is evident from his own account of the development of the JFU that he subscribed, as did many members of the educated middle and upper classes at the time, to certain Eurocentric views that in effect worked to maintain the dominance of white and brown elites in Jamaica.

In his 1967 MA thesis, "Development of the Documentary Film in Jamaica", Rennalls states that the country's visual education programme, in which the JFU was a key component, was primarily directed at Jamaica's small farmers, whom he identifies as the backbone of the island's economy. Describing the farmers as "predominantly of African origin" with ancestors "brought from the uncivilized, traditional and preliterate cultures of Africa", Rennalls notes the persistence in this population of "deep-rooted attitudes, predispositions, beliefs, customs and values which are not consistent with progress".[51] A primary concern of the JFU films, he points out, was "to bring the messages relative to social and economic development to the farmers, to engage their interest, redirect, channel and activate their attitudes and so involve them in the race to modernization".[52] Rennalls's comments indicate an intention to bring the farmers' creolized or African-based belief systems and practices into greater alignment with Western culture. Given such views on the part of the director of the JFU, it is hardly any wonder that he complains in his thesis of the existence of "a deep seated lack of rapport and empathy between the farmers and those concerned with the job of improving their lives". He states: "There seems always a gap that defies bridging, some deep down subliminal cords of consciousness that have not been touched, some deep rooted cultural values that resist the methods used by the films to reach them, to affect them and to bring about change."[53] Rennalls characterizes the farmers as having "split personalities",[54] describing them as outwardly responding eagerly to efforts at modernization while "deep down they remain firm in their old convictions".[55]

Rennalls's discussion in his thesis of the need to bring the small farmer into modernity suggests a sense of a national collective characterized by differences in cultural practices that correspond to race and class. This is in contrast to his succinct summary of the JFU's objectives which appears in the journal *Colonial Cinema*. Rennalls strikes a nationalist note in the colonial organ and conveys a sense of coherence and unity in the concept of a Jamaican national identity. Describing the Film Unit as playing a significant role in building a "New Jamaica",[56] Rennalls states that the policy of the JFU is "to produce films for Jamaicans, by Jamaicans, with Jamaicans, designed to assist in the solution of Jamaica's problems – educational, social, cultural and economical [sic]".[57] As will be seen in the discussion which follows, similar contradictions repeatedly emerge in the two independence films as the narratives explicitly assert a sense of unity while affirming social difference at a subtextual level.

As its title infers, *A Nation Is Born* is a film which seeks to "represent the nation to itself as a nation".[58] It associates a sense of national pride, exuberance and vigour with the independence celebrations, and emphasizes the presence and participation of children in the events as a symbolic expression of the youthfulness of the new nation and the prospect of future generations in building the country. Large numbers of Jamaicans are shown in the film: in parades and performances, and as spectators at events; urban and rural Jamaicans as well as persons across the social spectrum are seen. There is here a sustained attempt by the filmmakers to be inclusive in their representation of the citizens of the new nation. Most significant in this regard is the frequent use of medium shots and close-ups of faces in crowds at various events. This technique counters the anonymity of the crowd, conveying a sense of individual identity and presence rather than the notion of an anonymous, faceless mass. This fosters a sense of identification between spectator and film and, by extension, with the project of independence.

The documentary mode of both *Towards Independence* and *A Nation Is Born* accords these narratives of nation formation the illusory authority of "truth" as historical accounts of real events, while the use in the films of (male) narrators gives uttered statements about the nation further gravitas.

Disembodied and omniscient, the voice-over assumes authority in the film text as it explains, describes and interprets what the spectator sees on the screen. In both films, the voice-overs describe independence in lofty and grave terms. Independence is likened to a rite of passage, and the metaphor of the passage from childhood to adulthood is frequently applied so that the event is conceived as a kind of transcendental achievement that carries with it the weight of immense responsibility. In *Towards Independence*, for example, Reginald Maudling, secretary of state for the colonies, who chaired the 1962 London independence conference, lauds Jamaica's "political maturity" as an indication of the country's readiness for independence. The concept of the passage from youth to adulthood as a metaphor for independence also reflects, however, colonial (and local) misgivings about the emergent nation's ability to govern itself even as it infers that Britain, as the "parent" figure, had excelled at the task of governance in the colonies. In one instance, however, Norman Manley, then premier of Jamaica and one of the leaders of the joint delegation from Jamaica that attended the independence conference, rhetorically challenged the parent–child colonial paradigm by suggesting that Jamaica could teach Britain a thing or two about fostering racial integration. In his speech at the opening ceremony of the independence conference, captured in *Towards Independence*, Manley describes Jamaica as offering the world, and Britain in particular, an example of racial harmony as it had been able to weld a diverse heritage into "a harmonious unity".

Given the racial and ethnic conflicts that emerged in independence struggles in other parts of the world, it is not surprising that racial harmony is affirmed in both films as a sign of national unity and readiness for political independence. In his concluding remarks at the end of *A Nation Is Born*, the narrator identifies racial harmony as one of a number of characteristics that support the idea of unity and cohesion in the emergent nation. The narrator states:

> The spirit of unity, fellowship and goodwill which was demonstrated by Jamaicans wherever they gathered in their thousands shows that they are worthy of the independence they have achieved. It is a credit to their maturity that their emergence into independence is marked by such a display of reverence, dignity and peacefulness. But independence comes as both an opportunity and

a challenge: an opportunity to all Jamaicans to build, by their hard work and sacrifice, a racially mixed nation living in peace and harmony. An example for the world; a challenge to all of us to unite under one flag for a single purpose: the progress and prosperity of Jamaica.

In the film's visual representation of this racially mixed nation, however, there are few images of Jamaica's Asian minorities. Instead, the idea of harmonious mixing is asserted through images of Jamaicans that represent a broad spectrum of racial types on the black–white continuum.

The unity of the nation is also emphasized in both films' assertion of a homogeneous response to independence from Britain. Phrases such as "every man, woman and child"; "in every town and village"; "all Jamaica"; "in a thousand towns and villages all over the country"; "from one end of the island to another"; and "the common cause of independence" assert universal support for independence and seek to silence dissenting voices. This emphasis was necessary, in part, to assure the spectator that the conflict over the participation in and subsequent withdrawal from Federation in order to press for independence was indeed resolved.[59] *Towards Independence* closes with an image of the two political rivals, Norman Manley and Sir Alexander Bustamante, shaking hands and embracing, while earlier in the film, the narrator affirmed that "political differences were to play no part in the conference. Although Mr Manley and Sir Alexander hold divergent views on many subjects, independence was not one of them. In this, the main ideal, all parties were united."

This assertion of political unity was less than accurate, however. While, by all accounts, both government and opposition were able to quickly agree on the provisions of the constitution, newspaper reports reveal continuous public bickering over minor issues right up to the time of the 1962 London independence conference. There were other indications of dissent and disunity that the film also ignores, such as the severe heckling which Manley endured when he addressed the West Indian Student Centre in London at the time of the conference, and which, according to newspaper reports, left him "looking tired and shaken".[60] Also ignored was the small demonstration staged in London by supporters of the People's Political Party, a black nationalist party which was protesting its exclusion from the independence conference.

Given the state's strategic use of the JFU to promote the government and its programmes, as referred to earlier, such omissions are hardly surprising. They do indicate, however, a selective rendering of the historical narrative. Indeed, both *Towards Independence* and *A Nation Is Born* construct a narrative of independence that is truncated and foreshortened. Obviously, some selection and elision of events must take place in order to meet narrative demands, but beyond brief references to the West Indies Federation and a few superficial allusions to the "struggles of the past", in general, the films tend to conceptualize independence, ironically, almost as an ahistorical event with no detailed explanation as to how it came about. Thus, the anomaly that the 1962 independence conference, described as a momentous occasion in *Towards Independence*, is not even mentioned in *A Nation Is Born*. Greater historical resonance would have been achieved had the events in the two films been more explicitly foregrounded, either within the context of the preceding decades in which there was a gradual movement towards full self-rule or within the history of an ongoing black struggle for freedom, self-determination and majority rule that dates to slavery.

The latter perspective, in particular, was certainly not popular or dominant at the time and is a product of more recent Caribbean historiography which has recognized the role played by the black majority in resisting slavery and colonial rule. In a speech delivered prior to the London independence conference, however, Manley expresses a pointed sympathy with this perspective. His departure for London was framed by the *Daily Gleaner*'s front-page announcement that the premier was pressing for the first of August, the date of the abolition of slavery, to be designated Independence Day. In a message broadcast on radio after his departure for London he stated: "It is only when you are independent and truly free that you are free to treat all men as equals. So if Independence comes on August first it would be the wheel of history which made one full turn when slavery ended, making another full turn when nationhood began. There could be nothing like it I am sure, in all the pages of all the books in history."[61]

By the time Jamaicans were celebrating independence and the filmmakers were putting *A Nation Is Born* together, however, Manley was out of office, having lost the 1962 general election to Sir Alexander Bustamante and the JLP. Most likely, a film about independence explicitly linking it to emancipation would have been unthinkable to a JLP regime. Local newspaper reports indicate that in the tradition of the antagonistic politics which prevailed, setting the date for independence had become a contentious issue. Bustamante had publicly agitated for 23 May, celebrated in Jamaica as Labour Day, and as his popularity was largely derived from involvement in the labour movement, a 23 May independence day would have been of considerable political advantage. On his departure for the conference, Bustamante is reported as stating, "The 1st of August has no significance with Independence. Queen Victoria of blessed memory abolished slavery in Jamaica on the 1st of August 124 years ago. What significance has that with our Independence now?"[62]

More than likely, the historical emphases and perspectives in the films are simply a reflection of the influence of Eurocentric accounts of West Indian history which were dominant at the time and which did not recognize the black majority as a force in bringing about independence. Possibly, Bustamante's point of view, in which the achievement of independence was cut off from the history of the black majority's struggle and resistance to slavery, would have been the more popular one. Such thinking is reflected in the address of Donald Sangster who deputized for Sir Alexander at the opening of the London independence conference. Sangster, whose speech is partially recorded in *Towards Independence*, stated, "Jamaica has been independent-minded for a long time. You've only to read the reports of the parliamentary debates of two hundred years ago to realize that even then the colonials of those days wanted their own way of life." Ironically, Sangster makes no distinction between the twentieth century movement for political independence from Britain, with the attendant associations of majority black rule, and the agitation of white colonial assemblies during slavery for greater self-rule, which was associated with the increased oppression and control of the black majority. Whatever the reason, in detaching the event from its history, the films facilitate the negation of black agency, denying the black majority an active role in the achievement of independence and defining them as mere spectators to the process and passive recipients of its perceived benefits.

The representation of history is particularly problematic in *Towards Independence*, which is essentially a newsreel about the creation of the independence constitution. Simeon McIntosh asserts that the story of the origins of the West Indian independence constitutions is a critical aspect of the story of the political and collective identity of the Commonwealth Caribbean.[63] In *Towards Independence*, that story is told in such a way as to endorse the authority and dominance of Britain. This effect is achieved primarily through conceptualizing the process of moving towards independence (as indicated by the film's main title, *Towards Independence*) almost exclusively within the confines of the 1962 London independence conference (as indicated by the film's subtitle: *London Conference 1962*). Importantly, the film fails to acknowledge the existence of earlier successive constitutions, such as those in 1944, 1953 and 1958, which chart and define the movement towards independence as gradual and progressive. The film also pushes to the background significant steps in the process of writing the independence constitution which locate much of the document's authorship in Jamaica. Ironically, it is the chairman of the conference, Colonial Secretary Reginald Maudling, in his opening speech, not the narrator, who makes (brief) reference to these activities. Largely absent from the narrative, therefore, is a sense of the necessary local events that preceded the London independence conference: that is, the writing and debating of the draft of the constitution. Although these aspects of the process have since been severely criticized,[64] by failing to foreground them, the film erroneously locates the story of the writing of the Jamaican constitution – what McIntosh would describe as Jamaica's principal political text and its most prominent attempt at self-definition[65] – almost entirely within the framework of a nine-day event in London, presided over by the colonial authorities. In doing so, the film denies the role, however imperfectly performed, of legislators at home in the writing of the independence constitution. Thus, the perception of independence as a gift granted or given by the British, rather than actively struggled for and partially crafted by the colonized, is perpetuated, as is the idea of the total domination of the colonial power.

This perception is further supported by the film's emphasis on the motif of travel through the prominent foregrounding and the considerable running time accorded the Jamaican delegates' departure from Kingston and arrival in London. As there were three sets of departures (Manley and his party; Sangster and his party; Bustamante and his party), there are six scenes in this twenty-two-minute newsreel which document travel to London. Thus, a certain emphasis and importance is accorded the *idea* of travel and mobility (significantly by aeroplane rather than boat, the more common mode for the less privileged around that time). Here narrative structure reaffirms colonial paradigms of margin and centre, and the relative importance of each: the colonial subject must travel to the metropole in order to obtain his independence. Indeed, the film begins with what appears to be Manley's departure for the airport. Manley is shown descending the steps of a building and walking towards a group of people who watch him with open admiration and clap as he approaches; he greets them, shakes the hands of a few and walks out of the frame, while the group remains stationary, waving as he leaves. The voice-over informs us:

> The eyes of the world were on the Honourable Norman Manley, premier of Jamaica, as he prepared to leave his homeland for the most momentous of all conferences. The failure and practice of the Federation of the West Indies and its dissolution were common knowledge. Now Jamaica went to the conference table confident in her own future as an independent country and determined to bring the date of fulfilment as near as possible.

The narrator's hyperbole supports the myth of Britain's overarching dominance: the London independence conference is "the most momentous of all conferences" and is later described as "the most important few days of [Manley's] life, the days that would shape the future of his country and bring to reality the hopes of the people he served". The date of the opening of the independence conference, 1 February 1962, is similarly described as "a date which school children will be taught to remember for generations to come. It was the date that saw a new chapter in Jamaica's 450 years of recorded history." Ironically, few Jamaicans today are aware of the significance of this date, and, as stated earlier, it is not even mentioned in the later film, *A Nation Is Born*.

This persistent and underlying assertion of Britain's dominance in the process of nation formation in *Towards Independence* reflects Anderson's idea of the ambivalence of nationalism. It is also reflected in *A Nation Is Born* in the retention of colonial traditions and rituals that ironically herald the birth of the new nation. Obviously, part of the function of *A Nation Is*

Born was to educate Jamaicans about their new national symbols: the flag, the coat of arms and the national anthem, all of which are present in the film. Also evident, however, are the signs and symbols of the authority of the colonial power. Princess Margaret may have been referring to governance when she states in the film, at the sitting of the first parliament, that she had no doubt Jamaica would "uphold the traditions laid down by those who have gone before you", but the retention of much of the colonial parliamentary and other rituals – so evident in some parts of the film – is symptomatic of Munroe's observation that the attractiveness of continuity applied with particular force in Jamaica.[66]

The retention of colonial rituals and values is reflected in the differential roles, dependent on social status, accorded to participants in the independence ceremonies. The masses gather on the balcony at the airport to cheer Princess Margaret on her arrival, while an orderly line of prominent and privileged citizens is briefly, but individually, presented to her as she stands sheltered from the sun, beneath a canopy. The primary school children who dance in several inches of water on the field of the National Stadium are watched by an audience of dry, elegantly dressed spectators in the stands. It is important to note that in such instances the filmmakers are merely recording the activities, not determining the social hierarchy that informs them, but the filmmakers also actively reproduce similar values and perspectives as they construct these ceremonies into a narrative. In this narrative of the first independence celebrations, Princess Margaret is easily the most visible and identifiable individual. She is usually centrally framed, and more running time is accorded her participation in the activities than any other single individual, possibly including the new prime minister, Sir Alexander Bustamante. This is ironic, but possibly the filmmakers surmised that after the general election preceding independence, Princess Margaret might be a more unifying figure than either Bustamante or Manley.

There occurs, in a number of the segments in which Princess Margaret is shown, a spectatorial structure similar to that which Rice observes in the JFU's earlier production, *Churchill Visits Jamaica* (1953). In this film, Rice states, Churchill is framed centrally, watched by thousands of spectators, thus creating a clear relationship between leader and public. Further, the commentary suggests "a homogeneous group, unified in their support of Churchill and thus the Empire".[67] Similarly, in *A Nation Is Born*, the narrator comments on "the air of expectancy as the moment approaches for the arrival of Her Royal Highness, Princess Margaret", and the "thousands of spectators [who] line the route" of her journey from the Palisadoes International Airport to King's House. As a high angle shot shows people lining the roads, some running to keep pace with Princess Margaret's car, the lyrics of a mento song reinforce the idea of a homogeneous response to Princess Margaret as a universally beloved figure:

> We are proud and glad Princess Margaret
> That you have paid us another visit.
> What more can we wish?
> What more can we say?

While the narrative structure emphasizes the importance of Princess Margaret and Vice President Lyndon B. Johnson, the representative of the hemisphere's superpower, the United States, absent from the narrative are the voices of ordinary Jamaicans, the citizens of this new nation. The new citizens are readily seen in the film as members of the large crowds which turned out to greet Princess Margaret and participate in numerous other events. However, we never actually hear them articulate an opinion or point of view in the narrative. Instead, they respond through bodily actions. Immediately following the footage of the flag-raising ceremony and the playing of the national anthem, we see a high angle shot of a cheering crowd which appears to be joyously expressing excitement at the moment of the official birth of the new nation.

The switch from the regimentation of the flag-raising ceremony and what is constructed as a spontaneous bodily expression of approval from the crowd belies a tension that runs through the film between the formality of certain events and the far more relaxed activities and forms of celebration in which "ordinary" Jamaicans participate freely. In particular, a long sequence in the middle of the film that is more or less inserted between two formal events (the flag-raising ceremony at the National Stadium and the swearing in of the governor general) depicts how the "masses" celebrated on Independence Day. This sequence begins with a series of smaller, more informal flag-raising ceremonies around Jamaica,[68] followed by the various entertainment activities that had been organized throughout the country, such as street dances, road shows, cultural performances, sports and games. Here national culture is displayed – junkanoo, folk and creative dancing, popular music, performances by Louise Bennett – to assert Jamaica's plural cultural influences.[69] The sequence represents an expression of the energy, creativity, talent and culture of the people, but a social hierarchy is maintained: the sequence is introduced with the statement by the narrator: "Led by the Prime Minister and the Princess, Jamaica goes wild with excitement."

Towards Independence and *A Nation Is Born* are attempts to imagine the nation as a community, but through the repeated referencing of colonial values, divisive elements persist in the narrative that undermine the notion of the deep horizontal camaraderie Benedict Anderson refers to as one of the presumed features of the nation.[70] In these narratives, made at a time when Jamaica was poised on the threshold of change and transformation, the filmmakers looked as much to the past as to the future to define the new emergent nation. As representations of place, these films constitute explicit and self-conscious attempts to create narratives and myths to support identity formation and hegemony in the new collective. The motifs of social, political and racial unity seek to define Jamaica in ways that underplay the conflict and discord of both recent events as well as the distant past, while the maintenance of hierarchies normalizes assumptions about the social order and functions as a means of keeping people in their places at a critical period when change was imminent. These films' representation of Jamaica as a place marked by unity and harmony proved to be a fragile myth which would later be explicitly challenged in the independent narrative films that emerged in the turbulent decades of the 1970s and 1980s.

2
"BADDA DAN DEAD"
Resistance and Intertextuality in
The Harder They Come

Memba dem days when big fraid
Hole we everywhe we tun?
Ef dem hear a car back-fire
People sey a Rhygin gun!
—Louise Bennett, "Dead Man"¹

ON 31 AUGUST 1948, IVANHOE "RHYGIN"² Martin, a fugitive who had escaped from the General Penitentiary in Kingston and had been on the run for several months, made headlines when he shot his way out of a trap set by the police, killing one officer and wounding two others. Martin then made his way to a residence in Kingston, reputedly to kill the man suspected of informing the police of his whereabouts, and shot the three women he found there; one of them died. The story of the shootings hit the front pages of the two daily newspapers, the *Jamaica Daily Express* and the *Daily Gleaner*,³ on 1 and 2 September respectively, and Rhygin remained a hot news item for some six weeks until he was killed by the police on Lime Cay, off Kingston Harbour, on 9 October. The intense media attention bestowed on Rhygin a kind of mythic notoriety: thousands gathered at the morgue to see his dead body and rumours circulated after his death that he was still alive; Louise Bennett immortalized him in poetry and stories still circulate today that recount the intense fear and anxiety he produced, even in remote country areas where people feared that he might be hiding from the police. Granted the dubious distinction of Jamaica's first gunman, Rhygin has become an iconic Jamaican *badman*.

Jamaica's first fictional feature film, *The Harder They Come* (1972), directed by Perry Henzell and written by Trevor Rhone and Henzell, was inspired by the events of 1948 – Henzell's original script was titled "Rhygin". The film has played an important role in fostering ongoing interest in Rhygin and supporting his continued notoriety. Critically acclaimed, as well as popular with audiences, *The Harder They Come* has become an iconic representation of Jamaican life and has given rise to other narratives that continue to sustain the story of Rhygin. Largely because of the popularity of the film, Grove Publishers recruited Michael Thelwell to adapt the film to novel form, resulting in the publication of *The Harder They Come* in 1980, while the musical version of the film was staged in London in 2006. In this chapter I discuss *The Harder They Come* as a hypertext: a postcolonial reframing of the historical narrative of Ivanhoe "Rhygin" Martin. I am particularly concerned with the film's engagement with the cultural narrative of badness or badmanism and how it uses this as a means to probe issues of identity, resistance, and law and order in the new nation. I argue that in its reshaping of the Rhygin story, the film effectively interrogates elements of the colonial discourse within which 1948 reports of Rhygin were constructed and comments on the persistence of colonial values and social structures in post-independence Jamaica.

In her work on the contemporary romance novel, Catherine Roach describes romance as a "cultural narrative" which often functions as a foundational or idealized story about the meaning and purpose of life. Roach explains that by "cultural narrative" she means "a guiding story that provides coherence and meaning in many people's lives; a story whose truth value lies in the extent it is held to be true by people who shape their lives around that story, whether consciously or unconsciously".[4] Drawing on Roach's definition, I want to propose that badness, or badmanism, functions as a kind of cultural narrative in Jamaica that provides meaning and value for individual adherents, and, by extension, for the larger community. In Jamaican culture, therefore, badmanism takes on plural meanings and associations. A badman is not necessarily simply a person who resorts to uncivil, unlawful or antisocial behaviour; rather, badmanism can be understood as a performative strategy that is used to construct an identity which claims respect and affirms honour. When deployed by members of the lower classes within the context of the postcolonial society which continues to exhibit remnants of colonial hierarchies and values, the strategy of badmanism can take on the positive attributes of resistance to and defiance of unjust and discriminatory structures, particularly those of law and order that seek to ensure the dominance of elite groups and perpetuate the historical marginalization of the poor black masses.

Carolyn Cooper refers to contemporary popular culture to define badmanism; it is, she states, a "theatrical pose that has been refined in the complicated socialization processes of Jamaican youths who learn to imitate and adapt the sartorial ideological 'style' of the heroes and villains of imported movies".[5] Badness, however, is not merely an imported style or performance; Cooper acknowledges the deep cultural roots the phenomenon has in Jamaican society and also locates it in an "indigenous tradition of heroic 'badness' that has its origins in the rebellious energy of enslaved African people who refused to submit to the whip of bondage".[6] Cooper's linking of the contemporary mimicry of cinematic heroes and villains with rebellion against the injustices of slavery proposes how badness can be positioned within the postcolonial society as resistance to oppression. Obika Gray coins the term "badness-honour" in his impressive treatise on the Jamaican urban poor and their negotiation of and interaction with state power. Like Cooper, Gray defines the phenomenon in terms of cultural performance: "a distinct dramaturgy in which claimants to respect and social honour employ intimidation and norm-disrupting histrionics to affirm their right to an honour contested or denied".[7] Gray affirms that badness-honour is not a peculiarly Jamaican phenomenon, but rather one which occurs among the poor across all societies. It is, he states, a mundane but ubiquitous weapon of the weak, used "to secure a modicum of respect and power by intimidation".[8] Gray's linking of two seemingly opposed concepts, badness and honour, may seem paradoxical, but the term speaks to the ways in which adherents to this cultural narrative perceive that threatened or actual violence can function to elicit not merely fear in others, but can also accrue the positive attributes of honour and respect to those who perform this strategy, and, on a broader political and ideological level, function as an expression of resistance to the hegemonic impulses of dominant groups.

These perspectives on badness, which situate it within the historical resistance to oppression and strategies of empowerment employed by the poor, help to explain the ambivalence with which it is regarded in Jamaican culture. Particularly for marginalized social groups, it is both antisocial behaviour and a time-honoured strategy used by the poor, although not exclusively by them, to elicit respect. Such ambivalence was palpable in the responses to Rhygin's exploits in 1948. In newspaper reports, Rhygin was explicitly demonized as a bloodthirsty gunman, but the sensational news reportage also reflected a complex and deep-seated fascination with the man that bordered on admiration. That fascination surfaces in Louise Bennett's poem "Dead Man", which was published in the *Public Opinion* newspaper on 16 October, a mere seven days after Rhygin was killed by the police. Bennett's poem both denounces and pays tribute to the outlaw and, according to Cooper, balances "acceptance of the moral propriety of his necessary demise against the vicarious thrill of identification with his apparent indomitable badness".[9] Within the context of the sensational and explicit photographs of Rhygin's dead body that appeared in the newspapers (including one of him on a slab in the morgue, and another showing him sprawled on the beach at Lime Cay), and the timeliness of the publication of the poem in one of those newspapers, the title of the poem can be read as an ironic reference to Rhygin's descent from fearsome gunman to powerless corpse; death is the final and ultimate leveller: "But no care how man sey dem bad / Man kean badda dan Dead!" This diminishing of Rhygin is countered, however, in the final stanza in which, given the widely held belief in Jamaica in the existence of ghosts or duppies, even as a dead man, Rhygin still has the ability to inspire fear and terror:

> But ah wonder wat would happen
> To de picture – man Miss Sue,
> Ef wen him dah teck de picture
> Rhygin duppy did seh "boo!"[10]

In its coverage of Rhygin in 1948, the *Daily Gleaner* displayed a remarkable tenacity in keeping the fugitive on the front page throughout the six-week period he was at large, even after the other daily newspaper ceased to report on the lack of activity. What Thelwell describes as the media's "orgy of yellow tabloid sensationalism", led by the *Daily Gleaner*,[11] was inspired as much by the shocking nature of Rhygin's actions as by commercial considerations, for no doubt the sensational reporting offered the possibility of increased newspaper sales. Thus, Lynne Macedo asserts that the styling of Martin as a two-gun cowboy or gangster "seems to have been generated by the media as a means of attracting readership".[12] Indeed, only a few days after the initial shootings, the *Daily Gleaner* described Rhygin as "a one-man army with an itch in his trigger finger", and speculated that "Ivan Martin, in true Dillinger fashion – a fashion he had copied with his hair trigger revolvers and his constant target practice – would turn up at the burial of his victim".[13] One imagines the mixture of anticipation, fear and excitement such speculation would have produced at the policeman's funeral. The *Daily Gleaner*, therefore, even as it denounced Rhygin's actions, deliberately contributed to the notoriety and mystique surrounding him by casting him as a latter-day urban gunslinger in the style of the Western hero and gangster.

The newspaper's representation of Rhygin must be considered within the context of the *Daily Gleaner*'s long held reputation as the voice of conservative elements in the country and the hegemonic role it has played in shaping public opinion. Writing in 1981, Sheila Nicholson points out that as the oldest newspaper in the English-speaking Western Hemisphere, the *Daily Gleaner* exercised a virtual monopoly on information dissemination in Jamaica for much of its 144-year history and, further, that it has inevitably reflected the opinions and interests of the established wealthy institutions and groups that have controlled it.[14] It is not surprising, therefore, that the styling of Rhygin as a gunslinger was accompanied by the persistent dehumanization of the man, a mode of representation that seemed to address what must surely have been an anxiety among elites in the colony that his "indomitable badness" might inspire not merely admiration, but also further acts of lawlessness. One of the ways that the *Daily Gleaner* responded to this concern was to demonize Rhygin as a savage murderer. Repeatedly, rather than refer to him by name, the *Daily Gleaner* used the word "killer" to identify him, calling him "two-gun killer", "phantom killer", "gun-mad killer", "two-gun slayer", "Killer Martin", "cop-killer", "Carib Killer" and more.[15] More insidious was the newspaper's implication of his class and rural origins in his criminal behaviour. In a story published the day after he was killed by the police, the *Daily Gleaner* posed the question: "Who was "Rhyging [sic]?" and proceeded to answer it by referencing a history of poverty and dispossession: "Like many country boys, he drifted early to the city. He came by way of a provision truck, and when he was dumped out with the goods at the west-end country truck terminus, he stayed on."[16]

The allusion to garbage in the account of his arrival in the city is echoed in the caption of a photograph (appearing on the same page as the story cited above) which states, "'Killer' Martin lies on the flotsam-strewn beach on which he was cornered yesterday morning." Such descriptions were not only intended to convey the inevitable triumph of justice over a wrongdoer; they can also be understood as a deliberate attempt to strip the wrongdoer of his humanity. Thus, animal imagery prevails in the description of Rhygin's last moments: "Cornered at long last by the police he fought like a rat in a trap and like a rat he died"; later in the story he is described as having been "hunted from his lair".[17]

This "othering" of the criminal is extended beyond the individual to the group. Speculation by the press that Rhygin's extended liberty was due to the support he received in Kingston's west end where he "was regarded as a hero",[18] provided the opportunity to extend the vilification of the individual to an entire community and the labelling of its inhabitants as criminal and lawless types. Such assertions reflected the colonial authorities' continued historical othering of this community of poor black Jamaicans. A nineteenth century description of Smith's Village (a community in the western part of Kingston) states that while the area was becoming the resort of a better class of people, in "the old days it bore a very bad name and was . . . the home of wickedness and vice of the most depraved descriptions".[19] Such othering continues today, as will be discussed in later chapters in this book that explore the continued stereotyping of residents of the inner city as criminally inclined.

Although the newspapers limited their assertion of public support for Rhygin to the west end, it is quite certain that many beyond the borders of that community were also intrigued by the outlaw's activities and his talent at avoiding capture. Stories about Rhygin's seemingly magical ability to travel the city and elude the police were widespread, while thousands turned up at the morgue after he was shot, hoping to get a glimpse of his body. The *Daily Gleaner* writers' sensational and excessive use of cinematic allusion in the reportage on Rhygin possibly expresses something of their own repressed identification with the figure, but the newspaper reports do not themselves fully reflect the extent of what might be described as a kind of thrilling fear and fascination which Rhygin stirred, and which is more evident in oral histories and texts like Miss Lou's poem.[20]

In his account of the process of writing the novel *The Harder They Come*, Michael Thelwell describes Rhygin as a contemporary incarnation of recurring figures in Jamaican history which, "depending on your point of view", were regarded as "either rebel heroes or ungrateful and bloodthirsty savages".[21] Thelwell's statement inserts Rhygin into that larger ongoing narrative of resistance that has its origins in Jamaica's history of slavery and colonialism and, significantly, also infers how perspective informs attitudes and responses to badmanism: today's badman may be tomorrow's celebrated rebel hero. One such historical figure whose status and identity has changed with the times is Three-Fingered-Jack, or Jack Mansong, a runaway slave who attacked and robbed travellers and raided plantations in eastern Jamaica in the eighteenth century. Like Rhygin, Three-Fingered-Jack was repeatedly regenerated: in eighteenth and nineteenth century British fiction and theatre, in a twentieth century Jamaican pantomime, and, more recently, as the object of much academic interest. Variously depicted in plays and stories written by the English as either a Romantic hero in the style of the noble savage or a brutish threat to civilization, his acts of violence are now more often regarded as a form of resistance against the unjust institution of slavery.

The Harder They Come performs a similar kind of revision in its treatment of the Rhygin story and might be described as "activist" after Robert Stam's description of adaptations which challenge or interrogate their hypotexts, or source narratives, rather than attempt to faithfully reproduce some element of the original. In Stam's dialogical concept of adaptation, texts are continually transformed and worked on by later texts in "a complex series of operations" in which "the source text forms a dense informational network, a series of verbal cues that the adapting film text can then take up, amplify, ignore, subvert, or transform".[22] This process is evident in *The Harder They Come* in its use and treatment of the historical story of Rhygin. The collaboration between Rhone and Henzell resulted in a film which wrought substantial changes to the historical material, including the transformation of the protagonist, Ivan (Jimmy Cliff), into a creative subject (an aspiring singer) and ganja trader, and, notably, a change in setting to post-independence Jamaica.[23] Certain aspects of the plot reflect the Rhygin story: like Rhygin, Ivan is a country boy who migrates to the city; like Rhygin, he turns to crime, evades police capture and eventually meets his death at the hands of the police on Lime Cay.

One of the most significant elements of the original story with which the film engages is the idea of a populist response to Rhygin that ran counter to the dominant point of view. Ordinary people may have been afraid of the gunman but, as stated earlier, they were also intrigued by his resistance to law and order, even as newspaper accounts sought to depict that resistance as an uncomplicated expression of evil. The deliberate privileging of Ivan's perspective in *The Harder They Come* actively encourages spectator identification with the protagonist, a badman, and thus suggests an important site of intersection with the Rhygin story. The film creates a nuanced and complex portrait of Ivan that insists on the humanity of the figure of the badman. Ivan is a tragic would-be urban hero who uses violence as a means of resisting oppression and as a strategy through which he constructs an identity that demands respect and honour in a post-independence society marked by the retention of colonial values and hierarchies that define him, as a poor black man, as worthless and subordinate.

Ivan functions in the film as the site at which contesting ideologies and discourses converge. As postcolonial subject, he struggles to claim the benefits of full citizenship in a new nation in which elites continue to control the means of production, and as the dialectical forces of the postcolonial state play around and upon him, Ivan is subject to continuing transformation and change. In the film, he tirelessly reinvents himself to meet the demands of the dynamic environment of the postcolonial city, and transformation or reinvention of the self ultimately becomes a means of resisting the forces within that environment that seek to contain and then destroy him. As a hypertext, the film also functions as a site of intersection as it engages with elements of the Rhygin story as recorded in the pages of the conservative colonial newspaper, the *Daily Gleaner*, but privileges populist sentiments and perspectives. The film as text is also subject to transformation and resists stasis because it has the capability to produce diverse responses to Ivan that shift according to the context of reception. In what amounted to an acknowledgement of its dialogical nature, Henzell stated that while he had intended the film as a cautionary tale to overly ambitious young men about how dread Babylon was, several decades after its release, the film was more often regarded as a warning to Babylon about the rebellion of those whom it continued to marginalize.[24] In his essay "Historical Experience in *The Harder They Come*", Prakash Younger also affirms the film's dialogism, describing it as a palimpsest, a text that contains traces of narratives from various periods in Jamaican history. Younger identifies those narratives or stories as "the late 1940s when the events that inspired the film took place; the late 1950s and early 1960s when ska and reggae music developed out of a local taste for American rhythm and blues; and the early 1970s when the film was made, after the sociopolitical sea change exemplified by the Rodney riots of 1968".[25] Suggesting that the overall effect of the film is negotiated by the interplay of these three narratives, Younger prefaces his final analysis of the result of the "marriage" of these strands of history with the presumption that "relations would shift and vary, bringing some strands into focus, allowing others to fade away, in accordance with the specific dangers and needs of the moment of reception".[26]

The main thrust of Younger's essay is to demonstrate how these narratives, rooted in the local, are articulated in the film so that they resonate with the global audience. Of the narratives that Younger identifies, I am concerned primarily with the events of 1948 – their local resonance, rather than how they speak to a global audience – and what they contribute to the film's narrative of postcolonial Jamaica in the decade following independence. Younger's assertion of the film's dialogism, however, is key to my reading of the text, which engages with a popular response that seems to go against the grain of readings offered by a number of critics. Commentary on the film has typically tended to foreground the irony in the narrative and interpret it as diminishing any sense of accomplishment or victory that might be claimed for Ivan. The final sequence of the film, which depicts Ivan's demise and in which he dares the police to a shoot-out in the face of a most certain death, is often interpreted as Ivan's delusional embracing of the badman pose through reference to the cinematic gunslinger: a misguided retreat into make-believe induced by a too-intense identification with the fantasy and cultural imperialism of American cinema.[27] In opposition to such views, there stands Jamaican audiences' celebratory response to the film and their vigorous approval of Ivan's continued defiance, which suggests an alternative understanding of his last moments and indicates that, for them, there is much that is redemptive in his final gestures.

In her review of the film, American critic Julianne Burton refers to a *Rolling Stone* account which claims that patrons at the premiere of the movie were crammed three in a seat and were dancing in the aisles long before Ivan was gunned down in the final moments of the film. Describing Ivan's defiance in the final scene as "a hollow heroism", Burton reads the Jamaican audience's boisterous behaviour as an indication of the absence of critical engagement: "Such a response suggests that the immediate impact of the film medium might be stronger than its message, that the experience of seeing their lives portrayed on a screen might initially be perceived as an unqualified justification rather than a call to critical appraisal."[28]

The writer of the *Daily Gleaner*'s "Mello-Go-Round" column states that dancing took place in the musical interlude which preceded the film, rather than during the screening, but concurs that "Carib [Cinema] was jam-packed with Squeezing Room Only".[29] Like Burton, Trinidadian critic Gordon Rohlehr also proposes that "Ivan as gunslinger is, inevitably, an empty fantasy-ridden character", one who "begins to enjoy the chase in a strange way, and debases the spirit of his original protest by the triviality of his desires".[30] Rohlehr, however, does offer important insight into the audience's strong identification with the character:

> *The Harder They Come* does not preach, moralise or offer solutions. It prefers to look at what is. If an idea emerges at the end, it cannot be summarised in any easy moral formula. When I saw the film I noted how completely everyone around me identified with Ivan, and particularly with his defiant pose in the face of death. They didn't notice, nor did they mind the element of fantasy in his defiance. It may be that under that mask they saw something of their own daily desperation in the face of a system where the extreme gap between rich and poor is still maintained by class-legislation, and the constant threat of coercion which sometimes materialises in physical violence, and often assumes the absolute form of death on the streets.[31]

It is Kamau Brathwaite, however, who fully displaces the notion of a physically active but intellectually passive response to the film with the proposition that what took place at the premiere was revolutionary on a number of levels:

> The premier of the Jimmy Cliff roots/reggae film *The Harder They Come* (Kingston 1972) marked a dislocation of the socio-colonial pentameter, in the same way that its music and its stars and their *style*, marked a revolution in the hierarchical structure in the arts of the Caribbean. At the premier, the traditional "order of service" was reversed. Instead of the elite, from their cars moving (complimentary) into the Carib Cinema watched by the poor and admiring multitude, the multitude took over – the car park, the steps, the barred gates, the magical lantern itself – and demanded that they see what they had wrought. "For the first time at last" it was the people (the raw material) not the "critics", who decided the criteria of praise, the measure and ground of qualification; "for the first time at last", a local face, a native ikon, a nation language voice was hero. In this small corner of our world, a revolution as significant as Emancipation.[32]

Brathwaite identifies two distinct sites of political activity: the physical space of the cinema and its environs, within which the "multitudes", both literally and symbolically, overturned the critical and social values of the prevailing order; and the film text itself, which is concerned with the lives of the multitudes rather than the experiences of the elite.

In my reading of the film which follows, I draw on that boisterous, celebratory response to *The Harder They Come* that suggests, as Brathwaite states, alternate criteria of praise, to propose that even in the final scene of the film, Ivan's assumption of the role of badman is deliberate and purposeful, rather than delusional. I propose that it constitutes an act of intense creativity in which he uses the cinema as a metaphor to create an imaginative space that allows him to construct a narrative of badness-honour, that is, a narrative of resistance, even in the face of certain death at the hands of the agents of the postcolonial state. Ivan retains the posture of the badman to the very end. This is not empty fantasy or delusion; it is the character's steadfast adherence to a common cultural narrative often used by the poor to construct an identity that accrues honour and respect and affirms autonomy.

Ivan's initial and continued performance of the strategy of badmanism is depicted as a consequence of the failure of the postcolonial society to deliver on its promises of equality and economic opportunity for the black masses. An essential aspect of this perspective is the film's treatment of the police. In 1948, the *Daily Gleaner* referred to the police "as a protective wall between the lamb and the wolf", a shepherd "whose welfare and safety and success is wrapped up in the welfare, safety and success of the whole flock".[33] In its revisioning of the Rhygin story, the film portrays the police as a corrupt institution that plays a critical role in maintaining power within the hands of the elite. Thus, Ivan's flouting of law and order becomes morally acceptable as an act of political resistance by a member of the underclass who seeks to strike a blow against the remnants of an oppressive colonial system. In an essay that traces the emergence of the rude boy or badman ethos, Clinton Hutton points out that the creation of a lumpenproletariat in Jamaica occurred as a result of specific policies put in place by the dominant classes: "By denying emancipated Africans reparation for their enslavement, and artificially increasing the price of land up to sixty times the market rate for African-Jamaicans so as to strategically fetter black access, as well as using state intervention to prevent or to curtail black proprietorship, the post-emancipation elites engendered a class of African-Jamaicans with little option but to make a living primarily by antisocial means."[34]

The relationship Hutton describes between the engineered poverty and degraded social conditions of the black underclass and the emergence from their midst of a criminal class is powerfully articulated within a postcolonial context in *The Harder They Come* and is central to the film's representation of Ivan as badman. The film shows how the continued existence of forms of social and economic oppression in the new nation effectively maintains black Jamaicans in positions of subordination and economic disenfranchisement and suggests continuities with the demeaned status that was imposed on emancipated blacks in post-slavery Jamaica.

By depicting the new nation as one sharply divided by class, *The Harder They Come* explodes the independence promise of the creation of a unified and harmonious society and chronicles, a decade after political independence, the persistence of social and economic inequity. In the film, post-independence Kingston continues to resemble the colonial world that Fanon describes, in which natives and colonials experience the city in sharply divergent ways.[35] Throughout the film, the sense of a heinous and unequal distribution of wealth is conveyed through the juxtaposition of contradictory images. The long line of men seeking employment at a construction site; the bedraggled and destitute Ivan wandering the streets of Kingston looking for food; and most vividly, people scavenging in a garbage dump, are contrasted with the middle-class woman relaxing on her verandah; the luxury hotel with its uniformed guard; and the large white convertible (a recurring symbol of wealth and social status). These images of prosperity are accompanied by tropes of exclusion: the guard at the hotel chases Ivan off the property; the woman orders him to leave her premises and close the gate behind him; and when he first sees the convertible, he is separated from it by the glass window of the bus in which he travels. Ivan's struggle for identity is explicitly situated within this sociopolitical landscape, but when he decides to both literally and metaphorically "surge into the forbidden quarters"[36] by daring to claim his piece of the pie "right here, right now", his awareness of the wider political implications of his actions remains limited, as does his understanding of the forces which he challenges. Neither does he question or attempt to examine how the needs and desires which inform his actions are shaped and influenced by materialism, the primary feature of the very system against which he rebels.[37]

The duality of the city is integral in the construction of this ostensible irony. At the beginning of the film, as the camera follows the progress of Ivan's bus ride from the coast to the interior and into Kingston, the concern with the relationship between identity and place is introduced and the motif of the quest or journey is established and linked to Ivan's arrival in the city. Certain images proclaim the positioning of the urban space within an easily identified symbolic matrix: an upscale, high-rise apartment complex; a large billboard advertising life insurance proclaims "Talk With Philip Waite For A Better Life"; and a large white convertible which Ivan openly admires. Later, there is the ironic statement from a man who robs Ivan of his belongings when he gets off the bus that, "if you have money you can go anywhere". In contrast to the alluring images and, later, the exciting nightlife with which the city beckons and welcomes him, Ivan soon becomes acquainted with the seamier side of the city when, swindled and robbed of all his possessions and turned away by his mother who had preceded him into town, he wanders the streets destitute and penniless. Here Ivan experiences first-hand the despair, degradation and hopelessness of destitution that is also a feature of life in the city.

The stripping of his material possessions and reduction to despised and homeless vagrant is the first in a series of experiences in which Ivan's identity is challenged and his value as a human being eroded in the new space of the city. The second pivotal experience in this process occurs when Ivan is sentenced to eight strokes with the tamarind switch for wounding a man who had unjustly taken his bicycle, a valued possession that Ivan had lovingly and painstakingly repaired and restored.[38] Harris notes the overt sexual imagery of the flogging sequence but dismisses it as "little less than sadomasochistic, homosexual pornography".[39] In fact, the carefully constructed mise en scène in the sentencing and punishment sequence is essential to a postcolonial reading of the film. The wig and robes of the sentencing judge remind the spectator that the judicial system is a colonial legacy, while in the flogging scene, the dark body stripped and bound for the lash is reminiscent of the brutality of slavery. The framing of the flogging itself emphasizes Ivan's passivity and suggests the metaphorical performance of sodomy: an officer holding the whip runs towards Ivan, who is stretched and tied over a barrel, his naked bottom exposed for the lash; a jump cut repeats, and thus emphasizes, this action. The yellow trickle of urine indicating that Ivan has lost control of his bladder punctuates the explicit symbolism of the scene that conveys violation and the stripping away of manhood and autonomy. As with the theft of his possessions, Ivan again experiences a profound loss, although this time it is at the hands of a brutal and punitive judicial system.

Another critical moment in which Ivan's sense of self is challenged occurs when he attempts to sell his song to Hilton (Bob Charlton), the record producer. Ivan initially refuses Hilton's offer, but Hilton's monopoly of the music industry is so entrenched that Ivan has no choice but to accept the paltry offer. More than money is at stake in the transaction that takes place between the two men. Ivan's sole diegetic musical performance in the film, the singing of the title song "The Harder They Come" in Hilton's studio, occurs almost immediately after the flogging scene. The performance represents a resurrection of the self and reaffirmation of hope after the darkness and negation of the whipping. No longer the broken, beaten man who was flogged, Ivan in performance is renewed, confident, and sings with a barely controlled passion and intensity: "So as sure as the sun will shine / I'm going to get my share right now, what's mine." The performance affirms that while music for Ivan is certainly a commodity which he hopes will launch him on a path to wealth and celebrity, it is also, equally, the means through which he affirms his humanity as a creative and intense expression of his deepest desires and longings.

The integrity of the performance dissipates, however, when Hilton's voice cuts over the music, declaring he has heard enough. In the one-sided negotiation which follows, he offers Ivan a mere twenty dollars for his song. The mise en scène frames the interaction between Ivan and Hilton within a historical context, evoking the class and colour politics of the postcolonial period: the dark-skinned Ivan, sweating heavily from his labour (the performance), stands across from fair-skinned Hilton, who looks freshly dressed. Hilton will later use his control of the industry to suppress the song and keep it off the airwaves, and in so doing, attempt to teach "troublemekker" Ivan a lesson, that is, keep him in his place and remind him of his continued powerlessness in the new postcolonial arrangement. Hilton attempts to assume here the role of Prospero/Crusoe to Ivan as Caliban/Friday, as he tries to shape Ivan into what he presumes is an appropriate identity for a poor black man, that is, a person who recognizes Hilton's authority and accepts his own powerlessness and subordination.

Ivan's response to the postcolonial society's collective efforts to reduce and remake him as a broken, subdued and hopeless individual is resistance. He refuses to accept the boundaries of the psychological compartment into which society would contain him. Rather than surrender to its continued colonizing impulse, Ivan asserts his autonomy. He declines to occupy the space which those with power define as appropriate, and refuses to relinquish his belief in his inherent right as a human being and citizen to claim and define himself in this new place, the postcolonial city. Indeed, rather than turn his back on the allure and promise of the city, he meets the repeated threats of destruction, the attempts to render him powerless and submissive, with renewed efforts at transformation, continuously making himself over in an image that has value within this new space. Unable to become a star and earn a living through his music because of Hilton's exploitative hold on the industry, he turns to the underground economy and ganja (marijuana) trading. When he perceives that his activities there are also subject to exploitation by those who control the trade, he also resists. And when, in an attempt to contain his rebellion, police protection is withdrawn and he faces the possibility of arrest, he shoots the policeman rather than submit once again to the humiliation of corporal punishment.

Although it is an instinctive refusal to return to prison that initially thrusts Ivan into the role of outlaw, it is a role that he gladly assumes and delights in when he discovers that it has brought him public recognition. "Didn't I tell you I would become famous?", he boasts when it is broadcast on the radio that the police have launched a manhunt to track him down. Thus, Ivan consciously embraces a role that he had previously indignantly rejected when his mother urged him to go back to the country before he "tun criminal". The ordinary people of Kingston are in sympathy with Ivan and demonstrate their support. They identify him not as lawless killer, but as *badman*: a rebel against injustice, a small man bucking an exploitative and oppressive system. For them, this is enough. Commenting on the futility of Ivan's death at the end of the film, Burton questions the outcome of his actions: "To what end his martyrdom? Nothing has changed in shantytown", she states.[40] The cultural narrative of badmanism, however, does not necessarily require measureable, concrete change in order to denote positive meaning. According to the truth of this narrative, it is sufficient to resist. Thus, Ivan's song becomes an anthem of resistance: "But I'd rather be a free man in my grave / Than living as a puppet or a slave."

A series of scenes depicts Ivan's conscious and deliberate assumption of a new identity as he begins to imaginatively shape and define his role as badman. In one scene, he strolls confidently through the pool area of a hotel, presumably the same one from which he was chased when he was destitute. Now smartly dressed, he is the lone black local among the white bodies of the tourists. When he exits the hotel, he brandishes his gun in order to take possession of a large white sports car, similar to the one he admired when he drove into the city on the country bus, and drives with obvious pleasure and delight around what appears to be a golf course while we hear the repeated refrain, "You can get it if you really want / But you must try, try and try, try and try / You'll succeed at last."

The use of the song in this scene is instructive: the lyrics evoke the American dream that success is possible through hard work, but the narrative has already demonstrated that, in the postcolonial society, that adage is a myth for significant numbers of the new citizens. As Braune points out in her careful study of music in the film, the song assumes ironic undertones in this scene as Ivan's acquisition of the car, an important sign of affluence, is fleeting and illusory.[41]

As Ivan grows into the role of badman, it becomes identified not only with the idea of political resistance, but also, as illustrated in the car hijack scene, with the acquisition of the good life. The repeated use of two songs, "The Harder They Come" and "You Can Get It If You Really Want", on the soundtrack underscores this seeming irony in Ivan's actions by bringing to the fore, in the construction of the new identity of badman, the tension between individualistic materialism and consumerism on the one hand and, on the other hand, the desire for autonomy and equality, and the demand for respect, which bears the potential for political action that will benefit others. The lyrics of both songs refer to the attainment of an unspecified goal in the face of adversity and hardship. There is, however, a measure of ambiguity in the lyrics: that goal could be easily defined in material terms, but the songs also speak to such a spirit of perseverance, a willingness to suffer hardship and an assurance of eventual triumph, that desire and the quest itself take on spiritual dimensions and notions of the inevitability of natural justice. The irony underlying Ivan's desires is by no means clear cut: the dichotomy between materialism and the desire for equality is muddied rather than sharply defined. For in the city, affirmation of one's humanity is intimately bound up with wealth and the possession of material goods, as Ivan discovered when he was penniless. In the city, to be without is to be nothing and to be despised. Ivan's violence and resistance, then, are not aimed at annihilating the values and structures that define the city, but rather at challenging the exclusivity that defines those structures and which seeks to deny him the right and opportunity to participate in the promise of the new emerging society.

The cinema plays an important part in the film's construction of Ivan's new identity and figures heavily in his expectations of the city. On his first night in Kingston he goes to the Rialto to watch a Western with Jose (Carl Bradshaw), a hustler who will eventually introduce him to the ganja trade. Ivan later consciously imitates the gunslinger of the Western when he poses for photographs, guns drawn, ready for action and dressed to the nines in a photographer's studio. A montage giving the effect of a series of photographs is used to represent Ivan's photo session. These images are direct references to the Rhygin story: the use of black and white stills, the upside down images reminiscent of the photographic effect of the box camera of an earlier period, and the poses that Ivan strike are all reminiscent of the photographic images of Rhygin that accompanied the newspaper reportage of his activities. But in the middle of this quickly paced montage, several still shots are inserted that set themselves apart from the others in the sequence: they are in colour, and rather than showing Ivan in his gunslinger poses, they show him relaxing (or sleeping) in a lounge chair by the pool at the hotel, smiling over drinks with a woman, and in the recording studio. These shots, and particularly those of him in the recording studio, seem to be either outtakes or shots of Cliff out of character, possibly taken during breaks in the shooting process.

This self-reflexive montage, then, directs our attention to the various levels of artifice in the narrative: to the artifice of the camera and the apparatus of the cinema as they construct images and narrative for the spectator's consumption; to the artifice of the actor, Cliff, as he performs Ivan; and to the artifice of the *Daily Gleaner* in 1948 in its construction and dissemination of images of Rhygin. Most pointedly, however, the montage directs the spectator's attention to Ivan's artifice, to what is a conscious and deliberate assumption of a new identity: the persona of the gunslinger and badman.

By the end of the film, Ivan's identification with the hero of the Western has intensified, but it remains purposeful and deliberate. The film ends when Ivan is cornered on Lime Cay by the police (or possibly soldiers) and is killed in the ensuing shoot-out. In another self-reflexive sequence, flashbacks to the cinema scene at the Rialto are cut into the shoot-out scene. As Ivan fires at the soldiers, a flashback to the Rialto scene shows close-ups of the smiling, animated faces of the cinema audience as they watch and shout their comments at the action on the screen. Before the first flashback, Ivan is intent and serious, as the situation demands, but after he shoots and the initial flashback appears, he smiles and begins to stylishly dodge from tree to tree, to evade the soldiers' bullets: he appears to have assumed the persona of the gunslinger. The soundtrack from the Rialto scene – the excited shouting and cheering of the audience – continues to run under the visual track even when it cuts back to the shoot-out at Lime Cay, so that the sound of the cinema audience accompanies Ivan's actions on the beach. Out of ammunition and emptying the last shell from his gun on the sand, Ivan calls out to the soldiers, "Don't worry wi' the army business, one man just come out. Who is the bad man? Who can draw? Come on out who can draw!" Relinquishing his cover, Ivan moves out into the open and is shot dead.

In considering Ivan's imaginative summoning of the Rialto audience during the shoot-out at Lime Cay, it is important to note that in the initial Rialto scene, the patrons' shouted comments at the screen and their "inappropriate" laughing and jeering during a tense, dramatic moment constitute a form of critique, while Jose's repeated insistence that the hero can't die until the last reel indicates both knowledge of the genre's conventions and awareness of the constructed nature of the film text. The cinema audience which Ivan recalls in order to provide context and support for his actions on the cay, therefore, is not a passive group of spectators who are so caught up and lost in the spectacle of the Western that they are not able to distinguish fantasy from reality. Neither is Ivan himself lost in fantasy, indulging in a comforting but falsely conceived heroism. Rather, his is a deliberate act of creation that constitutes his final and ultimate act of transformation in which self and body become text and he creates his own ending. Ivan's final, victorious act of resistance lies in the act of creation itself, through which he announces a refusal to succumb to the authority of Hilton (and, by extension, the new elites) in the role of Prospero/Crusoe, and instead asserts his right as a human being, no matter how poor or marginalized, to order and decide his own fate. Like the artist he is, he does this by drawing on the limited resources available to him by subversively appropriating the genre of the Western and transforming it into a vehicle to support his continuing defiance.

That moment of the premiere of *The Harder They Come* in the Carib Cinema in 1972 must have seemed, at least to Brathwaite's "multitudes", full of irrepressible hope and promise. The patrons who had stormed the cinema had come there to watch a film which had been previously denied them and, amidst rumours that the premiere would be the only screening in Jamaica, they were determined to gain entrance.[42] The film was only then available for public viewing because the recently elected PNP government, led by Michael Manley, had removed a ban on the film imposed by a previous administration. Importantly, the banned film was not some foreign import, but the first Jamaican narrative feature and a Jamaican film to boot, which looked at the lives of "the multitudes", not the cocooned existence of those who dwelled uptown. The occasion of the premiere, therefore, celebrated and claimed narrative film, a vastly popular medium but one that had been up to that point largely foreign in origin, as a vehicle which now gave expression to Jamaican lives and Jamaican realities. In the film they were watching, Ivan was performing a similar act of appropriation as he imaginatively used the conventions of the Western and the cinema to create a space in which, as badman, he could continue to affirm autonomy and resistance and thus claim honour and respect.

Ivan's refusal to submit and accept defeat in the face of a more powerful opponent energized the Jamaican audience. What they celebrated was Ivan's *willingness* to resist, his spirit of badness that proved impossible to destroy. Perhaps for those in the forefront of that continuing narrative of resistance, who daily wage their own private, often invisible, seemingly hopeless battles against poverty, adversity and marginalization in an ostensibly uncaring and exploitative society, simply the ability to continue fighting, to prove oneself indomitable, even "badder dan dead", is more than sufficient cause to applaud.

3
THE TRICKSTER AS COCKSMAN
The Hotel as Contact Zone in *Smile Orange*

WIDELY CELEBRATED AS AN IMPORTANT JAMAICAN playwright, Trevor Rhone's accomplishments in the cinema are impressive but less well known. Rhone co-wrote with Perry Henzell the screenplay for *The Harder They Come*,[1] an achievement that is often overlooked; he wrote the screenplay for *One Love* (2003) and co-wrote (with director, Glen Salzman) the screenplay for *Milk and Honey* (1988),[2] a Canadian production that was partly filmed in Jamaica and for which he won a Genie Award. His signal accomplishment in cinema, however, is the film *Smile Orange* (1976), which he directed and co-wrote with David Ogden. A perennial favourite with audiences at home, *Smile Orange* is the screen adaptation of Rhone's immensely popular play of the same name, which was first staged in 1971 under the direction of Dennis Scott. Rhone's first big hit as a playwright, *Smile Orange* enjoyed an unprecedented run of 245 performances.[3] It returned to the Jamaican stage in 2009.

Smile Orange the film retains much of the original plot and dialogue of the play, but this faithfulness to the stage drama resulted in a visually unexciting film: in the long dialogues, the strictly functional mise en scène and the reluctance to depart from continuity editing, the sensibility of the playwright, rather than that of the film director or cinematographer, dominates. It is really the talented cast's strong performance, in particular Carl Bradshaw in the lead role of Ringo, which brings to life a screenplay layered with irony and funny from beginning to end. At the heart of the comedy is the figure of the trickster, Ringo Smith, a self-proclaimed playboy and hustler. His substantive post at the Mocho Beach Hotel is that of waiter, but Ringo earns additional income by providing special services of a sexual nature for the female guests who, he states, don't only come to Jamaica for the beach and sunshine.

Following *The Harder They Come* as Jamaica's second narrative feature, *Smile Orange* shifts the focus from the city to the north coast, the centre of the country's tourism industry, one of the primary earners of foreign exchange. Raymond Williams points out that the apprehension of a fundamental contrast between country and town is a long established but limited concept,[4] and rather than propose an artificial binary between the rural and urban space, *Smile Orange* deliberately dispels misplaced notions of an idyllic rural environment that resists change and exists outside the play of history. The film is set on the coast, but the focus is not the beach, that iconic landscape which has functioned as Edenic signifier and which is now a metonym for Jamaica and other Caribbean destinations in the pervasive discourse of tourism marketing. Rather, the film is characterized by a concern with interior spaces and, while some scenes do take place on the beach, our gaze is directed primarily towards the hotel rather than the iconic landscape that lies beyond. The film begins by setting in counterpoint two journeys that eventually culminate at the hotel: the aeroplane bringing tourists to Jamaica, and Ringo's long drive from his home in the hills to his place of work, the hotel on the coast. The hotel, therefore, functions in the film as something of a contact zone where locals (the hotel workers) and tourists meet. The two journeys, one associated with leisure and the wealth that affords mobility, the other, mundane but beset with difficulty, inform the relative status of the two groups as well as the underlying purpose of their interaction. In the contact zone of the hotel, tourists and locals re-enact a time-worn script that is informed by the history of slavery and colonialism and in which black labour is organized in the service of meeting the needs and desires of the tourists.

In *Consuming the Caribbean*, Mimi Sheller explores the centuries-long history of the imaginative fashioning of the Caribbean by the people of Western Europe and North America and the use of the region as a site for their projected fantasies and desires. Although at various periods the region has been associated in the European imaginary with death, disease and contamination, Sheller identifies the idea of the Caribbean as a tropical paradise as the prevailing iconic fantasy of the region. She states: "The

Caribbean has been repeatedly imagined and narrated as a tropical paradise in which the land, plants, resources, bodies, and cultures of its inhabitants are open to be invaded, occupied, bought, moved, used, viewed, and consumed in various ways. It is represented as a perpetual Garden of Eden in which visitors can indulge all their desires and find a haven for relaxation, rejuvenation, and sensuous abandon."[5]

Sheller makes it clear that this historical way of seeing the Caribbean perpetuates a politics of subordination in which the products, landscapes, visual cultures and, most significant, human bodies were understood as being available for the consumption of the north. This imagined concept of the Caribbean remains pervasive today, informing the discourse of tourism marketing and allowing northern consumers "to experience their proximity to Caribbean people as pleasurable even when it manifestly involves relations of subordination, degradation, or violation".[6] Eva Illouz confirms tourism as an activity that "presupposes an intensive exploitation of the landscape and its transformation into a commercial zone that can serve tourists' needs and desires. Tourism demands that natural landscapes, ethnic groups, or cities be organized – geographically and symbolically – to fit commercial exploitation (the 'travel package')."[7] Indeed, Ian Gregory Strachan affirms that the turn to tourism as a mainstay of threatened economies in the region is not accidental but directly tied to the historical influence of the slave plantation: "In a number of crucial ways, tourism has grown out of and sustains the plantation economy. The plantation laid the economic, political, cultural, and social groundwork that has enabled tourism to function so effectively in the Caribbean. As an institution of colonization, the plantation established a political and economic dependency on the metropolitan centers that tourism merely extends."[8]

Honor Ford-Smith proposes that these historical linkages are deliberately played upon in the representational practices of tourism which, she argues, "adapt old images of colonial domination and heterosexual relations to reproduce new forms of institutional and cultural racism".[9] Affirming a gendered discourse of tourism marketing that employs a language of seduction to offer the traveller a fantasy of superiority and privilege combined with heterosexual delight, Ford-Smith states: "The tourist brochures deploy images of domination precisely because it is in the implications of domination that the sense of privilege, superiority and pleasure associated with tropical tourism lies. The messages carried by the brochures deny any suggestion of violent domination while simultaneously drawing on discourses of colonialism so as to make domination seem a natural part of the feminized landscape."[10]

As women's spending power has grown and as they have become recognized as important consumers of leisure, the gendered language of tourism promotion has increasingly addressed this group. Thus, Ford-Smith refers to a television advertisement selling Jamaica as a holiday destination which features images of a "handsome smiling dread"[11] that hints at a sexual fantasy for white women.

Writing in 1995, Ford-Smith points to a dearth of research that links the economic reliance on tourism to the qualitative effects of the industry on the cultural relations it engenders, but notes that it is in the cultural sphere at everyday and symbolic levels that resistance to the colonizing narratives of tourism grows.[12] *Smile Orange* might be understood as visionary in terms of doing, as early as 1976 (and the play even earlier, in 1971), what Ford-Smith describes as the important and necessary work of confronting the ways in which "tourism reconfigures sexuality, racism and nationhood".[13] The film (and the play from which it is adapted, and which Ford-Smith comments on in her essay) explores the subtle and not so subtle ways that race relations in the hotel reflect the politics of subordination and resistance that characterized the plantation. In its exploration of this identity of place, *Smile Orange* challenges the essentially static representation of an idyllic, paradisiacal, rural landscape that resists notions of power and history. More specifically, it holds a mirror to the fantasy of privilege and entitlement constructed throughout Caribbean tourism advertising and reveals the seamy underside to the dream of the holiday on the tropical isle. *Smile Orange* characterizes tourism in Jamaica and, by consequence, the places that support it, as sites and spaces marked by contradiction and struggle.

Mervyn Morris's description of the play *Smile Orange* as "funny and deadly serious. . . . A devastating comment on attitudes the tourist industry harbours or can breed"[14] is equally applicable to the movie. Ringo's uncanny skill at turning adversity to his advantage provokes much laughter, but his methods also raise serious questions about collective values and the need for meaningful transformation in the post-independence society. The protagonists of *Smile Orange* and *The Harder They Come*, Ringo the trickster and Ivan the badman, suggest contrasting positions in terms of the postcolonial subject's consciousness of his own power and the still evolving movement from subversion to agency. (Although *Smile Orange* the film was released a few years after *The Harder They Come*, the play on which the movie was based actually preceded Henzell's film.) Certainly, Ivan's actions result in his death and the lasting benefits of this death may be debatable, but it is also clear that Ringo's trickery, while it may accrue some monetary gain for him, cannot stand as a model for the uplift and meaningful transformation of the community and, further, that such trickery is unequal to the task of fashioning a more equitable society.

Significantly, the opening sequence of the film introduces Ringo as a trickster but establishes his identity as such outside the environs of the hotel. At the beginning of the film, Ringo steals money from beneath his wife's pillow and then sneaks out of the house at daybreak wearing only his underwear and narrowly escaping her wrath and that of her two brothers. The sequence apprises the viewer of Ringo's problematic mobility, the nature of his domestic relationships and affirms his lack of patriarchal authority at home. (Later in the film, his wife and her brothers will repay Ringo's theft with a beating.) The long drive from the hills to the coast also signifies the hotel's removal from his domestic space; it is, in a sense, a world apart and one in which, as we will discover, Ringo assumes another, quite different identity. The emergence of this alternate identity begins on the drive to the hotel when Ringo first starts to assert himself as cocksman: he offers a young woman a ride then threatens to eject her from the car when she rebuffs his sexual advances. The woman eventually complies, and the scene shifts to the roadside bushes where she and Ringo undress and embrace, unknowingly, in a patch of cow-itch, a vine that, as its name suggests, produces an incessant itch in anyone unfortunate enough to come into contact with it.

Morris comments of the play that the roguish Ringo is constructed within the tradition of Anancy,[15] a trickster figure of African origin which features prominently in Jamaican folklore. The Anancy story constitutes a slippery kind of text that resists rigid moralizing. In her volume on Jamaican folklore, Daryl C. Dance states: "Anancy is generally a figure of admiration whose cunning and scheming nature reflects the indirection and subtleties necessary for survival and occasionally victory for the Black man in a racist society. Though most of the storytellers rejoice in his victories over the stronger animals with whom he is frequently in contest, they also recognize his immorality, his greed, his stupidity, his deceitfulness."[16]

Anancy represents not only a pragmatic approach to life but he also, as Dance suggests, speaks to the critical need on the part of a formerly enslaved and colonized people to employ a variety of strategies, including trickery, deception and role-play, as a means of surviving and contesting the remnants of a cruel and inhumane institutionalized system of oppression. Identification with Anancy on this basis permits a vicarious enjoyment and pleasure in his victories and triumphs to coexist with the recognition that his methods may be immoral, a conflict in values that is further mediated by ritual expression. In an interview with Dance, Jamaican folklorist, poet and performer Louise Bennett recounted the intense youthful pleasure of listening to Anancy stories, stating, "I knew Anancy as a child, and it was a *joy-y-y!* We loved to listen to the stories, we loved to hear about this little trickify man." But Bennett also points out that an important part of the storytelling was a ritual expression that renounced identification with Anancy's immoral choices: "At the end of each story, we had to say, 'Jack Mandora, me no choose none,' because Anancy sometimes did very wicked things in his stories, and we had to let Jack Mandora, the doorman at heaven's door, know that we were not in favour of Anancy's wicked ways."[17] As tricksters, therefore, both Anancy and Ringo represent ambiguity, the possibility of shifting meaning and multiple interpretive positions.

Ringo defines himself within this tradition of resistance by claiming his trickery as a politics of subversion: "Exploit the exploiter, God laugh," he states. In a subordinate position in a service-oriented industry that promotes itself as being in the business of satisfying the needs and desires of the consumer, Ringo must avoid open confrontation in his relations with both hotel guests and management. Subversion through trickery and role play is the preferred strategy for addressing any conflicts that arise. As Ford-Smith says of the play, "*Smile Orange* represents a stage of resistance in which survival is the central value. Resistance here is not confrontational. To confront overtly is to lose. The battle is constituted in an elaborate struggle between the official version of reality and the informal one."[18] Rhone also evokes the downside to the reliance on trickery as a strategy of resistance. Ringo's willing participation in transactional relationships with tourists leaves him vulnerable to being co-opted into a system of consumption that reaffirms his dependence and utility as a sexual commodity. And, more broadly, strategies of trickery and deception hardly constitute ideal values on which a community might define itself.

We are encouraged by Rhone's representation of the hotel as a modern-day expression of the ethos of the plantation to connect Ringo's strategic trickery to the historical use of similar methods by the enslaved. In the film, the tropical island as paradisiacal space is reimagined as a site where, quite explicitly, black labour is deployed to provide services and fulfil the desires of a white elite. Rhone certainly demystifies the white tourists – and they are all white, as they tended to be in the early 1970s – they are neither beautiful nor glamorous, and if they were rich they would probably be staying at a far better hotel. But as Jamaica Kincaid writes, no matter what the mundane reality of his life at home may be, the tourist is always perceived as being in a better position than the native of the place he visits.[19] Kincaid also makes a connection between the region's history of slavery and its investment in tourism, proposing that tourism's low-paying service jobs reduce individuals to "nobodies", mere units of production: "an institution that is often celebrated in Antigua is the Hotel Training School, a school that teaches Antiguans how to be good servants, how to be a good nobody, which is what a servant is. In Antigua, people cannot see a relationship between their obsession with slavery and emancipation and their celebration of the Hotel Training School (graduation ceremonies are broadcast on the radio and television)."[20]

The ethos of the plantation is further reflected in the playing out of hierarchies among staff, where racial divisions are also apparent. Like the overseer on the plantation, the appropriately named fair-skinned assistant manager, Mr Brown, is responsible for organizing labour – waiters, busboys, receptionist, lifeguards – in the interest of the (unseen) owner's profits and shows signs of assimilation into the dominant group in his speech (unlike the waiters, he does not speak Jamaican Creole) and in his choice of a white, non-Jamaican wife. The assistant manager occupies the intermediary position that Sartre envisioned as the role of the native elite in the colony that he describes as "hired kinglets, overlords and a bourgeoisie" branded with the principles of Western culture, "their mouths full with high-sounding praises, grand glutinous words that [stick] to the teeth".[21] Or, as Ringo more succinctly describes him, Brown is "a black jackass looking over a white wash fence".

As the appointed buffer between the black masses and the elite, Brown plays a critical role in maintaining the politics of the plantation at the hotel. His position as an *assistant* manager denotes his tenuous status: he is charged with day-to-day operations but has limited authority. His struggle to maintain the boundaries that demarcate power and subordination are continuously challenged and frustrated by the subversive efforts of the workers he supervises. The receptionist, Miss Brandon, constantly undermines Brown by steadfastly refusing to perform her job efficiently. More interested in gossiping about her relationship with one of the tourists and less concerned with monitoring the switchboard, Miss Brandon refuses to answer the calls Brown puts through, forcing him to walk to her desk whenever he wants to place a call or issue an instruction. On the home front, Brown's white wife would ordinarily be a marker of his association with the dominant group, but when it is revealed that she is sleeping with the gardener, further opportunities for subversion occur. Rhone's use of irony here is heavy but hilarious. Middle-class Brown's textbook anglicized enunciation contrasts sharply with the hotel workers' creole speech and is a sign of his higher social status. Mastery of the colonial language frequently bestows power in the former colony, but Brown's emasculation and lack of authority are repeatedly signalled through language. When he angrily instructs the gardener to "put more effort" into the job and work harder to please his wife, the gardener's cryptic response, "I'll work harder today to satisfy her", ironically redefines his work as tending the metaphorical garden of Mrs Brown's sexual delights.

Ringo effectively uses language as well as performance to subvert Brown's authority and disrupt the established patterns of dominance. He allows Brown to think he is asserting authority when in fact he is being played for a fool. In his interactions with Brown, Ringo is servile and fawning, lulling the assistant manager into a false sense of his own superiority and authority, and weaving a web of words that allows him to triumph over Brown, the less wily man. Summoned to Brown's office for a reprimand, Ringo skilfully extricates himself from the charge of refusing to serve the hotel's social director because she is black. He also uses the occasion to get ten dollars from Brown and secure the jobs of lifeguard and pool attendant for his two brothers-in-law who cannot swim. Ringo thus effects a shift in the politics of the master–servant relationship, performing a role in order to make Brown do *his* bidding.

Even as he affirms Ringo's actions as an expression of subversion within a politics of resistance, however, Rhone also proposes that such methods cannot support the transformation of society or function as the foundation on which to build the new nation. Ringo resists and disrupts an unjust and dehumanizing authority and, as trickster, he transforms the imposed identity of "a good nobody" into a subversive role that accrues some agency. But these methods are not fully liberating and, while strategic, only bring about a temporary shift in power. Ultimately, they function to consolidate and maintain the trickster in a subordinate position and reflect an inability to move beyond the limiting paradigm of the plantation's politics of exploitation. The trickster's forms of resistance lack the revolutionary potential to bring about lasting change, either in terms of dismantling the oppressive neocolonial system which continues to inform aspects of social interaction in the post-independence state, or by transforming the psyche of the citizens of the new nation. Rhone envisions the trickster figure as a product of the plantation who also participates in and trades on forms of exploitation as, for the most part, Ringo's subversion of authority involves depriving others of their money and ensuring material gain for himself. His insistence that the tourist (the white man) must pay for the historical oppression of the black man is quite literal: Ringo makes him pay in cash, which he promptly pockets. Indeed, Ringo's frequent referencing of a politics of subversion is to some degree merely a rhetorical device which only thinly conceals his greed, his exploitation of others and the extent to which these very methods help to confirm his own subordination. Ringo does not only steal from the rich; his first victim in the narrative is his wife, and his remarks at a crucial point in the film about black solidarity are undermined by his earlier refusal to serve the black social director in the dining room because, he explains, locals don't tip as well as tourists.

Like Brown, who has been groomed for his role as intermediary in the postcolonial society, Ringo as gigolo is occupying a role that, in a sense, has been predetermined by historical or external forces. In a long scene in which Ringo instructs Cyril in the coded language, gestures and conventions of the hotel sex trade, Rhone emphasizes the degree of role-play required by the gigolo. "Can I show you the sights, ma'am?" is both a statement of availability and a query as to the woman's desire for "de ting". Ringo insists that making the tourist pay for sex is one way of righting historical injustices and reversing exploitation, but his voluntary participation in such a scheme also means that he is complicit in defining his body as a commodity. Not surprisingly, then, his subversive intentions are somewhat muted by the latent sexual imagery that is used to describe the scramble for the tourist dollar. In a conversation with his friend and fellow waiter, Joe, Ringo states, "The white man love to see black people bow down, yu see man", but Joe replies, "Me touch ground as long as I can find a dollar bill down there." In contemporary Jamaica, "bowing" can refer to certain sexual acts, such as the male's performance of cunnilingus, that connote the loss of male dominance and a threatened masculinity within a hypermasculine and homophobic cultural context. "Bowing down" to pick up a dollar suggests a similar threatened masculinity and emasculation.

Ringo's claim to be a "c-man" (not a seaman or sailor, as Cyril at first mistakenly assumes, but a cocksman) appears to resist, at both the symbolic and literal level, the emasculation to which Joe appears to succumb. As cocksman, defined by the *Oxford English Dictionary* as "a man (reputedly) of exceptional virility or sexual ability", Ringo can proudly situate his pursuit of female tourists within the context of a culturally validated hypermasculine sexual performance. bell hooks sees such posturing as a strategy used by marginalized black men to accrue status in contexts where they do not have access to more traditional, economically defined expressions of patriarchal standing. She argues that the phenomenon represents a shift within advanced capitalism from an emphasis on patriarchal status to a "phallocentric model, where what the male does with his penis becomes a greater and certainly more accessible way to assert masculine status".[22] hooks states:

> With the emergence of fierce phallocentrism, a man was no longer a man because he provided care for his family, he was a man simply because he had a penis. Furthermore, this ability to use that penis in the arena of sexual conquest could bring him as much status as being a wage earner and provider. A sexually defined masculine ideal rooted in physical domination and sexual possession of women could be accessible to all men. Hence, even unemployed black men could gain status, could be seen as the embodiment of masculinity within a phallocentric framework.[23]

For black men in the former colony, such status is greatly enhanced when the object of sexual conquest is a white female. Polly Patullo points out that relationships between black gigolos and white female tourists may confuse race and class roles in the Caribbean in addition to providing black locals with access to hotel properties where they are not normally welcomed.[24] As an employee, Ringo already has access to the hotel, but his liaisons with the tourists do break a historical taboo, entrenched in plantation society, against sex between a black man and a white woman. This taboo was used to maintain the white male's ascendancy by controlling the sexuality of both white female and black male, but it also functioned as a means of legitimizing racial violence against black men. So that while the sexual politics of the gigolo–tourist relationship involves transgressing a prohibition imposed on female and black male bodies by white men, the transactional nature of this relationship erodes notions of power which might accrue to the gigolo. In the initiation scene, as Ringo instructs Cyril on the conventions of the sex trade, it is clear that the male occupies a subordinate position in relation to the white woman. In this scene, photographs and posters of women in various provocative poses are visible in the background, pinned on the wall as decoration to relieve the drabness of the hotel's working quarters. These images define women as objects of the male gaze and reflect Ringo and Cyril's similar diminished status as they construct themselves in a role traditionally reserved for women within patriarchy. As Ringo takes on the role of mentor and coaches Cyril, he shows the young man how to convey a certain deference when he approaches potential clients. This role-playing suggests that although they may gain access to the white female body, these sexual liaisons continue to reflect an unequal balance of power that rests on the women's superior economic status and the historical implications of authority embedded in her white skin.

Framed against the Caribbean's history of slavery and the attendant use of the black body as a sexual commodity, eroticism takes on new dimensions of meaning in the white tourist–black resident relationship, so that Ringo's claim to be a cocksman ironically threatens to locate him more securely in the ethos of the plantation. The phallocentric boast about his sexual prowess and the size of his penis can be understood as defining his masculinity in keeping with the colonial practice of distorting and fetishizing the black male body which, as Fanon states, has fixed the black man as a mythic symbol of sexual potency. Fanon suggests that at a phenomenological level: "For the majority of white men the Negro represents the sexual instinct (in its raw state). The Negro is the incarnation of a genital potency beyond all moralities and prohibitions. The women among the whites, by a genuine process of induction, invariably view the Negro as the keeper of the impalpable gate that opens into the realm of orgies, of bacchanals, of delirious sexual sensations."[25]

Within the framework of tourism and its important production site, the beach resort, black sexuality retains its notions of pleasure and abandon but loses much of its threat of violence and danger, which has also been attached to the construct of black male sexuality in racist and colonial discourses. The holiday resort provides a (relatively) safe, controlled space in which the white female can pay to indulge in forbidden sexual fantasies and fulfil taboo desires without fear. It provides her with the opportunity to explore and personally experience, within a protected environment, the myth of black virility. Thus the black male is incorporated into the hotel's holiday/travel package, allowing the tourist, as Illouz points out, to experience herself "within a safe, prefabricated image that the tourist industry has implicitly labelled 'adventure'",[26] without the attendant risks and discomforts of real adventure.

In order to preserve the notion of Ringo as a trickster who frequently manages to gain the upper hand and maintain the ambiguity of this performance, Rhone never explicitly shows Ringo in the role of commoditized sexual object of the white female gaze. In a nightclub scene in the film, it is the black female body which is signalled as available both as commodity and exotic spectacle. The scene is introduced with a close-up of the scantily covered buttocks of a black woman on the stage in the nightclub, moving rhythmically to the diegetic music; later shots repeat this erotic framing. From the dancers, the camera cuts to the audience in the nightclub: a white man and woman are most prominent in this shot and appear to be engrossed in the dancers' performance. The woman, watching the performance and smiling, clutches the man's arm as if she has noticed and is commenting on a particularly interesting feature of the dance. This coordination of images of the dancers and spectators in the nightclub defines the dance as an exotic performance that excites and arrests the gaze of the tourists through its strangeness and eroticism. The noticeable perspiration on the dancers' bodies, however, evokes contrasting associations. While the sweat increases the reflection of light and allows a sensuous contouring of the dark bodies within the dimly lit nightclub, emphasizing the erotic appeal of the dance, it also connotes the performance of labour and evokes the memory of the sweating bodies that worked the plantations' cane fields (as does Ivan's sweating body in the scene in *The Harder They Come* when he performs the title song). Thus, we are reminded that for the unskilled masses in the Caribbean, particularly those in rural areas, the options for employment are often limited to choosing physically strenuous work in the agricultural sector or the sometimes ethically dubious work available in the tourism industry.

One of the ways *Smile Orange* resists the seductive image of the Caribbean as paradise is by undermining the region's associations with romance. In one sequence, Rhone uses a montage technique to juxtapose three couples from the hotel, all of whom fall short of the romantic ideal: Cyril and Gladys, an American tourist, two Americans on their honeymoon, and Miss Brandon and her American lover. Cyril and Gladys's lovemaking on the beach might strike the viewer as a parody of one of Hollywood's most iconic love scenes – the Burt Lancaster and Deborah Kerr embrace in the surf in *From Here to Eternity*.[27] Instead of the romantic spectacle of the two toned bodies of the classic film, *Smile Orange* shows the naked, somewhat portly, middle-aged Miss Gladys and Cyril's rather clumsy attempts to straddle her. Rhone adds a further comic touch. After intercourse, Gladys runs into the sea and calls Cyril to join her, but he shouts from the beach, his lisp apparent, "Please, Miss Gladys, I can't thwim."

The two honeymooning tourists are equally laughable. The man insists on taking full advantage of a payment plan that allows him multiple choices on the menu, and, having gorged himself at dinner, he is rewarded with a case of acute indigestion that prevents him from living up to the expectations of a honeymoon night. The scene plays on notions of abundance and excess that both the tourism industry and colonial discourses have associated with the region and it evokes, at both the metaphorical and literal level, a sense of the tourist's consumption of the Caribbean. As the man's loud belching alternates with Miss Gladys's shouts and moans of pleasure, the film deflates the iconic setting of the tropical beach, constructing it as a site for farce and parody rather than romance.

Rhone's treatment of the third couple in this montage, Miss Brandon and the American, is far less playful. The two are shown semi-clothed in one of the hotel rooms, passing a ping pong ball from mouth to mouth. The mood changes suddenly when the man suggests, "Want to try that ping pong thing again in a different way?" The viewer is left to surmise exactly what the man means by "a different way"; Miss Brandon must wonder too, judging from the look on her face when he makes the suggestion and again when he throws the ping pong ball and hits her on the bottom. Miss Brandon, unlike Ringo, is unable to maintain even an illusion of control in this tourist–resident relationship. The ring the American gives her turns out to be a fake of no value and, instead of the promised plane ticket "to foreign", he leaves the hotel suddenly without informing her of his departure. The final image of Miss Brandon shows her sitting head down, looking dejected, as Mr Brown repeatedly asks, "What's wrong, Miss Brandon?"

Miss Brandon's activities affirm the equal involvement of the black female in the sexual exchange that defines the tourist experience at the Mocho Beach Hotel, but the outcome of the narrative suggests a failure on her part to skilfully negotiate the terrain of the modern-day hotel/plantation and successfully operate in the role of trickster. In contrast, Ringo is so crafty that his ability to turn misfortune into advantage is positioned as the climax of the film. This culminating incident is initiated when Ringo wins a considerable amount of money in a crab race by cheating. An American tourist loses badly, however, and after spending the night seeking solace in a bottle, he is so drunk the following morning that he falls into the swimming pool. The two life guards (Ringo's in-laws who got the job on his recommendation) cannot swim so they run off, leaving him floundering in the pool. Ringo arrives on the scene, and in the confusion, he too accidentally falls into the water. Also unable to swim, he is rescued by a female tourist, but it is too late for the other man, who drowns. Faced with the possibility of being held responsible for the man's death – having fixed the crab races and recommended his water-challenged in-laws for the lifeguard jobs – Ringo seizes on the mistaken perception that he had deliberately jumped into the pool, concocts a story that he risked his life in an attempt to save the drowning man and declares himself a hero. He tells Cyril: "Spread it around the hotel that Ringo risk his life to save the tourist. By this evening, radio. By tomorrow morning, newspaper: Ringo is hero. Then after that is promotion, eh sweet boy? When I get promote, I promote you too."

Ringo's story represents a fantastic manipulation and obscuring of the truth, both in terms of the actual occurrence of events as well as the larger realization that the dishonesty and deception that Ringo embodies is systemic in the hotel and can accrue serious and tragic consequences. Ringo leads the way in concocting this fantastic untruth, but his deception cannot succeed without the cooperation of others. Cyril and Joe are initially reluctant to participate in this final ruse, but when they realize that they can profit from the deception, they join in. Ringo also suggests that others who might challenge his story will, because of self-interest, readily accept the fiction of his heroism. The assistant manager, grateful for a story of bravery that will eclipse the more sobering and profit-plunging news of a drowning at his hotel, as well as his own responsibility in the affair ("Is him give the boys the jobs, you know", states Ringo), happily accepts Cyril's account of events and even rewards Ringo with a gift of cash. Further, as Ringo points out, the media will pick up the story, probably also happy for a "positive" headline rather than one that will have a negative impact on the all-important tourist industry. As Ringo declares, "When you get right down to it, everybody protecting his own thing. If is not money, is power."

The complicity of others in this deception indicates Rhone's extension of his critique of the trickster's values to the larger community. As suggested through the symbolism of the orange, which comes to represent the characters' involvement in the ethos of the hotel/plantation, Ringo's values and methods appear to be widely shared. Thus, Rhone defines the postcolonial moment as one in which the pressing demands of economic survival in the developing nation support the retention of the politics of the plantation and maintain a form of psychological bondage. Self-interest and the elevation of monetary and material gain above all else are some of the more insidious features of this system, while the declaration of a thief and liar as hero signals the moral and spiritual decay of the community. As in those folk stories when Anancy becomes the victim of his own trickery, a similar boomerang effect is at play in *Smile Orange*. Ringo gains materially from his deception but there is a greater loss at a less concrete level. Indeed, as the assistant manager rudely interrupts Ringo, while he is urinating, to give him his cash reward, one is struck by the sordidness of the transaction and also by the fact that Ringo continues to be defined as subordinate. The trickster may succeed in temporarily shifting the scales of power, but he is unable to bring about real and lasting change.

As the narrative draws to a close, a song paying homage to Ringo that was introduced at the beginning of the film is heard as Ringo receives the money and declares himself a hero. It also plays over a sequence that confirms Cyril's entry into the role of "c-man" and the ethos of the hotel/plantation. Featuring a sultry female voice, the song creates a cyclical movement as it links the end of the film with its beginning and suggests the perpetuation and continuation of the values that Ringo embodies:

> Ringo Smith is his name and survival is his game.
> Ringo, living by his wits,
> Ringo, hustler he never quits.
> Twisting, turning.... Cha! That man.
> He's slick.

On its initial playing, the song accompanies the early scene in which Ringo and the young woman who accepted a ride in his car embraced in the bushes only to find themselves in a patch of cow-itch. In that scene, two boys unseen by Ringo watch and laugh at his predicament, providing an irreverent contrast to the veneration suggested by the lyrics and tone of the song. Although the boys laugh at and mock Ringo, as voyeurs they are also engaged in an act of trickery as they spy on the two adults. Rhone seems to propose the two boys' voyeurism as a metaphor for the gaze of the spectator. Throughout the film, he draws the viewer into the narrative by evoking the celebratory laughter that expresses admiration and delight at the trickster's deception, but at various points, the narrative encourages mockery of Ringo, for example, as early as the cow-itch scene, and also when Ringo is finally caught and beaten by his in-laws for stealing his wife's money. Like the two boys, the spectator watches Ringo and laughs with him and at him, implicated in his actions because we applaud and enjoy his triumphant trickery and prevented from lapsing into the unrelieved adulation reflected in the song. Rhone leaves the viewer trapped in an Anancy web of discomfort and amusement, complicity and critique. Rhone intends this dilemma, but the folk tradition from which he draws offers resolution: the option to accept and live with ambiguity and to recognize it as part of the human condition: "Jack Mandora, me no choose none!"

4
REGGAE AND *ROCKERS*
Privileging the Local, Disrupting Paradigms of the External Gaze

AT FIRST GLANCE, THE INCLUSION OF *ROCKERS* (1978) in this discussion of Jamaican film might appear to be something of an anomaly. Written and directed by Greek national, Theodorus Bafaloukos, produced by an American, Patrick Hulsey, and shot by a largely non-Jamaican crew, one might question defining this film as Jamaican and wonder how this seeming "gaze[s] from the outside"[1] could possibly claim to "show us as we are". And yet, *Rockers* has become firmly entrenched in the body of work popularly defined and accepted as Jamaican film. The fact that the cast of the film reads like a veritable who's who of a less well-known group of reggae singers and musicians (some now deceased), who performed in the 1970s and who play themselves, certainly contributes to the film's "Jamaicanness", for *Rockers* functions, to some extent, as a historical artefact that records and preserves a pivotal moment in the development of Jamaican music. Beyond the composition of the cast, there is also something undeniably compelling in *Rockers*' gently humorous representation of inner-city life, while its focus on the Rastafari and its refusal to define the Kingston ghetto in terms of dysfunction lends a welcome diversity and complexity to the cinematic portrayal of place and identity in Jamaica. Indeed, perhaps more than any other film discussed in this volume, *Rockers* underscores the inadequacy of the origins of the director as a category for defining film and evokes the complex interplay of the local and the global.

Rockers is the story of an urban dwelling Rastafarian musician, Leroy, popularly known as Horsemouth (Leroy Wallace), who purchases a motorcycle to start up a record distribution business. The motorcycle is soon stolen by a criminal network headed by Marshall, a wealthy, black uptown businessman, and his second in command, Honeyball. Horsemouth's attempt to repossess the motorcycle is successful, but he is subsequently subjected to a vicious beating. Refusing to submit to this injustice, he organizes Rastafarian men in the community to launch a raid on Marshall and Honeyball's uptown homes, as well as the warehouse where they keep stolen goods. After absconding with practically every movable item they can lay their hands on, Horsemouth and friends, Robin Hood–style, abandon the bounty in various locations so that it can be claimed by the poor.

In his essay "'Jah No Dead': Modes of Resistance in *Rockers* and *Countryman*", Ed Guerrero addresses an underlying set of concerns that are relevant to my discussion of *Rockers*. Guerrero concludes his commentary on the two films by explicitly identifying the challenge that inevitably confronts the filmmaker working out of a location variously described as Third World, emergent, developing, peripheral or minoritarian, qualifications which may all be read, in this context, to construe a critical lack of national funding for film production, which creates a need for films to "cross over" into external markets in order to amortize production costs. Guerrero frames the dilemma in this way: "How does one build a viable cinema and gain mass media distribution for films made by repressed collectivities while deploying the most technology-dependent and capital-intensive of all mediums, usually in the most underdeveloped of locales and circumstances, without being totally coopted into the needs and purposes of dominant cultural values, markets, and media systems"?[2]

This multifaceted tension between the demands of capital, the priorities of the local audience and the requirements of the global marketplace resonates in many of the films discussed in this book. Keith Warner's somewhat reluctant acknowledgement of *Rockers'* achievements as well as Guerrero's more sympathetic reading suggest ways in which such tensions have been negotiated in this film. Warner describes *Rockers* as crude, stating that at times "the camera work resembles amateur home video shoots" while "much of the acting is lost in an unscripted babel of Rastaspeak that is not always fully captured by the subtitles".[3] He proposes, however, that it is precisely the unsophisticated look of the film that creates the impression of capturing "the essence of the true Rastafarian lifestyle, anchored as it is in the desire for a pre-technology simplicity".[4] Warner states that the "point of view of the entire film is Rastafarian, with the result that there is an anti-establishment tone",[5] but counters this with the somewhat paradoxical assertion that "one cannot escape the impression that what motivated its production was an attempt to capitalise on the emerging popularity of reggae on the international scene".[6] Unconcerned with what Warner sees as *Rockers*' crudeness, Guerrero's essay reveals a less ambivalent view of the film's negotiation of the tendency of market forces to impact aesthetic concerns and local cultural values. Guerrero sees *Rockers* (as well as *Countryman*,[7] which he also addresses in his comparative essay) as the artful mediation of a collection of binaries: the primitive or savage and civilization; development and underdevelopment; the metropolitan centre and the non-industrial periphery, which, he suggests, has contributed to the film's popular circulation in Western markets. He notes further, that such "issues take on deeper, more complex meaning when one interrogates these films' arguments, representational strategies, the narrative viewpoints of their heroes, and as well, the emancipatory impulse of the Jamaican audience to whom these texts also speak".[8] Arguing that *Rockers* and *Countryman* succeed as resistance texts, Guerrero asserts: "Both films offer counter-cultural expressions to what under-class Jamaicans in general and more specifically Rastafarians would perceive as a corrupt, oppressive, post-colonial social order held in place by the economic and cultural domination of the industrial societies that have figured so heavily in the island's history."[9] Like Warner, however, Guerrero qualifies *Rockers*' oppositional value, arguing that certain aspects of the film's resistance to dominant ideology are inadvertent. He states: "Both *Countryman* and *Rockers*, in *subtle and often unintentional, subtextual ways*, challenge the consumer audience's expectations of an exotic cinematic vacation, say, as so slickly rendered in the dominant cinema productions *The Mighty Quinn* (1989) or *Club Paradise* (1986)."[10]

Guerrero's assertion of resistance to dominant values in these texts is tied to the context of reception, but his reference to the "Jamaican audience to whom these texts also speak" suggests a privileging of the metropolitan perspective and a secondary consideration of the response of Jamaicans. In my discussion of *Rockers*, which privileges how the film might be understood by local viewers, I argue for a more highly developed and deliberate oppositionality. I propose that although the film was conceptualized by non-Jamaicans with obvious intentions of crossing over into overseas markets, it resists uncomplicated categorization as "a gaze from the outside". Indeed, Rockers privileges the local, both in its representation of the Jamaican urban space and the people who live there – specifically the Rastafari – as well as in its positioning of the spectator to foster identification rather than distance. The film's use of Jamaican Creole and dread talk (what Warner refers to as a "babel of Rastaspeak"[11]) is a key indication of its assumption of and appeal to a local spectator. Further, the methods used by the director to ensure the dominance of the vernacular speak to an attempt by a non-Caribbean filmmaker to use approaches to filmmaking that offer alternatives to the paradigms established by the exoticizing gaze that characterizes mainstream cinematic representations of the region. Undoubtedly, while much of the film's international appeal and commercial viability rest on its use of reggae, the narrative resists cultural appropriation by foregrounding the music's origins in Jamaica and asserting its function as a form of cultural resistance. In addition, the film uses self-reflexivity to draw attention to the process of incorporating reggae into the cinematic text and to the economic importance of the music, thus alerting the spectator to the increasing potential for commodification of this popular cultural form. The film combines this self-reflexivity, including instances of direct address to the camera, with realism, indicating a fusion of styles and aesthetics that represents an attempt to craft alternative ways of representing Jamaica.

One of the central planks of Rockers' oppositionality and its engagement with place from a Jamaican perspective is its resolute focus on the Rastafari. While a number of Jamaican films include Rastafarian characters, they tend to be either marginal to the narrative or problematic and seriously flawed. Such examples include the philosophical but fatalistic characters Pedro in *The Harder They Come* and Jahman in *Countryman*, as well as the violently patriarchal Luke in *Children of Babylon*. In some later films, *Third World Cop* (1999), *Shottas* (2002) and *Rude Boy* (2003), dreadlocks would become associated with gangsterism and urban violence. Rockers' treatment of this important and prominent group, however, recalls Manthia Diawara's discussion of the relationship between power and mise en scène in which he states: "Spatial narration in classical cinema makes sense through a hierarchical disposition of objects on the screen. Thus space is related to power and powerlessness, in so far as those who occupy the center of the screen are usually more powerful than those situated in the background or completely absent from the screen."[12]

Diawara's assertion of a hierarchy operating within mise en scène is made in reference to black independent filmmakers who have responded to distorted representations of black people and their absence from Hollywood films by seeking to "put on the screen Black lives and concerns that derive from the complexity of Black communities" and which "provide alternative ways of knowing Black people that differ from the fixed stereotypes of Blacks in Hollywood".[13] I am not attempting here to equate the institutionalized racism that exists in America with the kind of discrimination that Rastafarians have experienced in Jamaica. I do want to suggest, however, that in some ways, *Rockers* performs for the Rastafari community a function similar to what Diawara suggests black independent film has provided for African Americans in the sense that, in *Rockers*, the Rastafari are rendered fully visible and positioned at the centre of the screen and narrative so that they command the attention of the spectator.

Once despised and ridiculed for their appearance and beliefs, over time Rastafarians have gained increasing respect and acceptance in Jamaica, and indeed around the world. Rex Nettleford, one of the authors of a major study conducted on the Rastafarians in 1960,[14] describes a dynamic relationship between the Rastafari and the supporters of the status quo in Jamaica. He states that while members of the movement have often been treated as outcasts, elements of the group's belief system have found increasing acceptance in the wider society. He points out that around the time of the publication of the 1960 report, the Rastafari were widely regarded as "stupid, irrational and unlawful", "criminal, lazy, irrationally emotional, hopelessly mad and dangerously violent".[15] By the late 1960s, however, Nettleford notes that there was a more widespread embrace of Rastafarian attitudes, ideals and even practices, such as the wearing of locks, the smoking of ganja, the commitment to Africa and a yearning for knowledge of the African past. Writing in 1970, Nettleford attributed the continued survival of the Rastafarian movement to the persistent relevance of their dissatisfactions with Jamaican society to issues that continued to concern other Jamaicans. He states: "The widening gap between rich and poor and the attendant deepening of class differences, the failure of political leaders to find effective answers in the wake of independence, the disinheritance following on increasing foreign ownership of key resources, all served to give the Rastafarian 'rumblings' a rationality and a continued centrality to the quest for identity and for economic security among the black majority."[16]

The Rastafari have not only sustained their significance within Jamaica, the movement has grown into a worldwide phenomenon. Like Nettleford, Nathaniel Samuel Murrell identifies a trend of increasing acceptance and points out that the movement has become "recognized not only as one of the most popular Afro Caribbean religions of the late twentieth century ... but also as one of the leading cultural trends of the world".[17] As a cultural movement, the global popularity of Rastafari has been propelled by the tendency of youth to identify with its ethos and philosophies of resistance and, importantly, by reggae music. Nettleford describes the Rastafari, therefore, "as visionaries bearing the message of liberation and redemption through music";[18] Murrell concurs, identifying reggae as the most powerful force behind the international spread and popularity of Rasta culture.[19]

Rockers is a provocative expression of this phenomenon, the global spread of Rastafari and reggae, and arguably more than any other Jamaican film, *Rockers* and its mode of production evoke the interplay of the local with the global. Director Bafaloukos and his production crew's journey to Jamaica to make *Rockers* in the late 1970s was generated, in part, by the commercialization of reggae and its export, along with Rastafari, beyond Jamaica's shores. Through its international distribution and enduring popularity, *Rockers* has, in turn, helped maintain the global dissemination of reggae and Rastafari,[20] but the film's alignment with a local point of view and sensibility is a critical element in its acceptance as a Jamaican film (rather than a foreign-made film about Jamaica) which has in turn contributed to its popularity and acceptance as an authentic representation of Jamaica and the Rastafari. The images of the Rastafari and inner-city Kingston that dominate the film will be unfamiliar and perhaps even "strange" to some spectators, but within the narrative, Rastafari is not constructed as exotic: here, the presence of the Rastafari in the urban space is unremarkable. Many of the major characters are Rastafari, as well as most of the minor characters and extras, and although in the film members of the faith encounter prejudice and discrimination, within ghetto spaces they are accepted and integrated members of the community. There is very little sense in the film of what Jane Bryce, in her comparative critique of two adaptations of *Wide Sargasso Sea*, describes as a foreign or distanced point of view which positions the spectator as if "engaged in a species of cultural tourism". Rather, there is the sense in *Rockers* that a local audience is assumed, one which is "familiar with the terrain, watching an aspect of its cultural history brought to 'life' on the screen".[21]

Indeed, the paradigmatic identification with the outsider that Guerrero suggests is inscribed in the opening scenes of *Countryman* (1982), is absent in *Rockers*.[22] While in *Countryman*, the arrival of two Americans on the island initiates a chain of events that form the plot of the film, in *Rockers*, non-Jamaicans appear only very briefly in one scene. In fact, *Countryman*, a film directed by a Jamaican which also focuses on the Rastafari, dissuades us from the prejudice that cultural perspectives are necessarily determined by the national origins of the filmmaker. Describing *Countryman* as an adventure fantasy, Gilroy states that it is

> a tale of Obeah and adventure . . . based on a simple inversion of the Robinson Crusoe myth. "Friday", recast in the form of a rasta hermit-fisherman endowed with magical powers that originated in his total harmony with the natural world, saves and protects two young white Americans who fall into his Eden as a result of a plane crash. They are unwittingly involved in the drug business but with his help are reunited with their families and sent back to the US once the villains, the military wing of Michael Manley's socialist government, have been put in their place.[23]

Gilroy's more substantive point has to do with the appropriation of black cultural practices, specifically music, for use in capitalist ventures that elide the origins of these practices. He points out that "the gradual involvement of large corporations with a broad base in the leisure industries in the selling of reggae stimulated important changes reflecting a conscious attempt to separate the product from its roots in black life". Gilroy implicates Island Records in this process, asserting that the company became involved in film production (*Countryman* and *The Harder They Come*) as part of a strategy to create markets for reggae outside of Jamaica.²⁴

While Bafaloukos's use of reggae in *Rockers* is implicated in the film's commercial viability, it speaks to a rather different orientation and approach than that which Gilroy ascribes to Island Records. Certainly, there are occasional moments in the film where, as Warner points out, the action seems set up to lead to a performance,²⁵ but there is only one instance where this is blatant or jarring. This is Gregory Isaacs's performance of the song "Slave Master", which seems to be an insertion of actuality footage. In contrast to this singular awkward moment, are numerous instances where music and musical performance, as organic elements of the film text, are used to develop thematic concerns, express local cultural values, create social commentary and critique dominant perspectives. Bafaloukos resists the colonizing impulse of appropriation by actively locating the production of reggae in Jamaica: by affirming its origins in the inner city and its connections with another source, the Rastafari. The film's reflexivity also comes into play here, for there are numerous references to the creation, performance, production, distribution and consumption of the music which constantly remind us that music encompasses the spiritual, cultural *and* commercial. Notably, this reflexivity does not extend to signifying the overseas origins of the director and production crew; it does function, however, to draw the spectator's attention to the process of filmmaking and its incorporation of reggae into the cinematic text.

Bafaloukos's first (and only feature) film, *Rockers* emerged from his fascination with reggae and a desire to "do something" on Jamaica.²⁶ In the special twenty-fifth anniversary DVD reissue of *Rockers*, Bafaloukos states in an interview: "'Fan' is maybe really not enough to express how I felt when I became aware of the music. It was really something that really spoke directly to me. . . . I saw right away that something was going on [in Jamaica], [it] was not just your regular music scene, [it was] something original. . . . it was dread. . . . Its main attraction for me . . . is it is authentic, it is for real." Bafaloukos ventures that it is the film's use of reggae which accounts for its continuing popularity and confesses that "if there was anything I did, I became a conduit at the right time in putting [reggae] on film."²⁷ But Bafaloukos's role as "conduit" may be extended beyond reggae to the narrative focus of the film itself: the life of the urban poor in Jamaica and the Rastafari. *Rockers* might be said to reference the neorealist tradition, therefore, not only in its use of the quest motif with the stolen mode of transportation as the desired object, as occurs in Vittorio DeSica's classic film *Bicycle Thieves*,[28] but also in its attempt to use the cinematic medium to make visible the experiences of the "ordinary man". Indeed, through a combination of techniques, the film gives the impression of projecting onto the screen everyday life as it was lived by ordinary people. The use of unembellished locations, the handheld camera, long takes and the leisurely pace of editing with seemingly reluctant cuts, all work to create the impression that the filmmaker has captured a scene that he has simply wandered upon, rather than a carefully constructed cinematic moment.

While a close look at the film easily reveals the craft and artistry involved in the construction of its images, the feeling of spontaneity and improvisation is not entirely based on illusion. It results, in part, from what might be referred to as a process of translation that Bafaloukos used to film dialogue. In contrast to *The Harder They Come*, in which dialogue tends to be brief and succinct, *Rockers* is marked by the use of extended, loosely evolving dialogue that, importantly, is delivered almost entirely in Jamaican Creole and dread talk, the latter being a form of speech that Velma Pollard describes as a lexical expansion of Jamaica Creole.[29] The use of the vernacular as the dominant mode of expression suggests that Bafaloukos was not intent on addressing only the needs and desires of the overseas market, the crossover audience. Dread talk also infuses the film with the oppositional qualities of a form of speech which is said to reflect "resistance to perceived oppression (both historical colonial prejudice and current economic disenfranchisement) and the sense of the overwhelming potential spiritual redemption that Rastas can achieve".[30] Bafaloukos asserts that the film was fully scripted and the shooting schedule carefully organized and adhered to, necessarily so because of production and budget demands. Without that structure, he states, "We couldn't make a movie at all, [we] would have a lot of footage, but no movie." In order to maintain Jamaican Creole and dread talk as the mode of expression, Bafaloukos used a process of translation. Prior to shooting, he used the Standard English script and "talked the scene through" with the actors involved, but then had them translate the dialogue and perform the scene in Jamaican Creole and dread talk when the cameras started to roll.[31]

I want to suggest that Bafaloukos's reliance on the Jamaican cast to "translate" the dialogue opened up spaces of creativity and agency in the film for the actors, who for the most part were not professionals but musicians and singers playing themselves. The dialogue, often meandering and repetitive, sometimes open-ended, speaks to a degree of improvisation, while the body language – the gestures and postures that accompany the dialogue – has a naturalness and authenticity that suggest such movement was not initiated through the instruction of the director, but rather, evolved naturally. It is not a great leap, then, to conclude that what took place was translation in its most creative sense: a process of interpretation, in which the musician/actors not only *translated* the script into Jamaican Creole and dread talk, but also used the process to insert their own ideas into the narrative within the framework of the existing script.

Bafaloukos's method of working with the Jamaican cast erodes the idea of the director as auteur and the film as the expression of his or her artistic vision. *Rockers* asserts instead a kind of communal or collective vision and sensibility for the film in which space is created for the input of the Jamaican participants. Unlike what occurred with the *Lieutenant Daring* controversy, the director did not simply arrive from abroad and impose his preconceived fantasy on the island. It may have been Bafaloukos's lack of experience as a filmmaker, his professed love for the music and culture as well as his awareness of his status as outsider that informed what appears to be a willingness on his part to be, as he calls it, a conduit, and allow the subjects of the film to not only speak for themselves in their own language, but also, in a sense, to *be* themselves. The musician/actors' own sense of agency is implicated here as well. Bafaloukos reported clashes with Leroy Wallace who plays the lead character, Horsemouth, while Kiddus I, a singer who performs in the film, recalls that the Jamaican cast consisted of "strong-willed men" who could not be easily controlled.[32]

Bafaloukos'collaborative approach to directing is underscored by Bev Braune's account of an episode that occurred during the filming of *The Harder They Come* which, by contrast, indicates Perry Henzell's far more exacting expectations of actors' performances:

Regarded as the most important line in the film: "Every game I play I lose", said by Elsa (Janet Bartley), had thirty-six takes. In his aim to "get the line out" of the performer, Henzell admitted that he drove her until she "broke down and cried in frustration, after which she was left energyless", so that in the thirty-sixth take the words "Every game I play I lose" were said without the personality of the performer shadowing them.[33]

In contrast, Bafaloukos seems to allow the actor to actively participate in deciding how to style the performance. When singer Gregory Isaacs, a reggae crooner known as "The Cool Ruler", is consistently cool, blasé and stylish in the film, whether he is walking down the street, opening a safe in the middle of a heist, or telling off tourists when they refuse to pay for a service rendered, the Jamaican spectator understands that Isaacs is performing himself or, more precisely, a version of himself: a public persona that holds specific meaning for the Jamaican audience. Bafaloukos's use of well-known musicians and singers to play themselves is important in this regard: it certainly draws attention to the reliance on the popularity of reggae to boost the film's appeal, but it also intensifies the idea of the actors' creative input in the production. This sense of the musician/actor's identity informing the role or character, rather than the narrative defining a character that must then be performed as directed (as occurred, for example, in *The Harder They Come*), is heightened by the film's inclusion of a number of performances of reggae music. These musical performances, like the "translated" dialogue, can also be considered as creating spaces within the narrative that function as sites of authority and autonomy for the Jamaican musician/actors and thus constitute a significant element in the film's ability to project a Jamaican sensibility and perspective.

The creative input that the Jamaican cast brings to the film encompasses encoding their performance with the style, nuance and meaning appropriate to the culture. In the scene where Horsemouth purchases the motorcycle from his friend, Jah Tooth (Gregory Isaacs), the musician/actors' creative input is apparent in their performance of cultural conventions and practices. When told the cost of the motorbike, Horsemouth protests loudly and bitterly that he lacks the necessary funds. The ensuing argument between Horsemouth, Jah Tooth and bystanders (including Horsemouth's good friend Dirty Harry) is understood by all involved as a form of role-play: a kind of ritual exercise of protest and counter-protest as part of the negotiation that must accompany activities of trade. Loud voices and poses of antagonism notwithstanding, there is no real hostility between the friends. The body language of the men speaks to their understanding of the cultural codes which govern this exchange, rather than reflect the instructions of the director. Eventually, Horsemouth buys the motorcycle for $200 less than the original price and rides off, but not before Dirty Harry (Richard Hall), ignoring Horsemouth's further ritual protests, proclaims himself a "key bredrin", and jumps on the back of the bike.

Bafaloukos's visual style facilitates the musician/actors' agency and improvisation, for the camera appears to simply allow this tableau to play itself out, framing the argument first in a medium shot and then a long shot. There are no close-ups or shot/reverse angle shots that would locate the sequence within a classic narrative style and which would impose emphasis on one or another speaker or force the spectator to look at faces in isolation. That is, rather than positioning the spectator in relation to the exchange in accordance with mainstream editing practices, the viewer is constructed as if he were an actual bystander, a kind of fly on the wall who simply watches the argument develop.

A similar approach is employed in the opening sequence which announces a distinctive visual style and clearly establishes Bafaloukos's intention to privilege the local. The film opens with a long shot, maintained for the duration of the scene, that shows a group of Rastafarians in a thatched shelter, presumably in a rural location, singing and playing the drums and a guitar, smoking and passing around a chillum pipe. As an establishing shot, the image positions the spectator not so much within a physical landscape and location, for the environment beyond the thatched shelter is not visible in the tightly framed shot, but within a space that is culturally defined. A drummer in the foreground announces, "Jah, Rastafari!" and a minute or so later, a Rastaman with long, heavily matted locks and beard detaches himself from the group and moves towards the camera, sits directly in front of it and welcomes the spectator in dread talk, proclaiming, "Greetings and love to one and all. In I presence I preme coverage of I heights". The speech performs the conventional narrative function of framing and introducing the action, but the direct address disrupts the illusion of realism, and in effect proclaims the intention of the filmmaker to construct a fictional narrative. In this initial scene, the film declares its location outside mainstream cinema through both the subject in the frame, which would have been unfamiliar to many outside Jamaica, and in its editing practices. The static long shot (just over three minutes in duration) in which the men are framed, and the Rastaman's muffled delivery which is barely intelligible, again suggest an alternative aesthetic to classical narrative conventions. The language of the greeting is as important as its message. The use of dread talk anticipates its dominance throughout the narrative, as well as the local perspective the film will adopt, while the message of love and cooperation asserts the importance of these values for the Rastafari community and offers the story that is to follow within the spirit of this moral framework.

Music provides a bridge between the prologue or opening scene, and the scene that follows which thrusts Horsemouth out of the anonymity of the communal "I and I" of the Rastafarian group and identifies him as protagonist and a well-known and respected member of the urban community. The melody performed in the prologue continues with only a slight break, which facilitates a change from drums to brass instruments and coincides with a cut which moves the location to Kingston, where we see Horsemouth walking through an inner-city community or yard. This music is revealed as diegetic when, in a single take almost three minutes long, the camera follows Horsemouth as he walks through the neighbourhood and comes upon the source of the music: Dirty Harry and three others playing saxophones and horn in a corner of the yard. At the outset, therefore, the film identifies two sites for the production of reggae – the Rastafari faith and the inner-city yard – and also connotes the music's multiple functions. The Rastafarians' performance is powerfully spiritual: the song, with its Amharic title ("Satta Amassagana"), its wistful quality and proclaimed longing for "a land far, far away", as well as the drumming, evokes the historical, emotional and cultural connections with Africa, and, in particular, the Rastafari's desire for repatriation to the Ethiopian homeland. While the urban scene presents music as part of the fabric of daily life in the yard, it also points to its economic importance within the urban space, for the group of performers are studio musicians practising for a gig, and a conversation soon develops about recent earnings from this work.

The opening sequence is also notable for its fusion of self-reflexivity and realism. Bafaloukos switches from the direct address to the camera in the prologue to a style associated with cinéma-vérité in the urban scene. In the latter, the long take, the mobile camera that gives the impression of casually following Horsemouth and capturing his greetings to friends, informally offered and returned, all combine to suggest the natural occurrence of events. This illusion of realism masks the careful planning that must have gone into the shooting of the scene, however. In the short distance that Horsemouth covers as he walks through the community, the spectator is treated to a comparatively busy visual environment that includes a football game, the exterior of several dwellings, a conversation between Horsemouth and a friend (Trusty), the neighbourhood men standing around, clotheslines strung with colourful garments, and Horsemouth's eventual arrival in the circle of musicians. When Horsemouth stops to talk to Trusty, movement in the frame is maintained by the men playing football, artfully framed in the space between Horsemouth's body and the wall of Trusty's house.

Like many Jamaican films, *Rockers* is concerned with issues of existence in the Jamaican urban space, but it foregoes sensational, commercially informed representations of the more disturbing aspects of ghetto life, such as gun violence. While the mise en scène reveals that inner-city Kingston is plagued by the usual problems that affect cities in developing countries such as unemployment, overcrowding and poor housing, the film focuses on another, often ignored side of urban life. Emphasizing cohesiveness, the film depicts the community as a site of cooperation where, despite the evident poverty, male relationships are defined by loyalty and nurturing and supportive structures rather than violent, self-destructive interactions. This view of the ghetto community, less exciting and less provocative than the narratives of dysfunction often associated with such spaces, emphasizes the common humanity of the residents. The film's rejection of popular but sensational ways of framing the Jamaican experience speaks to the attempt to affect a paradigm shift in the way that external filmmaking entities have historically constructed the Caribbean.

The positioning of the Rastafari and reggae music within the urban community, and the affirmation of the interrelation of the Rastafari and the production of reggae, are fundamental to Bafaloukos's construction of the Jamaican ghetto as a site of positive social interaction and cultural resistance. Fulani suggests, in her comparative analysis of *Rockers* and *The Harder They Come*, that the central positioning of the Rastafari within the process of music production provides the basis on which the narrative constructs a transformative role for reggae:

> *Rockers* shows reggae as an outgrowth and an expression of the Rastafarian spirit of collaboration. . . . Where *The Harder They Come* shows music as a means to achieve stardom and wealth, *Rockers* presents music as a force for healing, for unity and resistance. Several scenes in the film show the people of the ghetto coming together to share the pleasure of good music and to forget their cares temporarily.[34]

The film seems to acknowledge, therefore, that while reggae is a commercial product that can be fit within a globalized capitalist practice, it also fulfils essential non-material needs for those who create it and for those who constitute its local audience. Reggae music, the film suggests, is an active and vibrant cultural force that binds performers, musicians, consumers, and even producers into a community of participants for whom it functions, like narrative, as a means of expressing and interpreting experience, and imposing order and meaning on a chaotic and often unjust world. *Rockers* speaks, therefore, to a complex network of interactions and causative relationships that exist between the Jamaican urban community, the Rastafari and reggae music.

By actively foregrounding the role of the Rastafari in the production and performance of reggae, the film emphasizes reggae's rootedness in a tradition of resistance and protest, but also conveys that reggae is but a contemporary expression of a long-standing tradition of cultural resistance. In one scene, Horsemouth happens upon a revivalist baptism at a river. His grandmother is among the participants, and while she expresses concern at Horsemouth's Rastafari faith, it is also clear from the music and dance that form part of this expression of religious worship that, like the Rastafari, it resists dominant cultural values. Indeed, beginning with the prologue, Bafaloukos uses music and song to construct a discourse of opposition to dominant ideologies. This idea is masterfully enacted when Dirty Harry and Horsemouth visit an uptown nightclub but are asked to leave because they are Rastafarians. They become disgruntled because the deejay is playing American rhythm and blues and stage a "Rasta takeover" in which Dirty Harry gains control of the deejay booth and begins playing rockers, that is, reggae music. As Guerrero proposes, here "cultural confrontation and resistance are cast in the most fundamental terms: those of clashing musical ideologies as well as styles of dress and appearance".[35]

Throughout the film, music is used to "chant down Babylon". Gregory Isaacs, in his performance of "Slave Driver", threatens to burn the "slave master's" plantation, while Peter Tosh's "Stepping Razor", played as extra-diegetic music over a montage showing the men in the community gathering for the heist, powerfully invests otherwise benign images of Rastafarian men with a sense of threat. The film's use of music by Peter Tosh in this scene is significant: known for his radical politics and uncompromising stance against racism and other forms of oppression, his militant music has proved less amenable to the appropriation and commodification that Cooper suggests has occurred with the music of Bob Marley.

Other songs are less radical in their postulation of resistance and, rather than threaten violence, evoke Rastafari's intersection with Christian theology and assert a belief in the eventual establishment of an alternative world order that will reward righteousness and punish evil. In this worldview, Guerrero states, "social justice is achieved not so much by confrontation and struggle with corrupt institutions and bureaucracies as by submission to Jah's will, which is always equalizing and redemptive".[36] Within the narrative, rather than asserting a kind of helpless, fatalistic acceptance of destiny, these songs can be seen as supporting non-violent yet resilient forms of resistance. McFarlane points out that the Rastafarians' belief in the eventual fall of Babylon and their anticipation of Jah's reign "connotes strength of character and will . . . as well as a new and enlarged (extended) sense of time".[37] Burning Spear's a capella rendition of "Jah No Dead", which Guerrero describes as "powerfully resistant and affirmative",[38] marks a quiet, still, spiritual moment in the film during which song, spliff and brotherly solidarity provide comfort and sustenance for Horsemouth at a time of intense distress after his motorcycle is stolen. In Kiddus I's "Graduation in Zion", the threat of Jah's judgement replaces the threat of violence but the tone is one of admonition rather than submission. Here, as with Inner Circle's performance of "Dreadlocks Can't Live in Tenement Yard" to a racially mixed audience at a hotel, we are again made aware of the worldly dimensions of the music, or rather, the music business. "Graduation in Zion", initially performed in the studio during a recording session, is then heard over images showing the manufacture of 45 rpm vinyl records. These images and the studio setting suggest a tension between the music's spiritual message and the commercial and industrial processes that underlie the performance. This is further underscored when the scene shifts to Horsemouth and the producer, Jack Ruby, discussing a business transaction outside the studio in which money is exchanged. The idea of reggae as a commodity is also suggested in the hotel scene. As the band plays, a tourist remarks, "What is this? It certainly isn't calypso", implying that reggae, like calypso before it, may be stripped of its local meanings when it is appropriated by the tourist industry for the entertainment of visitors.

Indeed, the film constructs the hotel as Babylon and in opposition to the urban community. Marshall, the head of the criminal network, owns the hotel, Honeyball is his manager, and the hotel seems to be the base from which they operate their illegal activities. It is at the hotel that Horsemouth encounters the most intense forms of discrimination. Most disturbing is the uncharacteristic passive manner that Horsemouth adopts when he applies to Honeyball, who appears to be of Middle Eastern descent, for a job with the hotel band; all the tensions of the class and colour conflict of the postcolonial state are played out in the exchange as Horsemouth humbles himself and endures Honeyball's crass tirade in order to grasp an opportunity to earn his daily bread.

In another scene set at the hotel, Horsemouth is pushed down by an angry Marshall who catches him talking to his young daughter. Rather than fighting back, Horsemouth reclaims his dignity by expressing his consternation to the viewer. This declaration, the second instance in the film of direct address to the camera, is highly ironic. Claiming that he will not retaliate in kind because he is a Rastafari and a man of peace, Horsemouth acts out a ritual cultural performance of bravado and unwillingness to resort to violence, often displayed by the male when the success of actual physical confrontation is not assured. Class prejudices and politics underlie

Marshall's actions, but his attack may also be informed by his daughter's relative youthfulness. These two incidents underscore Horsemouth's subordinate status within the environs of the hotel, a space defined by Babylonian capitalist structures, discriminatory practices and the exploitation of labour.

Horsemouth's plan, put into action early in the narrative, to purchase a motorcycle in order to get into music distribution and gain more control over the products of his labour, is widely viewed as a progressive enterprise that will strike a blow against the expression of similarly oppressive forces in the music business. Horsemouth sees the venture as both a direct assault on monopolistic capitalist structures as well as a bold business move that will provide much-needed income. The endorsement of the project by members of the community and, importantly, their cash donations towards the purchase of the motorcycle, help define the venture as a communal rather than individual effort, and locate it outside normal capitalist practices.

Horsemouth's motorcycle also forms part of a pattern of visual motifs in the film that speak to the intersection of Rastafari, resistance and reggae within the Jamaican urban community. Immediately after purchasing the motorcycle, Horsemouth visits the neighbourhood artist to have him paint the Lion of Judah in a prominent place on the gas tank. On a practical level, the painting makes the motorbike distinctive and easy to identify when it is stolen. In addition, the stylized painting is also a well-known emblem of Rastafari pride and faith that signals, McFarlane suggests, the conscious and deliberate rejection of the amoral methods of survival practiced by the trickster, whose symbol is Anancy the spider, in favour of more positive and progressive values. He states: "Symbolically, the lion suggests nobility, self-confidence, strength, pride, and moral fortitude in the face of oppression.... a forceful self-assertiveness, a roaring sense of personhood seeking justice, and a dreadful challenge to cowardice."[39] Emblazoned on the motorcycle – the symbol of Horsemouth's progressive entrepreneurial effort – the Lion of Judah restates the connection between Rastafari, resistance and reggae.

In its assertion of the integration of Rastafari in the urban community, *Rockers* does, however, sound a note of discord in its construction of gender politics. The relationship between Horsemouth and his partner, Madgie, is one of continuous strife and reflects both the tensions of their economically marginal existence as well as problematic patriarchal attitudes towards gender relations and male parenting. The attention paid to this domestic conflict helps ensure that *Rockers* does not lapse into an idealized account of the Rastafarian lifestyle and faith, providing yet another romanticized cinematic version of the Caribbean. While Horsemouth's Rastafari faith is not a specific problem in his relationship with Madgie, who does not wear locks, it does seem to either inform or support certain attitudes towards his role in the family which are a constant source of tension in the union.

The final scene of the film is paradigmatic of the couple's differences. The morning after the raid, Madgie, like the other ghetto dwellers, is excited at the consumer goods that seem to have miraculously appeared overnight and which are now up for grabs to those who are fleet of foot. Tired after a night of righteous pillaging and more interested in getting some sleep, Horsemouth remains in bed and ignores Madgie's eager cries when she discovers the bounty. The scene alludes to the couple's divergent interests and concerns: Madgie is focused on the family's material welfare and on meeting her children's needs for food and shelter; Horsemouth's primary interests lie outside the domestic sphere in the cultural and political concerns of the wider community. Thus, conflict between the two is constructed around a series of binaries: male and female, public and domestic, spiritual and material.

Horsemouth's disdain for the process of acquiring and accumulating money is a constant bone of contention in the relationship. Madgie finds little comfort in his assertion that "Jah will provide", with the result that her enduring anxiety about money and the details of survival place her in a confrontational role with the frequently absent Horsemouth. She declares, "Di yout dem no ask you fi food, dem ask me fi food." (The children don't ask you for food, they ask me for food.) Madgie's concerns about everyday survival are by no means divorced from the larger issues that have to do with the exercise of power in which Horsemouth is interested, but her complaints are construed by her partner as distractions which serve to impede his supposedly loftier pursuits. In one memorable scene, Madgie berates Horsemouth (whom she calls Leroy) about his absence from the home and seeming lack of concern for the family: "Every night you gone, why you can't stay with us one night? I worry over you, yu know Leroy. I don't care about myself, I just check for di yout dem. You walk around like yu don't check for di yout dem. Suppose anyting happen to you outta street now? What happen to di yout dem?" (Every night you are gone, why can't you stay with us one night? I worry about you, you know Leroy. I don't care about myself, I just care about the children. You walk around like you don't care about the children. Suppose something should happen to you out on the street? What would happen to the children?)

Horsemouth responds to Madgie's specific and practical concerns about the quality of his interaction with the family philosophically:

> Mi know say you worried, yes, but what, Jah will always provide for everyone. . . . See all my yout dem, jus culcha mi ah teach dem, yea culcha. Don't care what all di weak-heart say, mi ah go teach my yout dem, culcha. For yu see some people out deh . . . is vanity Madgie. I tell yu dat! Vanity, clothes, food, house, money. That's all them care bout yu know. Yu see me? Mi is a man, sey mi is like a messenger come to carry Jah works out deh. I show yu dat as my dawta, yu know. Come to carry through Jah works! So yu see mi? Mi nah too worry bout dem tings yu know. . . . Me? I going look after my youts dem, I going mek sure dem have culcha. Yu see what mi ah deal wid?

> (I know you are worried, yes, but what, Jah will always provide for everyone. . . . See all my children, it's just culture I am going to teach them, yea culture. I don't care what all the weak-hearts say, I am going to teach my children about culture! For you see, some people out there . . . they're about vanity, Madgie. I am telling you that! Vanity, clothes, food, house, money. That's all they care about you know. You see me? I am a man, I say I am like a messenger come to carry out Jah's works out there. I show you that as my daughter [woman], you know. I've come to carry through Jah's works! So you see me? I don't worry about those things, you know. . . . Me? I am going to look after my children, I am going to make sure they have culture. You understand what I am dealing with?)

Ironically, as Horsemouth denounces the markers of middle-class achievement – money, shelter, clothes and even food – as vanity, he is in the process of changing into one of the many fashionable outfits he sports throughout the film. In fact, Horsemouth seems to go home primarily to change his clothes, spending little time interacting with either Madgie or their children. His neglect of his family is blatant and Madgie's pleas and complaints generate a great deal of sympathy in the viewer.

Despite the inconsistencies underlying Horsemouth's declarations, however, not least of which is that the values of the culture cannot be communicated to children through absence, his response cannot simply be dismissed as a series of excuses for paternal neglect. Horsemouth's assertion of a legacy of culture for his children is concomitant with his rejection of assimilation into middle-class Jamaican society and Western consumer culture. There is a certain practicality here: the structures of the Jamaican postcolonial state are not geared towards enabling social mobility in the poorest of the urban poor; rather, deficient educational institutions, social discrimination and prejudice, and the lack of robust welfare programmes help maintain the poor in marginal situations. Typically, a ghetto family's opportunities for social mobility are slim. Rather than enter the proverbial rat race for increased wealth and social status, the terms of which have been predetermined and in which he has little chance of success, Horsemouth instead steadfastly refuses to compete. More importantly, his rejection of materialism signals a refusal to participate in the processes of deracination and deculturalization that often accompany upward mobility and assimilation into the middle class, and which for the black man can be an education in self-hate. Instead, Horsemouth embraces the alternative: the celebration of the ancestral link with Africa and immersion in a concept of community that is defined by sharing, cooperation and brotherhood. In a society that Nettleford describes as "still enslaved in the social structure born of the plantation system in which things African, including African traits, have been devalued",[40] Horsemouth succeeds, through Rastafari and reggae, in defining himself in ways that accrue value, dignity and pride.

5
LOVE AND SEX IN BABYLON
Nation and Desire in *Children of Babylon* and *One Love*

TRINIDADIAN CULTURAL CRITIC PAULA MORGAN CLAIMS that the desire for romance is universal. She asks, "Why does each society, even the most realistic, the most cynical, insist on creating its own romantic fantasies?"[1] Romance may well be ubiquitous – the romantic comedy is one of the most popular and commercially viable of film genres – yet romantic fantasy is sorely missing from the field of Jamaican feature film. As earlier chapters have demonstrated, characters like Ringo in *Smile Orange*, Elsa and Ivan in *The Harder They Come*, Madgie and Horsemouth in *Rockers*, all confirm the illusory and fleeting nature of both love and romance rather than attempt to persuade us of its transcendental and transformative possibilities. Indeed, there are few Jamaican films that are centrally concerned with romance or even, on a more realistic level, with the intricacies of sexual relationships. *Children of Babylon* (1980), directed by Lennie Little-White, and *One Love* (2003), directed by Rick Elgood and Don Letts, constitute a qualified departure from this pattern. Both films are explicitly concerned with the complexities of heterosexual bonding, but also use what might be referred to as the quest for coupling to explore ideas about community.[2]

Faithful to the structure of the classic romance in which the plot develops around the protagonists' negotiation of the obstacles to their union, *One Love* is a story of young love that reclaims the tropics – specifically, Jamaica – as a site for the expression of normative sexuality. *One Love* draws on the fantasy of the romance to affirm a vision of unity and harmony for the heterosexual couple, their community and, by extension, the nation. In *Children of Babylon*, the desire for bonding in the heterosexual pair also lies at the heart of the narrative and is symbolic of the quest for national unity. Here, however, the traditional romance trajectory gives way to the formation of multiple relationships that feature the exchange and circulation of partners and, ultimately, failure to realize a lasting union.

Belinda Edmondson points out that the narrative pairing of romance and ideas about the broader community or nationalism is not novel in the black literary tradition.[3] Indeed, Claudia Tate, whose work Edmondson cites, observes that African American female authors in the nineteenth century used "black Victorian love stories" to participate in contemporary dialogues about racial justice and sexual equality.[4] Edmondson asserts, therefore, the existence of continuities between such writing and other more explicitly nationalist genres, stating that "for the black communities of the diaspora, romance, eros, and nationalism have always been connected".[5] Edmondson explains that the first black romances in the nineteenth century probably focused on social upliftment over eroticism because of the problematic representation of black sexuality as rapacious, threatening or demonic in European, American and white West Indian writing. Consequently, Edmondson affirms the need to recover eroticism in the black romance and bridge what she describes as the subgenre's "historic schism between agape and eros".[6] In its attempt to claim a normative sexuality for the black heroine, *One Love* betrays the signs of erotic suppression that Edmondson refers to, but in *Children of Babylon*, eroticism is used as a deliberate strategy to explore issues of identity and concerns of national unity. My primary focus is not eroticism (nor the lack of it), but rather that other element which, as Edmondson, Tate and Ann duCille contend, has always been an enduring concern of the black romance, that is, the articulation of ideas about the black community. For African American authors, that community was defined as the members of a racial minority who were the target of discriminatory practices and legislation; in the two films discussed in this chapter, community is defined within the context of nation.

In *One Love*, the transformational potential of romantic love is closely associated with ideas of nation. In the final scene, the requisite happy-ever-after ending of the classic romance features the reconciliation of the male and female protagonists, which in turn becomes a metaphor for the healing of the community and the resolution of conflict and difference. Rastafari and Christians, two previously warring factions of the community, together perform a song which cements this metaphorical association:

> Maybe one by one
> We can see that something can be done.
> With a little peace from everyone
> We can make a stand, we can heal this land.

In contrast to the utopian vision of nation asserted in *One Love*, *Children of Babylon* is a darker, more tragic comment on the failure of the quest for unity, at the level of the heterosexual couple as well as on the broader social scale of the national collective. In this film, the attempts and failures to develop lasting and stable unions are part of a narrative strategy to explore differences of class, gender, race and culture within the nation which constantly threaten to disrupt the bonds of community. The liner notes to *Children of Babylon* rather insistently declare that it "is not just another pictorial essay about love and life in the Tropics. It is a timely social comment which illustrates the contradictions which arise in a society stratified by economics and class determinants".[7] This statement affirms the film's opposition to a genre of rather predictable stories of love and passion set in the tropical zone, but in doing so also infers a hierarchy in which heterosexual bonding as a subject is deemed less worthy of attention, less politically charged, than topics of a more explicit historical or social nature. The inference recalls Edmondson's observation that the nineteenth-century black romance focused on issues of nationalism rather than eroticism, and perhaps the makers of *Children of Babylon* found it necessary to assert the film's concern with social issues precisely because of its erotic content, which at the time of the film's release was thought to be quite sensational. But it is precisely through the mechanism of the erotic heterosexual relationship that *Children of Babylon* explores and makes visible troubling questions of power, domination and conflict in postcolonial Jamaica. This chapter, then, explores how both films, drawing on ideas associated with romance about the resolution of conflict and the forging of unity, use the heterosexual union as a metaphor through which ideas about another union are explored: the imagined community of the nation upon which also rests affirmations of cohesion, a shared purpose and a shared identity.

In both films, the rural environment is critical to the exploration of ideas about nation. Moving away from the disturbing paradigms of urban life that concern the "city films", *Children of Babylon* and *One Love* are both set in rural Jamaica. For several of the characters in *Children of Babylon*, the countryside functions as a respite from the demands of city life, but the location of much of the action in a great house and its environs ensures that the rural landscape brings the spectator to a closer recognition of the process of history, rather than function to obliterate it. The concern here is not the apparent beauty of the surface, but the history that informs the landscape and which, as Glissant affirms, is spread out beneath it.[8] Thus, in the film the great house repeatedly evokes the memory of a divisive and cruel past which continues to intrude on the present and affect individuals' interaction with others as well as how they see themselves. The initial scenic depiction of the rural landscape progressively gives way to an increasing interiority as the main character is progressively contained within and even confined to the great house and its environs.

In contrast, throughout *One Love*, the rural landscape is used to support a picturesque representation of Jamaica. Although the DVD notes describe the narrative as "set in the environs of Kingston, Jamaica", in fact, the presence of the city is elided from the film. Here, the scenically framed countryside is deployed to construct the romantic relationship as symbolic of a new, more harmonious society which counters the tropical dystopia of colonial romance literature. In its attempt to rewrite one stereotype of Jamaica, however, *One Love* reproduces another: the film's representation of the rural space indicates resistance to the colonial representation of the tropics as a site of degenerate sexuality and moral corruption, but it also fashions the kind of scenic landscapes that are reminiscent of tourism advertising and marketing.

CHILDREN OF BABYLON

As one of Jamaica's early narrative features, *Children of Babylon* occupies an important place in the story of Jamaican cinema. Little-White claims that his film "broke away from the stigma that Jamaica was a place of ghetto and rude boys".[9] More precisely, *Children of Babylon* and the earlier film, *Smile Orange*, directed by Trevor Rhone, represent a departure from the model established by *The Harder They Come* in which the urban setting and popular Jamaican music are defining elements of the film text. Little-White's boldness in daring to depart from a pattern which was established as commercially viable needs to be recognized. Both Rhone and Little-White make use of the anti-romance, rural environment and opt for original soundtracks, but while Rhone's film would have been an easy sell to Jamaican audiences who had gone to see *Smile Orange*, the play, in record numbers, *Children of Babylon*, as an original screenplay, had no such assurance of success.

In *Children of Babylon*, five characters, Penny, Rick, Luke, Dorcas and Laura, are thrown together in a great house over a period of several months, with the passage of time marked by successive images of leaves torn from a calendar. The racial and social composition of this group, as well as the way in which its members are bound together in the great house and connected to that space, suggest they function as a metaphor for Jamaican society and the nation. The characters precisely correspond to Rex Nettleford's description of class and colour hierarchies in Caribbean plantation societies which conceptualises a pyramid with white masters at the apex, black labour at the base and a buffer class of free coloureds between the two extremes.[10] George Beckford observed in the early 1970s that, four generations after emancipation, this basic structure of plantation societies in the New World remained largely intact.[11] The group of characters in the film reflects this undesirable stability and mirrors not simply Jamaican society of a bygone period, but also the divisions and hierarchies of the modern nation which have been informed by that history.[12] The liner notes of the film introduce this idea, describing the characters in terms of their socioeconomic status and the historical roles associated with their class:

> Laura is the absentee landlord who still controls the institutions which determine the lives of the people. Penny represents the overseers who have assumed the role of the bourgeoisie in the absence of the owners. The overseers administer the state and have the power to manipulate and use the masses. Rick, the mulatto, is a part of the nouveau riche who seek for all the material trappings of the "motherland". The lumpen proletariat is evidenced in Luke who parallels those field or yard slaves whose main ambition is survival at any cost.

Dorcas is the house-slave who continues to live in the shadow of the glory but never sees the light.[13]

While the liner notes describe the film as an "epitaph for the more than 300 years of colonialism", the narrative affirms a far more dynamic phenomenon than the word "epitaph" might suggest. Colonialism may have officially ended with independence, but the interaction of the five characters suggests how the legacies of colonial rule continue to be felt even as political change affects historically prescribed social roles and identities. Treating the group of characters as a microcosm of the nation, Little-White presents a tragic vision of the quest for national unity as individual relationships are increasingly marked by disharmony, betrayal, exploitation and, eventually, violence. Little-White emphasizes socioeconomic and cultural differences within this microcosm, proposing that the legacies of colonialism – too great and too burdensome to throw off – threaten to thwart the project of national unity and cohesion.

The opening montage of the film introduces the notion of difference and heterogeneity within the national collective. Rick (Don Parchment), who is an artist, travels from Kingston to a friend's great house in the country in order to do work for a major exhibition to be held overseas. The initial stages of his journey are remarkable for the sense of contrast they create by showing the varied faces of Jamaica. Rick's journey takes us from the middle-class suburb where his home is located to the heart of the city with its modern, multistoreyed glass and concrete commercial buildings. As he moves out of the city, images of the dilapidated dwelling houses of the poor are followed by views of the buildings of the old colonial capital which, although actually in ruins, are framed by the camera to appear majestic and impressive.

On his way to the country, Rick offers a ride to an attractive young woman, Penny (Tobi Phillips), who plans to conduct interviews with rural women as part of the research for her PhD. On arrival at the great house, Penny meets Luke (Bob Andy), a handyman on the estate, and Dorcas (Leonie Forbes), a servant. Not unexpectedly, Rick invites Penny to stay at the house for the duration of her visit to the country; she agrees, and a sexual relationship soon develops between the two. At first, Penny's stay is idyllic, but it is disrupted by the arrival of the owner of the great house, Laura

(Elizabeth deLisser). At Rick's suggestion, Penny goes back to the city, but when she returns to the great house earlier than expected, she discovers that Rick is sexually involved with Laura. Penny finds solace in Luke's company, but Rick is greatly angered when, after Laura's departure, expecting a resumption of his affair with Penny, he discovers Luke in her bed. A fight ensues between the two men and Penny moves out of the main house to take up residence with Luke, who lives in the servants' quarters. Luke, in turn, spurns Dorcas with whom he had a prior, rather exploitative relationship; this rejection leads to Dorcas's suicide. As Penny begins to slip into the role of domestic drudge (for Luke) that Dorcas once occupied, the relationship deteriorates. Seeing himself in this new relationship as head of and provider for the household, Luke tries to look for a job, but is repeatedly refused work because of his locks which identify him as Rastafari. Growing frustrated and angry, he vents his resentment on Penny and becomes increasingly domineering and abusive. Penny tolerates this until he comes in drunk one night and rapes her. She leaves the estate the next day.

Children of Babylon came to the screen in 1980 at the height of a period of intense political conflict in Jamaica. In the late 1970s, the introduction of democratic socialism by the government of Michael Manley and the resulting opposition by certain groups in Jamaica, as well as the US resistance to socialism in the region, led to an especially turbulent period in Jamaican history that was marked by escalating violence, increasing political polarization, a failing economy and social unrest. While little direct reference is made to contemporary events, the film reflects the turmoil of the period in the conflict and tension that characterize personal relationships in the film. Much of this tension hinges on issues that emerged in the popular ideological debates at the time: the viability of Marxism versus capitalism as models for economic and social development; the neocolonial character of American domination in the region; causes of Third World underdevelopment; and the legitimacy of the Rastafari's faith-based cultural and political protest. The contemporary Jamaican spectator, therefore, would have tended to see the conflicts between characters as an expression of the contentious social and political issues that confronted the society at the time and which often functioned as divisive elements within the national body.

Carl Stone defines the 1970s in Jamaica as the post-independence or second stage of the decolonization process; a period, he states, that was marked by "all the local class pressures and external stresses that accompany efforts by small Third World states to redefine some of the external economic and power parameters that stifle development".[14] Stone notes that these pressures and stresses on the international and domestic fronts generated a return to ideological politics. He points out that although there was little concrete evidence of the development of far left policies by Manley's PNP administration, nevertheless, as relations between the Manley government and the United States deteriorated, conservative local and foreign interests converged "to create political hysteria" in order to block the government "from proceeding with what appeared to be a commitment to radical leftist changes".[15] This action succeeded when the PNP was voted out of office in the 1980 general election and replaced with a capitalist-oriented, pro-America JLP administration led by Edward Seaga.

That election campaign was a prolonged and violent one that saw over eight hundred people killed. Brian Meeks points out that, on reflection, it "was the last election in which the great majority felt that the government was a prize; that the process of supporting a party and winning an election was the vehicle which would bring 'better', whether that better be defined as the mythical future of socialism or the mythical past of plentiful, '1960s' capitalism'".[16]

Children of Babylon anticipates the sense of disenchantment, loss of idealism and the retreat from politics and ideology as a solution to the country's social and economic problems to which Meeks refers. More than simply a cautionary tale warning of the potential dangers of "sexual slumming", therefore, *Children of Babylon* can be seen as a film about the loss of innocence and idealism on a personal level, as well as at the level of the community. Steeped in the rhetoric of leftist ideology, Penny is made to confront the deep divisions that mark Jamaican society as well as the failure of political ideology to resolve those differences. Penny's disillusionment and her failure to bring about transformation unfolds within the context of personal relationships, but the dynamics of these relationships pivot on the same issues of social, cultural and gender difference that preoccupied the nation at the time. Thus, her experience resonates as a narrative of Jamaica in the 1970s and corresponds to the attempt by the postcolonial state to transform old paradigms and structures. Penny's arrival at the great house suggests a disruption of the old order. She attempts to initiate change, both in her transgression of traditional sociosexual boundaries as well as through her unsuccessful efforts to persuade other characters to adopt more politically radical positions. Penny's sexual relationships with men outside her social group, Rick and, more overtly, Luke, can be seen as the expression of a desire to achieve social integration by attempting to erase class distinctions and boundaries and bridge cultural difference. Her sexual relationships, therefore, can be understood as symbolic of the aspiration for national unity.

The various iterations of coupling and uncoupling in the narrative underscore the inherent complexities of these relationships, particularly within a context of social stratification. This subject matter allows for the inclusion of images of nudity and lovemaking that were controversial at the time and which must have functioned to drive interest in the film. *Children of Babylon* is certainly not guilty of eliding eroticism. More broadly, however, the focus on intimate relationships facilitates the exploration of social and cultural differences in Jamaica and the implications they have for the forging of a unified nation. As characters in the film form sexual relationships across social barriers, such differences are brought into sharp relief and reveal aspects of subjectivity which in turn subvert or challenge the idea of the nation as homogeneous. By confirming the existence of cleavages and tensions in the national body, these differences threaten the myth of unity. The film brings into focus, therefore, what Stuart Hall describes as "the recognition of the immense diversity and differentiation of the historical and cultural experience of black subjects".[17] While Hall emphasizes the variety of black experiences across the diaspora, *Children of Babylon* insists that diversity of experience also exists within the boundaries of the geo-political space defined as nation.

The title of the film infers the potential for unity or community as well as dispersal, and thus difference. Commonly used by the Rastafari, Ennis B. Edmonds explains that the term "Babylon" draws on biblical references to the deportation and servitude of the ancient Hebrews. At its most immediate level of signification, Edmonds states, "Babylon" as used by the Rastafari refers to "the gut-wrenching experiences of suffering and estrangement faced by the 'underside' of Jamaican society" that arise out of economic hardship, political marginalization and, significantly, cultural alienation. At the sociopolitical level, Edmonds notes, Babylon refers to "the ideological and structural components of Jamaica's social system, which institutionalizes inequity and exploitation. . . . Babylon is the complex of economic, political, religious and educational institutions and values that evolved from the colonial experiment."[18]

The characters in the film are, therefore, *children* of Babylon in that their common cultural and psychological inheritance is the divisive and alienating values of colonialism and the hegemonic institutions that maintain them. As individuals, however, each character's experience of those institutions and forces differs. As Hall states, there is difference and diversity in the "ways we are positioned by, and position ourselves within, the narratives of the past".[19] What the film brings into sharp relief is the extent of such differences as they occur across the various strata of the social pyramid that Nettleford describes. Caught up in and part of what Hall refers to as "the continuous 'play' of history, culture, and power",[20] the characters in the film are also cast as children of Sisyphus as they struggle, with little success, to position themselves in relation to the narratives of the past in ways that foster greater unity and understanding. Little-White thus identifies one of the challenges of building the postcolonial nation as the individual's difficulty in overcoming historically determined cultural and social barriers in order to form lasting, mutually beneficial relationships across those boundaries.

Setting is important in conveying a sense of how current realities are informed by the past. Except for the opening of the film and a brief scene midway through the narrative, all action takes place in the countryside, primarily within the confines of the great house and its large estate. This location is significant: the great house in the film functions as a kind of crossroads (as did the plantation) – a space in which characters from various socioeconomic and cultural backgrounds are brought together so that their lives collide and intersect. In African mythology, the crossroads is a liminal space that offers possibilities for transformation, but like the old house of the Gothic text, the great house in *Children of Babylon* is a powerful evocation of the past and the idea that the past continues to project into and affect the present.

Specifically, the great house evokes the period of slavery, where lie its origins. In Little-White's great house, the viewer is struck by the inability of the characters to escape the prison or prisms of history and forge new narratives that support freedom, unity and harmony. Instead, historical relationships of unequal power endure, as seen in the perfect reproduction of the hierarchies of the social pyramid of plantation society. As a symbol of Laura's wealth and status, the great house is a potent reminder of what Carl Stone describes as the illegitimate origins of the bourgeoisie's wealth and privilege in repressive slave society.[21] In one scene when Laura rides on horseback, her formal riding costume complete with whip and hat, her upright, self-assured posture as she surveys her large estate and the horse, define her as a modern version of the colonial planter or, more precisely, the absentee landowner. In her relaxed attitudes towards pleasure, Laura is also reminiscent of the decadent, hedonistic planter of the colonial romance. She visits Jamaica, it would seem, solely to indulge in a little rest and recreation that includes sex and smoking ganja. Unlike Penny, she is unperturbed by the idea that she is not Rick's sole sexual partner and is willing to "share" so long as she is able to have time with him when she wants.

Little-White often uses cross-cutting within the interior of the house to emphasize social and cultural differences among the characters and so reinforce the idea of the great house as a crossroads. In one sequence, he evokes the inequities of plantation society and emphasizes cultural difference by juxtaposing images of Dorcas, Luke and Penny in their various quarters. The sequence shows a picture of Christ prominently displayed in Dorcas's room, while Luke smokes a ganja spliff in his room with a picture of Haile Selassie visible in the frame. Penny's far more comfortable accommodation is in marked contrast with the spartan servants' quarters.

The unequal distribution of material resources and persistent poverty is not the only legacy of colonialism, however. Its lasting psychological impact is also conveyed when, in another sequence, the narrative cuts from the scene showing Laura riding on horseback, to her bedroom in the great house where Dorcas, wearing one of Laura's dresses, her face inexpertly painted with the other woman's make-up, mimics her white employer. As Dorcas peers into the mirror and pretends to be Laura, a voice-over (significantly, in Laura's voice; we never hear Dorcas's voice, not even in this interior monologue) conveys the black woman's thoughts. Dorcas's masquerade expresses a deep longing to be white and to possess the beauty and privilege she – as well as the society of which she is a part – associates with whiteness. Luke catches her in the act and pours scorn on Dorcas's mimicry, but his abusive tone and cruelty, and especially his use of a racial epithet – he calls Dorcas a monkey – ironically also express a rejection of blackness and the internalization of colonial attitudes on Luke's part.

As a new convert to Rastafari, Luke suggests potential change: the possibility of a radical response and resistance to the colonial narrative, but his actions and beliefs, and in particular his attitude towards women, indicate that he remains trapped in the paradigm of the plantation. Luke's affirmation of patriarchy through reference to Biblical injunction reflects a recognized intersection of Rastafari and Christianity, but he is a particularly offensive representation of Rastafari's patriarchal leanings, even as he retains little sense of the radical political resistance and awareness also associated with the movement. He vociferously declares to Penny, "The head of the woman is I and I, man!" When she dares contradict him, he slaps her. His treatment of Dorcas suggests a retreat from progressive ideology and a willingness to exploit a lonely and vulnerable woman who longs for intimacy and kindness. He tells Penny that he simply uses Dorcas as a means of sexual release: "Both of us here and I man nature want release, so we do a thing." ("Both of us are here and my [sexual] nature needs release, so we do a thing.") Luke's use of the plural pronoun suggests that he and Dorcas share the same understanding of the relationship. The narrative shows otherwise, however, both in Dorcas's lack of participation and pleasure in Luke's rough and clumsy attempts at intercourse and, most poignantly, in her suicide after his rejection. Indeed, Luke's relationship with Dorcas echoes the planter's historical sexual abuse and exploitation of the black female, while the misogyny that surfaces in his interactions with both Dorcas and Penny suggests Eurocentric models of patriarchy that can be conceived as a legacy of colonialism.

In contrast to the other characters, Penny shows a willingness and desire to bring about transformation and signals an intention to disrupt the prevailing order, but her efforts meet with limited success. She argues heatedly with Rick, a pragmatist who has a decidedly materialistic and capitalist outlook, but their frequent and passionate exchanges never reach resolution. Each remains locked within a particular perspective, unwilling to acknowledge the salient truths of the other's argument. Penny criticizes him for "selling out" to foreign interests rather than using his talent to build the nation; Rick responds that while local collectors willingly display his work in their homes and offices, they are reluctant to pay for his art. On her arrival at the great house, Penny disregards the unspoken rules that preserve class difference in Jamaica and tries to initiate conversations with the servants. Her overtures to Dorcas are unsuccessful, but she manages to create a friendship with Luke that later develops into a sexual and, eventually, domestic union. This evolving relationship signals the breakdown of the class barriers that discourage certain kinds of social and sexual contact between a female member of the elite and a lower-class black man. The social gulf between these two characters is metaphorically conveyed when Luke drives Penny to her home in uptown Kingston and two ferocious dogs prevent him from entering the property. Penny's blithe unawareness of the dogs' attack, however, hints at her ignorance of the real and concrete nature of social prejudice and divisions in Jamaica and how they affect the poor, as well as the contradictions of her own bourgeois existence as she preaches equality and the need for change but continues to enjoy the privileges of the upper middle class.

As the relationship between Luke and Penny develops and certain barriers crumble, others emerge which prevent harmony and reassert another kind of hierarchical system, one based on gender. In a synopsis of the film, director Little-White states: "Penny's social background prevents her from adjusting to the strict doctrinaire philosophy of Luke's religion" (that is, Rastafari).[22] Little-White's comment reflects a patriarchal bias as it infers that the success of the union rests on Penny's ability to adapt to Luke's demands even though Luke becomes domineering and abusive. Prior to his domestic union with Penny, Luke rejected capitalism, the accumulation of wealth and any participation in political activity. When Penny affirmed that he should own the estate because he worked the land, he replied: "What the use I kill myself? I have a piece of land that give I food; I don't have to pay no rent. Bwai, the only thing that I want is to see Africa." Luke experiences a radical reversal of values, however, when the presence in his household of a woman of elite status, and what he perceives as his "ownership" of her, elevates his patriarchal standing and thus requires the performance of certain forms of masculinity. After Penny moves into his room, he declares, "My woman mustn't work out. You is my queen and if I can't give you everything you need, I is not a man." ("My woman mustn't work outside the home. You are my queen and if I can't give you everything you need, I am not a man.) Thus, Luke feels compelled to seek regular employment and earn a wage to support Penny even though she is not financially dependent on him.

The relationship between Luke and Penny introduces radical shifts and changes, but these are not transformative in a positive way. A temporary reversal of the traditional racial power structure is certainly achieved, but this does not lead to greater freedom, harmony or understanding. Instead, one form of oppression is exchanged for another. Defining his manhood and patriarchal rank in relation to the elite status of the "browning", Luke expresses his new-found dominance in tyrannical control of his prized "possession". Penny cooks and cleans as she keeps house for Luke, her "batty-rider" shorts exchanged for the dress of the Rastafari sistren because Luke insists on a more modest wardrobe. Such images are signs of her loss of autonomy and increasing containment within patriarchy as she exchanges the role of intellectual for domestic worker. Sex, previously erotic and mutually pleasurable with Rick, becomes a duty that is performed for Luke's sole pleasure. When she speaks up about her own needs, Luke retorts that "only babies suck woman titty". Luke's domination eventually extends to violence, forbidding her to use contraceptives, and rape, when he refuses to respect her stated desire not to engage in sex. As Penny experiences a progressive loss of privilege, the narrative effectively shifts focus from the more overtly political leftist ideological debates, with which she had been explicitly concerned, to questions of gender politics, particularly within the context of a patriarchal Rastafari movement.

As indicated earlier, Little-White's representation of Rastafari is problematic. More than simply a narrow-minded perspective of Rastafari, however, the characterization of Luke speaks to a larger problem in the film that has to do with Little-White's unwillingness to grant even minimal agency and self-awareness to his lower-class characters: Luke's misogyny is as severe as Dorcas's social marginalization and psychological alienation. Burdened by a trifecta of misfortune, Dorcas is mute, unable to bear children and was abandoned at the estate at birth. Luke's rejection results in her suicide, an act construed as an expression of extreme hopelessness and despair. Prior to the suicide, Dorcas performs a ritual that seems to be grounded in folk mythology in which she casts pointed glances at a large knife. Rather than using the knife to exact revenge on Penny or Luke, however, she takes it into the bush and directs the urge towards violence at the despised self; in the morning she is discovered hanging from a tree. The sequence lacks unity in that the significance of the knife is not readily apparent but, more important, it also deprives folk culture of its traditional role as a form of resistance for the lower classes in the face of hardship and adversity.

The sense of Dorcas's social marginalization is reinforced by her marginality in the text as she is literally written out of the narrative after her suicide. Following her death, the other characters are briefly sad and regretful, and then Dorcas is forgotten as the plot shifts focus from her tragic demise to the troublesome unfolding of Luke and Penny's relationship. This narrative marginalization of Dorcas precludes the assertion of female solidarity in the film and, with it, one of the bases on which calls for unity that transcend social difference might be built. Penny's gradually emerging demeaned condition as Luke's woman mirrors Dorcas's experiences, but Penny does not explicitly acknowledge their shared vulnerability as women in a patriarchal society. Indeed, even after her relationship with Luke turns abusive, Penny persists in pursuing leftist ideological paradigms as a means of critiquing the Jamaican postcolonial experience. In the face of the daily subordination she suffers with Luke, she does not identify brutal patriarchal oppression as her more pressing and immediate reality. The morning after Luke slaps her, she says to Rick:

> After all the years of political independence we still haven't left the plantation. This place is really the total picture of what we are. This estate and that great house, it's just like Jamaica. The building continues to crumble while those like you continue to get fat. Thanks to who? The absentee landlord, Laura. She's no different from our imperialist masters, whether they be countries, multinationals, the IMF [International Monetary Fund] or the World Bank. You sit here waiting for meagre handouts. The plantation is alive and well and is Jamaica.

Penny certainly articulates a valid perspective of the postcolonial dilemma, and one that resonates throughout the narrative, but her words ring hollow. Here, her preoccupation with global structures seems to function as a deliberate distraction from the more urgent and immediate concerns of the patriarchal politics that inform her personal circumstances.

Penny's failure to forge a more explicit connection between her domestic situation and what she refers to as "the plantation", that is the history of colonialism and the re-enactment of unequal relationships in the modern global economy, suggests either an unwillingness or inability to articulate ways in which the personal is political. As a Marxist, she is not open to the feminist politics that would allow her to make such connections and which would also force her to question her self-sacrificial response to Luke that entails the acceptance of his abuse. The narrative, however, does evoke linkages between Luke's marginalized socioeconomic condition and his misogyny. Immediately after Penny's speech on the global political economy, we are shown images of Luke in his fruitless search for employment. When Luke comes home that night, he rapes Penny, forcing himself on her despite her pleas that he is hurting her. For Luke, following the script of the low status male in patriarchal society, the female body becomes the site at which he offers resistance to subordination and expresses what he defines as manhood in a society which discriminates against both his black skin and identity as Rastafari.

Penny's sojourn in the land of the oppressed, however, is only temporary; unlike Dorcas, her wealth affords an escape. When she is no longer able to endure Luke's tyranny, she leaves – the morning after she is raped – to resume her life in Kingston. On the morning of her departure she is wearing the shorts Luke had forced her to discard, but she is sober and subdued. When she bids Rick goodbye, he offers to give her one of the paintings he has done over the summer, including one that shows Penny as she was on her arrival at the great house: happy, confident and self-assured. Penny's silent refusal of the gift is ambiguous. It is not clear whether it signals a desire to obliterate the painful memories of the summer and leave behind anything that would remind her of her failed attempts to bring about change, or whether her refusal reflects a hard-earned maturity and wisdom and a rejection of the naivety of the woman in the picture, the idealist, who thought change could be easily achieved. Neither interpretation is without disconcerting implications. If Penny has gained wisdom and insight, it would appear to have come through the degradation and humiliation of rape and abuse. If she has turned her back on the idea of bridging the chasms of social divides in Jamaica, then Little-White has signalled the dream of national unity as an unobtainable objective. Whatever the reason for her refusal of Rick's painting, it is Penny's silence that is most disturbing. Once the articulate intellectual, by the end of the film, she retreats from words and from communication and is effectively rendered as mute as Dorcas.

ONE LOVE

In contrast to *Children of Babylon*'s dark ending which seems to deny the possibility of national unity and the healing of history's traumas, *One Love* offers a utopian vision of nation, drawing on the courtship plot to affirm the ability of love to heal, transform and transcend difference. In the film, Serena (Cherine Anderson), the daughter of a rigid Christian fundamentalist pastor, falls in love with Kassa (Ky-Mani Marley), a Rastafarian musician. Serena's father, Pastor Johnson (Winston Stona), objects to her socializing with people outside the faith, and most emphatically forbids her to have contact with Rastafarians. The plot develops along the lines of the traditional romance and also echoes *Romeo and Juliet*, as Serena and Kassa's relationship is opposed by their respective communities of Christians and the Rastafari. Love prevails, however, and the film concludes with the reconciliation of the estranged lovers and their betrothal. This happy-ever-after ending, a standard feature of the romance, is symbolic, signifying not only the resolution of conflict between the two would-be lovers, but also between the two factions in the community. The film's scenic framing of the rural setting supports the symbolic resonance of the betrothal: associated with natural imagery that suggests rebirth and regeneration, the young couple represents the possibility of a new nation unfettered by old, divisive and destructive ways of thinking. Despite the emphasis on youth and rebirth, however, in important ways the narrative maintains a conservative agenda that signals the retention of traditional values. The film's closure affirms marriage as the ideal arrangement for the eighteen-year-old heroine; it also brings the previously rebellious Rastafari hero into alignment with dominant values and ideology. Ultimately, marriage contains both protagonists within patriarchy.

The film's intertwining of romantic love and a utopian vision of nation that rests on social harmony is reflected in its title, inspired by Bob Marley's iconic song about universal brotherly love: "One love, / One heart, / Let's get together and feel alright."[23] The metaphorical connection between romance and nation is established in the film's opening sequence as the song is played over a high angle shot that moves over the ocean towards a heavily forested coast. The version of "One Love" we hear features female voices singing selected lyrics from the song: the chorus quoted above and also the lines "Give thanks and praise to the Lord / Feel alright". This traditional religious phrasing in a song made famous by a Rastaman underscores the connections between Rastafari and Christian tradition and dogma, and thus prefigures one of the main concerns in the narrative, that is, the affirmation of the bonds of community within the context of seeming social and cultural difference.

Situated within the scenic framing of place in the film's opening sequence, the song "One Love" also opens up other constellations of meaning. As the sequence reproduces the updated iconic images of the island paradise – the ocean, the coast, a small hut with thatched roof, the Rastaman playing his drum and, later, a panoramic shot of the mountains bathed in early morning mist – the song evokes a well-known advertising campaign by the Jamaica Tourist Board which also combined picturesque images of Jamaica with a version of "One Love".[24] This campaign set representations of racial harmony (through the grouping of actors of different races) against lush, scenic Jamaican landscapes. Commenting on this campaign, Honor Ford-Smith argues that in the print versions of the promotion, the referencing of the song by the slogan, "Come to Jamaica and Feel Alright", "subtly indicates that Reggae and Rastafari, once signifiers of protest and oppositional identity, are now part of a hegemonic alliance in support of the friendly apparatus of tourism".[25] Similarly, Carolyn Cooper locates the promotion campaign's use of the song within a trend towards the commercial appropriation of Marley's musical legacy, stating that "the revolutionary Tuff Gong Rastaman has been commodified and repackaged as our 'One Love' apologist for the Jamaican tourist industry".[26] Cooper also argues for a complex reading of the lyrics of "One Love". She proposes that the song questions the possibility of actually achieving "one love" (what we might think of as a universal expression of love for one's fellow man), rather than unequivocally asserting it as an attainable objective or ideal. For many across the globe, however, the song has come to represent a celebrated and uncomplicated call for peace and unity; and, thanks to its use in the Jamaica Tourist Board campaign, it has also become associated with a facile assertion of racial harmony in Jamaica.

The *One Love* filmmakers likewise draw on Marley's song to affirm the bonds of community in Jamaica. Like the Tourist Board commercials, the film carefully skirts more contentious issues of difference: race, partisan politics and class distinctions – factors which have created deep divisions in Jamaican society – are elided from the narrative. Kassa and Serena are culturally different because of their respective faiths or religious values, but although one lives in a large house and the other in a thatched hut, there is little sense of class difference. Part of an idyllic, romanticized natural landscape, Kassa's hut speaks of charm rather than poverty, while his brown complexion and his speech imply middle-class origins. Rather than the troublesome and contentious arena of class, therefore, tension and conflict in the narrative are limited to the less disruptive and polarizing spheres of prejudice against the Rastafari and the patriarchal tendencies in fundamentalist Christianity. At the time *One Love* was made, however, the Rastafari in Jamaica were largely accepted and were hardly treated with the degree of scorn and derision that characterized the public response when the movement first emerged.[27] In fact, as stated earlier, Rex Nettleford reports, "By the late sixties there was much more widespread embrace of Rastafarian attitudes, ideals and practices among bona fide members of the wider society." The wearing of locks and Afrocentric clothing, the smoking of ganja, the conscious reference to oneself as a black man rather than a negro, an unashamed commitment to Africa and a yearning for knowledge of the African past are just some of the Rastafarian practices that Nettleford identifies as gaining increasing acceptance in the 1960s.[28] Certainly, some of these practices were so common by the 1990s that they were no longer specifically identified with the Rastafari movement. Yet the film emphasizes a cultural gulf between the Rastafari and the Christians by suggesting that members of the movement are still socially ostracized and the object of overt prejudice.

The film is, as co-director Rick Elgood states, "pure fantasy, a dream",[29] and the representation of the rural landscape is critical to the film's construction of this dream. Filters, diffused lighting, panoramic shots and scenic locations create a soft, beautiful rendering of the countryside, which in turn reflects the innocence and purity of the protagonists' relationship and the promise their union represents for a new and unified Jamaica. Not only the physical landscape is rendered picturesque; in the film, life in rural Jamaica is also made to appear quaint and charming, suggesting a nostalgic return to some mythic, romanticized, less complex time as rural poverty and underdevelopment are either erased or made to appear scenic. The film's mode of production is implicated in this picturesque representation of the rural environment. Access to funding through a co-production treaty with the European Union is reflected in the film's high production values: this is not imperfect cinema, aesthetics of underdevelopment nor a film with a gritty "Third World" look. Rather, the use of expensive, high-quality film stock ensured superior picture quality, and the technical skills and resources provided by Norway, the co-production partner, resulted in a visual reproduction of place that in many instances recalls the images of a glossy magazine or a tourism product.

As occurs in *Children of Babylon*, a sense of place is concretized in the narrative by a cluster of images that are created through a journey. In *One Love*, a vehicle goes from town to town announcing, by loudspeaker, a music competition with a substantial cash prize. The competition is an important aspect of the film's subplot, but as the vehicle moves through the landscape, the spectator is also furnished with defining images of place. Although the competition appears to be national in scope, in this early staging of place, the city is elided. The vehicle drives along country roads and through what appears to be small villages or towns providing images of lush vegetation as well as quaint and charming tableaux of country life: a mento band plays in the doorway of a shop; a domino game is in progress in another doorway; a donkey cart laden with grass makes its way down a country road. Soft mento music plays over some of these images, intensifying the nostalgic effect. One of the images in the sequence, however – that of a wall of speaker boxes piled at the side of the road – renders the mento music asynchronous. In this brief moment, the film's idyllic transformation of place is brought into critical perspective as the nostalgic, extra-diegetic mento attempts to silence what the image of the speaker boxes signal: the presence of dancehall music, a more controversial, socially conscious and contemporary genre that practises a disruptive politics of noise.

The location of a black Jamaican romance within this representation of place suggests an intention on the part of the film to counteract certain aspects of colonial discourse pertaining to black sexuality. In her exploration of the history of the literary and visual representation of the Caribbean, Mimi Sheller carefully elucidates the ways in which the region has been repeatedly imagined by western Europe and North America as "a perpetual Garden of Eden in which visitors can indulge all their desires and find a haven for relaxation, rejuvenation, and sensuous abandon".[30] Within the context of these ways of seeing the Caribbean, various myths about black sexuality emerged that functioned to maintain European dominance, in part by justifying white men's access to black women's bodies as well as their violent responses to black men. As Barbara Bush notes, during the period of slavery, Europeans labelled the black woman promiscuous and affirmed that she was always amenable to the sexual advances of white men.[31] Black men, on the other hand, were seen as sexually aggressive. These myths of black sexuality defined black people as inappropriate subjects for the traditional romance; in such stories, normative sexuality was the preserve of the white protagonists. It is not surprising, then, as Edmondson points out, that early white Caribbean romances either depicted black sexuality as rapacious and threatening, or it was simply elided; in colonial stories of love and passion, she states, "good black women and men were asexual".[32]

One Love actively seeks to redress this discursive tradition. The film revives notions of the Caribbean as paradise through the idyllic representation of the rural environment, but while minor characters, such as the avaricious back-up singer Claudette (Kelly Barrett), may echo colonial stereotypes, the heroine remains firmly within the boundaries of normative sexuality as defined by patriarchal Christianity. Kassa wants a monogamous relationship, but as a Rastafarian he associates marriage with the evils of Babylon, and for him it is not a prerequisite for a long-term, stable relationship. Serena, however, is adamant that marriage must precede sex and she is the agent who brings Kassa into alignment with these conservative Christian values. In order to attain the heroine, Kassa must marry her, and he does. Thus, the narrative places great value on female chastity and marriage is defined as the preferred site for sexual activity. By locating Serena within the romance's traditional role of "virtuous" heroine, the narrative signals the didactic intention to refute Jamaican cultural norms of common-law union and childbearing without benefit of formal marriage vows.

While Serena functions within the narrative to promote chastity and marriage, and presents a version of femininity that is ultimately subordinate to male authority, Kassa represents a new expression of masculinity that embodies values of kindness and tolerance which are defined as necessary to the achievement of a better society. The film begins by contrasting the new masculinity with its more traditional, intolerant and authoritarian variant, exemplified by Pastor Johnson, Serena's father. In an early sequence we see Serena in a church, part of a congregation that engages in a ritual of shaming in which two members, male and female, are loudly denounced for fornication. Serena appears uncomfortable with this ritual, which functions to police sexuality by publicly exposing and humiliating offending church members. The scene cuts from the loud accusations and heightened emotions in the church to a serene, tranquil image: a close-up of water dropping from a leaf, making concentric circles in the river below as sunlight streams through the trees in a beautiful and idyllic natural setting. Kassa emerges from the water and hears Serena's disembodied voice singing sweetly, "I'm alone; I'm so alone. . . . One heart." This framing of the two protagonists serves as a critique of formal religion and the patriarchal authority which informs it by contrasting the dehumanizing church ritual with the peace and serenity of the natural environment. The juxtaposition of the two scenes and the two sites, the church and the river, suggests that true communion with God or spirit may be more readily found outside the church, in nature. The sequence also associates Kassa with the natural world and symbols of purity and rebirth.

Despite its emphasis on marriage and female chastity, the film is critical of the church's excessive attempts to police sexuality. In particular, Pastor Johnson's efforts to control Serena expose him as domineering and misguided. As both religious leader and father, Pastor wields significant authority over his daughter and uses religion to mask the colonizing impulse he manifests towards her. He refuses to allow Serena to attend music school and insists on her marriage to Aaron (Idris Elba) in spite of her doubts and protests. Serena is no shrinking violet, but she finds it difficult to oppose the powerful combination of patriarchal power which her father embodies: a potent fusion of religious and parental authority. When Serena expresses doubts about marrying Aaron, Pastor attempts to invalidate her desire for autonomy by defining it as opposition to God's will. He exhorts, "You don't see what's happening? Satan has weaved his way into your heart and is using you to destroy my credibility, to destroy the church." Pastor, both in his role as father and spiritual guide to his daughter, shows signs of moral corruption as he conflates his personal ambitions with what he identifies as God's will.

The opening sequence of the film thus initiates a pattern that emphasizes the contrast between the two men: Pastor is associated with the social world of the church that is defined by hegemonic and oppressive structures; Kassa with the natural world and what will emerge as a more relaxed and open approach to sexuality, greater tolerance of religious difference and acceptance of female equality. The differences between the two men – one the heroine's father, the other her suitor – are also defined as generational, thus Kassa, as a more compassionate, less domineering man, is an alternative version of masculinity that must replace the old one in order to ensure a more tolerant and cohesive community.

The construction of the young couple as a symbol of the new nation and a more utopian society appears to cast romantic love in a subversive role and endow it with the potential to oppose, even transform, patriarchy. Early in the narrative, romance threatens to displace religion as a primary signifier or ideological construct which lends meaning to life. Catherine Roach asserts that the story of romance is "perhaps *the* most powerful narrative at work in popular culture" and suggests, as stated earlier, that it functions in Western society as a cultural narrative: "a guiding story that provides coherence and meaning in many people's lives".³³ This proposition surfaces in *One Love*, where romantic love not only suggests a magical connection between the protagonists (Kassa hears Serena's voice when she is in church and he is in the river), it also restores their zest for life and reawakens artistic sensibilities after they experience depression and withdrawal following the death of loved ones. Significantly, neither Christian church nor Rastafari livity has been able to provide this healing.

Indeed, at its outset, the narrative seems poised to claim romance *and* eroticism as a rejuvenating and appropriate sphere of experience, not simply for the black female, but for the black female of specific sociocultural origins. Serena's modest clothing, unprocessed hair and sheltered home life help identify her as what Jamaicans commonly refer to as a "decent Christian girl", for whom, like Richardson's eighteenth-century heroine, Pamela, virtue is defined largely in terms of her chastity.³⁴ The scene in which the two lovers actually meet, however, is rich in romantic and erotic symbolism. Brought together in a recording studio, a series of reverse-angle shots visually isolate Serena and Kassa as she sings: "There's no one I found who can love me without condition, / Gave his own son for me, / I'm so happy to be alive." While Serena sings, the camera creates the illusion, by juxtaposing Kassa's reflection with Serena's image, that she is addressing him. The lyrics of the song reference love of God, but the image, coupled with Serena's heartfelt performance, evokes eros, or erotic love. The juxtaposing of these two different expressions of love seems to validate romantic and erotic love, inferring that it is a gift from God.

This promise of eroticism is never fulfilled, however. The narrative's insistence on the containment of sex in marriage effectively purges this romance of erotic content. Like heroines of an earlier century, Serena is frequently chaperoned, effectively reducing her opportunities for erotic involvement. On the single occasion when she is alone with Kassa in private, they kiss, but as soon as Kassa's hand strays to forbidden zones, Serena affirms that sex (and even petting) is off limits. Kassa, in turn, is no predatory male or romantic rake, a figure in the classic romance whose sexual aggressiveness creates a space in the narrative for erotic content. Rather, the respect and gentleness with which he treats Serena are significant elements of the new masculinity that he represents and which the film valorizes.

The film's marriage ending also functions to further diminish the subversive potential of romantic and erotic love. At the end of the film, Serena is betrothed to the man she loves, rather than the man her father chose for her, presumably signalling a victory for romance and female autonomy. In fact, the final scene is key to both protagonists' containment within patriarchy. Kassa's proposal, a public declaration of love before hundreds of people is, as they say, the stuff that romance is made of. However, his commitment to a formal union that will be sanctioned by the church and recognized by the state also marks the Rastaman's capitulation to "Babylon" and his alignment with the patriarchal hegemonic structures of the church. The betrothal also marks the curtailment of the female's rebellion against her pastor/father. Serena glances at her father before she accepts Kassa's offer of marriage, signifying her continued respect for his authority, her acceptance of patriarchy and her resumption of the mantle of obedient daughter after her rebellion in the name of love. Importantly, the marriage ending also ensures that the female's struggle for autonomy remains within specific parameters. Although Pastor Johnson has stymied Serena's development by denying her the right to attend music school, the narrative does not entertain the possibility of Serena forsaking marriage altogether in order to pursue a career or develop her talent. In this sense, romantic love and the desired outcome of marriage can be seen as deeply conservative rather than a force for change.

The spectator's acceptance of this conclusion to the romance which defines marriage for eighteen-year-old Serena as a "happy-ever-after" ending is encouraged by the closure the scene brings to several strands of the narrative. Primarily, the final scene is the culmination and climax of the romantic trajectory: the stage in the narrative at which the estranged lovers are reunited and the future of their relationship assured. This is the structural and ideological juncture at which the (romance) narrative has worked to place the spectator: the point of affirmation that love conquers all. A climactic musical performance, the culmination of the subplot concerning the music competition, also informs the scene's closure. The performance not only gives a Jamaican cultural stamp to the conclusion of the romance, it is also intensely pleasurable, making full use of the talent of the actors who play the protagonists (they are professional singers) while close-ups and medium shots show off their good looks to maximum advantage.

As commonly occurs in romance narratives, the marriage ending takes on symbolic connotations of social unity. In *One Love*, the betrothal of hero and heroine signifies the healing of social conflict between the Christians and Rastafari and the emergence of community. The marriage ending also cements the metaphorical link between the romantic couple and the film's vision of nation, affirming that love can heal hearts as well as nations. The musical performance functions as a metaphor for community and the triumph of love and acceptance over prejudice as the two previously opposing factions constitute a community on stage: Rastafari reggae band and church choir blend voices and musical styles in a demonstration of tolerance and integration before an approving audience. When Kassa falters on stage, unable to perform because of his estrangement from Serena, she walks on, begins to sing and inspires him to continue. The church group, also entrants in the contest but lacking their keyboard player because Aaron has been arrested, lend their voices to the performance. The moral is clear: two groups sound better than one. The lyrics of the song reiterate the ties of community by locating the notion of unity and nation building within the context of a spiritual quest: "What am I to do today / So I can leave this world tomorrow? . . . Jah is my inspiration, my dedication / My motivation is to heal a nation."

One Love's dream of a joyful resolution of conflict is in sharp contrast to *Children of Babylon*'s refusal to offer a happy ending and embrace an unrealistic response to the social divisions and tensions that confront Jamaican society. In the final scene of *Children of Babylon*, the female protagonist leaves the great house alone, dejected and disillusioned, quite the worse, it would seem, for her experience over the summer. In *One Love*, the heroine is enfolded in a loving, supportive community, part of a couple that has been transformed into a symbol of unity. These final scenes emphasize how very different these two films are in their intentions, their construction of heterosexual relationships and indeed, in their representation of the nation that is Jamaica.

6

NEGOTIATING PATRIARCHY
The Erotic Performance of *Dancehall Queen*

THE STOP AND START NATURE OF film production in Jamaica is reflected in the significant gap between the two feature films released in the 1980s – *Children of Babylon* (1980) and Dickie Jobson's *Countryman* (1982) – and the first feature released in the 1990s, *Dancehall Queen* (1998). Rick Elgood and Don Letts, who operated out of the United Kingdom, were recruited to direct *Dancehall Queen*, which revived the model that proved so successful in first *The Harder They Come* and then *Rockers*, in which popular music and its performance play an integral role in the narrative and the commercial viability of the film. By the 1990s, dancehall had overtaken reggae as the most current expression of popular music in Jamaica. The engagement with dancehall music signals a significant departure from earlier films: *Dancehall Queen*, like its predecessors, is a story of urban struggle, survival and resistance, but it is also vitally concerned with the politics of pleasure and erotic performance.

The first Jamaican feature film to focus on a working-class female protagonist, *Dancehall Queen* engages with a range of gendered concerns: motherhood and single parenting, sexual abuse, the politics of fashion and female erotic performance. This story of a marginalized black woman who overcomes the obstacles and challenges of a violent patriarchal society is the stuff that feminist empowerment narratives are made of. Marcia (Audrey Reid), a street vendor and single mother of two struggling to break out of the cycle of poverty and her dependence on men, discovers the dancehall as a space of opportunity within the limited choices available to lower-class women. *Dancehall Queen* explicitly valorizes Marcia's eventual rejection of patriarchal conventions and ways of thinking that define her needs as subordinate to those of men, but the use of the erotic performance of the dancehall as the catalyst for her resistance to patriarchy constitutes a complex narrative manoeuvre.

As a narrative of place, *Dancehall Queen* focuses on the dancehall as a specific site at which a gendered identity is performed. Sonjah Stanley Niaah defines dancehall in ways that speak to its existence "beyond the musical genre to encompass a wide creative economy, global network and culture" and, further, sees it as "developing from, and coterminous with, its reggae predecessor".[1] Similarly, Norman C. Stolzoff describes dancehall as an "active cultural production, a means by which black lower-class youth articulate and project a distinct identity in local, national and global contexts".[2] In *Dancehall Queen*, however, although dancehall music and culture are associated with diverse economic activities, rather than permeating through Jamaican society and beyond, dancehall is largely portrayed as a cultural phenomenon that is performed within a bounded place.

Distinguished by its fantastic fashion, the Jamaican dancehall of the 1990s featured visually striking costumes that utilized bright colours, bold patterns, tight, close fitting garments, and lacy, shiny and sheer materials artfully used to barely cover the female body and emphasize its erotic qualities. For some, the dancehall's spectacular fashion and erotically charged dance is a carnivalesque expression of freedom; for others, it is a form of female objectification.[3] Carolyn Cooper sees the dancehall as a space of autonomy for women:

> This dancehall affirmation of the pleasures of the body, which is often misunderstood as a devaluation of female sexuality, can also be theorized as an act of self-conscious assertion of control over the representation of her person. Woman as sexual being claims the right to sexual pleasure as an essential sign of her identity. Both fleshy women and their more sinewy sisters are equally entitled to display themselves in the public sphere as queens of revelry.[4]

Donna P. Hope also characterizes the dancehall as a space of freedom that permits alternate expressions of femininity, but maintains that such expression remains framed within patriarchal conventions. She points out that although the "erotic displays of female sexuality project a subversive narrative, the embodiment of [these] dancehall models, dancers and queens remains locked within the boundaries of patriarchy.... The sexual displays and suggestive gyrations of the dancehall queens titillate male sexual fantasies and feed into male perceptions of women as sexual objects."[5] Bibi Bakare-Yusuf's description of the dancehall as a phenomenon marked by its hybrid nature, irreducible plurality, complexity and ambiguity[6] acknowledges the contradictory nature of the space but does not attempt to privilege a single perspective. In an essay on the spectacular fashion of the dancehall, she notes: "It is important to remember that dancehall fashion operates within a patriarchal economy which positions women as the object of male desire and control. The extent to which the explicit celebration of women's sexuality challenges the power relations between the sexes is therefore limited. Dancehall fashion should, however, be understood as both an expression of female agency and the opportunity for male scopic mastery."[7]

Michael Reckord's review of *Dancehall Queen*, perhaps unwittingly, reveals something of the multiple fields of contestation with which the dancehall, and consequently the film, are concerned. Writing soon after the movie's release, Reckord noted: "Our latest local motion picture, 'Dancehall Queen', has lots of mass appeal. There were large numbers of ordinary folk at Carib 5 (I'm judging from their dress and speech) and they vociferously enjoyed the movie. This does not mean the film is good. It's vulgar, both in the sense that it is 'of the common people' and tasteless and lewd."[8] In his distancing of himself from the "ordinary folk" and the "common people", through reference to difference in speech, deportment and dress; in his claim for a more discerning assessment of the film; and in his scribal response as opposed to their bodily one, Reckord reveals the dialogic qualities of the film and how reception and meaning might vary among individuals and social groups. The endorsement and enjoyment of the "ordinary folk" situated in opposition to the writer's middle-class sensibilities, values and disapproval, alert us to *Dancehall Queen's* subversive intentions: its attempt to challenge hegemonic social values and validate cultural and aesthetic practices associated with dancehall and the lower classes.

By showing women in the dancehall joyously expressing and performing their sexuality, taking great pleasure in declaring themselves erotic subjects and revelling in the performance as well as the attention they receive from both men and women, *Dancehall Queen* defines this cultural phenomenon as transgressive and facilitating alternative expressions of female identity that defy middle-class norms. As Cooper affirms, Marcia "unashamedly revels in the male gaze. No feminist anxieties of 'objectification' disturb her."[9] However, the film also exploits the opportunities this erotic dance offers for the expression of an objectifying male gaze, for the figure of the dancing female is made to accommodate the persistence of conventional cinematic codes that define the dancer as erotic object and visual spectacle. The film thus raises questions about mediation, that is, the consequences and impact of the camera's entry into the relationship between performer and spectator; it confronts us with the critical question of the degree to which the transgressive and subversive potential of this particular cultural practice is capable of surviving the transformation from live performance to recorded event, and subsequent transportation outside its cultural context and environment. The specific question explored in this chapter then, is how successful *Dancehall Queen* is in its attempt to attach notions of empowerment and agency to the dancehall's erotic performance, given its use of a genre – narrative film – which has historically been identified with ways of looking steeped in patriarchal culture.

Stuart Hall's concept of negotiation in the communicative act avoids the rigidity of Laura Mulvey's iconic work on the dominance of the male gaze in narrative cinema by allowing us to understand the representation of the erotic performance of the dancehall in the film text, as well as the live performance, as sites of contesting ideologies where a struggle over meaning occurs. Mulvey theorizes that mainstream film's coding of the erotic into the language of the dominant patriarchal order assumes a male spectator, prescribing a passive role for women, that of image, and an active role for men, that of bearer of the look. Hall proposes however, that in communication, "decoding within the negotiated version contains a mixture of adaptive and oppositional elements: it acknowledges the legitimacy of the hegemonic definitions to make the grand significations (abstract), while, at a more restricted, situational (situated) level, it makes its own ground rules – it operates with exceptions to the rule".[10] Elaborating on Hall's formulation, Christine Gledhill affirms that the value of the concept of negotiation is that it avoids an overly deterministic view of cultural production:

"For the term 'negotiation' implies the holding together of opposite sides in an ongoing process of give-and-take. As a model of meaning production, negotiation conceives cultural exchange as the intersection of processes of production and reception, in which overlapping but non-matching determinations operate. Meaning is neither imposed, nor passively imbibed, but arises out of a struggle or negotiation between competing frames of reference, motivation and experience."[11]

Gledhill points out that cine-psychoanalysis theories, such as Mulvey's, which assert that the narrative organization of films is patriarchal and thus that the spectator constructed by the text is masculine, "offer largely negative accounts of female spectatorship, suggesting colonized, alienated or masochistic positions of identification".[12] In place of Mulvey's formulation of the seemingly unassailable dominance of patriarchal ideology,[13] Gledhill proposes a struggle over meaning at the point of both production and reception, which offers an approach to understanding the relations between media products, ideologies and audiences that allows for greater critical participation and autonomy on the part of the (female) spectator. Consequently, the concept of a negotiated reading can support *both* a critical response by the spectator *as well as* notions of pleasure, and female erotic performance in *Dancehall Queen* may be conceived as expressing not simply the dominance of one ideology or another, but rather as the convergence of contesting ideologies.

In *Dancehall Queen* this struggle over meaning and the convergence of contesting ideologies play out in the fantastic figure of the woman in the dancehall. The plot insists that the dancehall's erotic performance supports opportunities for the liberating expression of alternative erotic identities for the female, but the film retains dominant modes of looking which encourage objectification, framing female erotic performance in ways that resemble fetishism, and supporting what Bakare-Yusuf refers to as male scopic mastery.[14] The erotic performance, therefore, becomes an embodied paradox: the expression of what Sturken and Cartwright refer to as conflicting ideologies coexisting in tension,[15] and best understood, not as *either* empowering *or* objectifying, but as both.

The concept of negotiation can be thought of in different ways in regard to *Dancehall Queen*. At one level, it is a useful theoretical concept through which ambiguity in the narrative may be understood and explained. Within the narrative, the term can also be used to describe the process of give-and-take in which Marcia must participate as she "negotiates patriarchy", or finds her way through or around the obstacles and barriers that have been erected by the patriarchal society in which she lives, and which threaten the well-being of her family and thwart the achievement of prosperity. Strategies of trickery and deception are an important aspect of Marcia's negotiation of patriarchy. Like Ringo in *Smile Orange*, Marcia is a trickster figure and uses her wits, rather than direct confrontation, to get the better of the powerful men who threaten her well-being. Her physical transformation in the dancehall, what Cooper refers to as shape-shifting,[16] allows her to assume multiple personas which, in turn, feature in her strategies to undermine these men. Embedded in the plot, notions of trickery, deception and shape-shifting constitute a trope that, by signifying ways in which meaning becomes uncertain and unstable, also informs the concept of negotiation as a struggle over meaning which results from the friction of contesting discourses.

Cooper's observation that the shape-shifting afforded by dancehall's spectacular fashions links the film to the much older cultural form of the folktale[17] suggests yet another dimension to the perpetual negotiation of meaning in the text. As a contemporary, cinematic version of the folk narrative, the trickster tale, *Dancehall Queen* shows how Jamaican film recycles, revises and renews time-honoured cultural practices. Framed as an urban tale that is introduced by the contemporary version of the traditional storyteller, the dancehall deejay, the structure of the film confirms continuity between the old and the new: film, dancehall culture and the folktale. In the opening montage, the deejay, Beenie Man (who plays himself), is seen in the process of composing the movie's title song, "Dancehall Queen", as he sits with pen and paper, singing and writing the ballad that he will perform at the dancehall queen contest that takes place towards the end of the film. Essentially, then, the film unfolds as a flashback that is introduced by Beenie Man, the urban, latter-day counterpart to the traditional raconteur, while his song assumes the function of the folk ballad as it tells a story about contemporary figures and events:

> Contest a gwaan fi di dancehall queen,
> Who a wear di crown? Nuh di one Olivine,

Hell and powder-house when "Miss Lady" come een,
Den everybaddi start scream, seen?
Where di girl come from nobody don't know.
She's a devil angel and she's a go-go,
Is this girl human or she's a yo-yo?
Ask mi I don't know.

(There's a dancehall queen contest going on
Who wears the crown? The one Olivine
Hell and powder-house when "Miss Lady" comes in
Then everybody starts screaming, understood?
Where does the girl come from? Nobody knows
She's a devil angel and she's a go-go (dancer)
Is this girl human or is she a yo-yo?
Ask me, I don't know.)

The performance of the dancehall deejay, like that of the dancer, may also constitute a site of negotiation and contesting ideologies. This is fantastically illustrated in the first dancehall scene in the film, introduced by a recording of Junior Demus's song "Shot Mek Yu Wiggle". As the music comes up, the deejay declares, "Remember, di man who mek di gun mek a wicked sump'in, you know. . . . Devil!" From this clear initial denunciation of violence and the gun, the song lyrics proceed to create a metaphorical bridge between gun violence, the movement of the dancers and the dancehall:

Shot mek yu wiggle
Ah no sump'n fi yu giggle
For di man who build di gun him build a dangerous sump'n.
Shot mek yu wiggle
Ah no sump'n fi yu giggle
Some bwai mus be tink ah ay diggle diggle

([Gun]shot makes you wiggle
It's not something to giggle about
For the man who made the gun made a dangerous thing.
[Gun]shot makes you wiggle
It's not something to giggle about
Some boys must think it's "hey diddle diddle" [something childish or trivial].)

Here the word "wiggle" metaphorically conveys the pain and distress the gunshot causes as well as a bodily response to the gunshot, that is, the shot causes the affected person to feel pain and it also makes one move about (or "wiggle") in pain and discomfort. Heard over images of dancers, male and female, performing various rhythmic, often erotic movements (they too are "wiggling"), it becomes apparent that the lyrics also play on the idea of the gun as a phallic symbol, so that "shot" and "wiggle" also refer to the sexual act. This interplay of movement, image, music and lyrics affirms the dancing bodies as kinetic metaphorical expressions of, paradoxically, both (gun) violence and pleasure (sex). The scene suggests that the dancehall functions for the community, in part, as a coping mechanism, a place where both everyday experiences as well as the violence and terror of this harsh environment are mediated through music and performance. It signifies, as well, a close connection between the dancehall and the streets, that is, the life of the community beyond the walls of the performance space. The dancehall may be constructed in the film as an alternative mode of expression and authority that expresses the community's creativity and capacity for joy and beauty in its many forms, but it is also linked with violence, as is further supported in the cross-cutting between Marcia's performance in the dancehall queen contest and the fatal encounter she engineers between Priest (Paul Campbell) and Larry (Carl Davis), the two men who are her antagonists.

As a metaphorical expression of the interplay or convergence of sex and violence in the lives of community members, the erotic performance of the dancehall also articulates Marcia's own struggle against patriarchal control. Marcia's negotiation of the male-dominated society begins at an early age: thrown out of her parental home and forced to leave school when she became pregnant, it is oppressive patriarchal attitudes that cut short her education, initiate her slide into poverty and predispose her to a condition of dependency. When the film opens, Marcia's baby-fathers are "absent without leave", and she relies to a large extent on the wealthy Larry for help with the bills, in particular, school fees for her older daughter, Tanya (Cherine Anderson). Marcia's dependence on men is not only financial; there is psychological dependence as well, for she displays attitudes that indicate an acceptance of male supremacy and male privilege. This is most evident in her response to Larry's attempt to initiate a sexual relationship with Tanya who, ironically, is fifteen, the same age at which Marcia became pregnant. Sanctioning Larry's demands and colluding in the reduction of her daughter to mere sexual commodity, Marcia reminds Tanya that it is Larry who pays the bills and urges her to cooperate. "Jus' try to go along wid di programme as much as possible," Marcia counsels, "when Larry deh bout the place things run right." (Just try to go along with the programme as much as possible; when Larry is around, things go well.) When Tanya protests, Marcia insists, "Just put this inna yu pipe and smoke it: I'm yu madda so yu do what I say!" (Just put this in your pipe and smoke it: I'm your mother so you will do as I say.) The irony of Marcia's invocation of parental authority is palpable and underscores her failing as a parent. For as she attempts to rationalize her actions by claiming economic necessity and pragmatism, Marcia fails to prioritize her daughter's well-being.

Larry is not the only predatory male who seeks to violate the domestic space. Marcia and her family are also threatened by Priest who, unknown to them, was hired by Larry to kill Sonny (Donald Thompson), a close friend of the family. Priest threatens Marcia and her brother, Junior (Mark Danvers), in order to dissuade them from "turning informer", that is, identifying him to the police as Sonny's killer. Caught between Priest's threats and harassment by the police, who pressure him to reveal what he knows, Junior has a breakdown, leaving Marcia to care and provide for the family on her own. Junior's emotional response to Sonny's death and his subsequent psychological collapse suggest a "hysterical", feminized response, and thus, a reduced status within the patriarchal social system. For Marcia, however, he occupies an important position in the home by virtue of being the only man in the house. The combined pressures of Sonny's death, the loss of Junior's support and Larry's financial contribution, as well as Priest's threats and harassment, constitute a critical period for Marcia marked by anxiety and fear, the collapse of the family structure and the loss of income. These problems that confront Marcia and her family function to define the social environment as one in which men exercise "badness" – violence, coercion and aggression – to determine status and power.

Under the collective weight of these events, Marcia faces a crisis of huge proportions. Bereft of male protection and patronage, she realizes that she must assume responsibility for her family's well-being. The idea of the dancehall as a possible solution to her money problems is initiated by the revelation that the erotic figure of the dancehall queen constitutes a persona that she too can assume, and which can accrue significant wealth for her. She witnesses the approbation accorded Olivine (Patrice Harrison), the reigning dancehall queen, when she is involved in a traffic accident, and notices not only that Olivine drives a new motor car, but also how "ordinary" she looks when not dressed in her dancehall finery. As Marcia's friend, Winsome (Sandra Isaacs), remarks of Olivine, "She can only paint up her face and wine up her batty, and she have money, you know, she can buy anyting."

The connection between male desire and male patronage also underlies the film's treatment of Larry's sexual demands of Tanya. In one of the exchanges between mother and daughter on the subject, Marcia is silenced and apparently shamed when an incensed Tanya declares, "If you think Larry is such a great meal ticket why didn't you sleep with him?" Hanging her head, Marcia mumbles, "Is you 'im want." (It's you he wants.)

Dancehall fashion allows Marcia to remake herself into an idealized and stylized version of femininity that is desired and valued by Larry and other men. Heavily made up, wearing a blonde wig, high heels and a gold lamé short-pants suit, Marcia is transformed into what Larry describes as "one sexy bitch" whose "legs lead straight to heaven". The costume is worn with the attitude to match: Marcia as the "sexy bitch" is sassy, flirtatious and gives the impression of sexual availability. This version of femininity is far removed from the Marcia we saw previously, who paid little attention to her physical appearance and whose manner was direct and no-nonsense. While some suspension of disbelief is required to accept that the transformation wrought by the dancehall costume is so radical that Larry cannot recognize her, it is clear that when she inhabits this new persona, Marcia becomes an object of male desire.[18] As dancehall vixen, Marcia commands certain forms of power over men and is able to manipulate Larry and extract financial support, something she could only do previously through the promise of her daughter's body. Marcia's assumption of the dancehall persona should not be thought of, however, as simply a willingness to be contained within a role deemed appropriate by patriarchy, rather it represents a strategic negotiation of patriarchal structures which allows her to reap benefits for herself. When Tanya first discovers her mother in dancehall fashion and exclaims, "Mama, that's not you," Marcia replies, "You're right, it's not me. But I have a plan and it's going to make life better fi all ah wi."(You're right, it's not me. But I have a plan and it's going to make life better for all of us.)

It is clear, however, that the benefits Marcia derives from the dancehall are not solely economic, even though monetary gain is the initial reason for her participation. Bakare-Yusuf uses the term "carnal power"[19] to describe Marcia's new-found desirability, and this new form of power is accompanied by the flowering of confidence and self-esteem. Dancehall participation allows Marcia to express her sexuality and articulate an aspect of the self that was previously dormant and undervalued; it thus facilitates the creation of a more holistic identity. This flowering of a previously repressed sexuality is defined as a female-centred process of rebirth, for Marcia is assisted by other women: her friend Winsome, Miss Gordon (Pauline Stone Myrie), the dressmaker and, most important, her daughter, Tanya, who plays a critical role in bringing about Marcia's ultimate conversion into the confident woman who emerges from the dancehall at the end of the film.

Role switching frequently occurs between mother and daughter, who are separated in age by only fifteen years, as Tanya often assumes the role of parent, guiding and encouraging her mother and insisting on a higher moral standard than that which Marcia has set. When Olivine attempts to sabotage Marcia's performance in the dancehall queen contest by exposing her as a street vendor, it is Tanya who is the voice of wisdom when she declares: "Why you think she trying to frighten you off? Is because she know you better than her. And you're not ashamed of who we are, are you?" The cooperation between mother and daughter in Marcia's transformation into a confident dancehall queen plays an important part in rebuilding the trust that was destroyed when Marcia betrayed Tanya to Larry. Again, the irony is evident: Marcia replaces her daughter as the desired object of the male gaze, but the underlying notion of female-derived benefits from male desire remains intact.

Marcia's participation in the dancehall leads to the construction of two interlocking personas which Marcia moves between and displays selectively. She is the "sexy bitch" to Larry when he sees her in dancehall fashion and in the dancehall she becomes known as the "mystery lady", a participant whose identity and origins are unknown. To family and friends, however, she is Marcia, mother of two who makes her living as a street vendor. Towards the close of the narrative, around the climactic dance contest sequences, these three identities are openly declared and revealed to all as manifestations of a single subject. Importantly, at the end of the film, Marcia emerges from the dancehall, not dressed in the fantastic fashion of the sexy bitch or mystery lady, but as Marcia the street vendor, and proudly takes her place with her family at her vending cart as the supportive crowd cheers her on. Marcia's deliberate resumption of her "everyday" identity at the close of the narrative broadly indicates an ultimate acceptance of self and origins, the integration of a fragmented identity and the flowering of confidence and self-esteem. Marcia is not solely defined by her pose as the sexy bitch or the mystery lady – nor indeed is she only defined by the fact that she is a mother and works as a street vendor – but the dancehall makes these masks available to express otherwise silenced aspects of the personality. Thus, the narrative affirms a complex, multifaceted subjectivity for its female protagonist. It also infers that Marcia has acquired something far more valuable than the generous cash prize she is awarded for winning the dancehall queen contest. The shedding of oppressive beliefs associated with patriarchal ideology and colonial attitudes allows Marcia to see both herself and her daughter as worthy of respect and having intrinsic value as black women. It is this confidence and independence, as well as the belief in herself and abilities as a woman, the narrative infers, not simply the prize money, that will ensure a brighter future for Marcia and her family.

At a conceptual level, therefore, the film's attempt to valorize the liberating aspects of the dancehall's erotic performance and use it as the context for Marcia's empowerment and emergence from patriarchal restrictions is both clear and credible. It is in the visual representation of this idea, however, that the film's negotiation of the contesting ideologies at play in the dancehall becomes less certain and assured. In its exploration of the articulation of various forms of spectatorship that occur in the dancehall around female erotic performance, the film constructs the dancehall as a space where creativity, performance and participation are fuelled by looking: in the dancehall, being seen and acknowledged connote status, even certain forms of power and authority. However, while elements of self-reflexivity suggest a deliberate intention to interrogate modes of representation of the female body, contradictions arise as elements of patriarchal ideology are asserted in the film's retention of conventions that promote an objectifying male gaze.

The film's attempt to draw attention to modes of spectatorship can be seen in the second dancehall sequence; this is the first instance when Marcia enters the dancehall as a full participant. In this sequence, there is a brief interaction between two women: one walks past another who looks at her in a pose that exaggerates both the act of looking as well as an expression of amazement at what is being looked at. In another part of the sequence, a woman holds her flattened palm above her eyes, a gesture that seeks to bring attention to the act of looking and also indicates the extraordinary nature of that which the viewer beholds. These images of women watching other women in such an exaggerated fashion occur in a sequence that shows female dancehall participants, clothed in erotic costumes, performing erotic dances. The montage speaks, therefore, to the idea of the female as both spectacle and spectator in the dancehall, and further suggests spectatorship as an active rather than passive event, and even as a performance in its own right.

The dramatic climax of the film, the dancehall queen contest between Marcia and Olivine, constitutes a dynamic playing out of the performance and spectatorship that occur in the dancehall, as the two women perform erotic dances on an elevated stage before a large crowd. The contest puts to rest the simmering rivalry between the two women, which has been defined throughout the narrative as a competition for the gaze and approbation of dancehall patrons, including that of a photographer. During the women's performances in the contest, alternating shots of the dancer and the watching crowd briefly show a videographer and the photographer in the audience recording the performances. Cross-cutting further reveals that the performances, duly captured by the video camera, are transmitted live on television and are watched at home by Marcia's younger daughter, Tasha (Anika Grason), and Tanya's boyfriend (Warren Harris). This self-reflexive cross-cutting between the live action and television spectators who watch the performances at home suggests different forms of reception and spectatorship. The young man's exclamation when Marcia appears on the television screen, uttered in disbelief to Tasha, "That's your mother?", certainly calls our attention to the transformative nature of the dancehall's sartorial practices, but also to the importance of the mediating role of the camera as it frames and reproduces performance for the spectator who is removed from the live event – a function also performed by the film itself, as noted earlier. Thus, we are reminded that the cinematic and televisual apparatuses render the image of the dancing erotic body vulnerable to appropriation and consumption by countless spectators whose gaze the performing subject is powerless to confront, rebuff or even acknowledge.

Such formal strategies suggest *Dancehall Queen* as the type of text which acknowledges what Hall describes as the complexities and ambivalence of representation and which "accepts and works with the shifting, unstable character of meaning".[20] In her reading of *Dancehall Queen*, Bakare-Yusuf elaborates on the techniques employed in the film to counter conventional modes of representation and create alternative ways of seeing. She argues that the film moves beyond the patriarchal conventions of dominant cinema and reconstructs the erotic female as subject rather than spectacle by disrupting the active/passive polarization of the performer and audience.[21] She points out that in the contest scenes, where those watching the performer actively respond to what they watch, reciprocity between performer and observer closes the distance necessary for objectification, so that, Bakare-Yusuf asserts, the performer ceases to be an externalized object and a fetishized mode of activity that implies and enforces an equal and attendant mode of fascinated passivity on the part of the audience. As there is no gap between the stage and active audience in the contest scenes, she argues, the diegetic audience is much more like a crowd, a site for potential activity and engagement:

> The dancehall queen represents the audience as a representation of themselves. The performing woman embodies and mirrors her community. In this sense the embodied agency of the dancehall queen involves an erotics of community. The community of the crowd is folded within her every movement. Her dancing body is the subject of the performance and the means by which the crowd can reciprocate by expressing its own identity. As an erotic

site the stage performance, therefore, allows for the jubilant celebration of female carnal power as a unique opportunity afforded by the culture. This celebration does not slip back into pornographic images because the community itself is presented within the audience. The crowd contains celebrating women as much as appreciative men. An erotics of community replaces pornography because both sides of the stage are engaged in active dialogue or communion.[22]

Bakare-Yusuf's notions of reciprocity, identification and community refer specifically to the dynamics between the dancehall performer and the diegetic crowd/audience, but do not take into account the impact of the camera on this dynamic, that is, the extent to which a community of erotics and notions of reciprocity remain viable in the relationship between the cinema spectator and the image of the performance. For the cinema audience, the camera mediates between performer and spectator offering possibilities of disruption and alienation that do not occur within the framework of the live performance. In the contest scenes, therefore, while there are instances where shot/reverse-shot editing attempts to position the spectator within the diegetic participatory "crowd" and works to encourage identification with the crowd and thus, the dancing women on the stage, there are also significant occasions where this identification is disrupted. Through cross-cutting, both Olivine's and Marcia's performances are fragmented and constructed as interruptions of highly dramatic, crucial moments in the narrative. This not only tends to disrupt the process of spectator identification with the dancer and the diegetic crowd who watch the contest, but it also conforms to a pattern that Mulvey identifies in which woman, in her traditional exhibitionist role as passive visual spectacle, interrupts or brings the narrative to a halt.[23] Just before she takes the stage, Olivine informs Marcia that she has discovered and informed the crowd that Marcia is just an "ordinary little street vendor". Shots of Olivine's performance interrupt the playing out of Marcia's emotional refusal to compete in the contest and her gradual understanding that members of the crowd not only accept her lower-class status but identify with it. Similarly, when Larry and Priest finally meet in an anticipated confrontation that Marcia has engineered, cross-cutting frequently shifts narrative focus from the fatal fight between the two men to Marcia dancing on the stage.

Indeed, from the point of view of the spectator who sits before the screen, rather than that of the diegetic "crowd" which watches the dancing women and participates in the performance, what emerges is not a "community of erotics", as Bakare-Yusuf proposes, but rather an awareness of the frequent use of patriarchal visual codes and conventions in the construction of the erotic performances that constitute the dancehall queen contest. Modes of representation which visually fragment and dismember the female body are prevalent: close-ups and medium shots isolate or direct attention to specific parts of the body and the camera tilts to selectively direct the spectator's gaze up or down the female body. Such modes of looking, including the occasional use of canted framing, suggest fetishism and, being unique to photography and cinematography, create a perspective of the dancing women's bodies that resides outside the arena of live spectatorship.

In particular, during Olivine's performance, choreography and framing combine to emphasize the erotic in a specific and explicit manner. As she dances, Olivine frequently grasps her crotch, while a preponderance of low angle shots, close-ups and medium shots are used to direct attention to the pelvic area and buttocks. At the very beginning of her performance, Olivine strides to the front of the stage and stands almost directly over the camera, so that she is viewed from an extreme low angle, and the (cinema) spectator's perspective is that of someone who is looking up her short skirt. She then drops to a stooping position and opens her legs to reveal her scantily covered crotch, while the camera's low angle shot emphasizes this area of the body.

Indeed, the use of such patriarchal cinematic codes are present in the framing of erotic female performance throughout the film. In the first dancehall scene, Marcia does not dance among the other participants but stays on the sidelines observing the dancers. Even while shot/reverse-shot editing suggests Marcia as the diegetic spectator, the erotic display is framed according to the conventions of an objectifying male gaze: the dancers' bodies are often fragmented as close-ups and medium shots focus on the torso and isolate the breasts, the pelvic area and the buttocks in particular; low-angle perspectives dominate, emphasizing the torso and calling attention away from the dancers' faces.

It must be noted, however, that throughout the film, Marcia is largely excluded from this mode of representation. In the contest sequences, not only is Marcia's performance less risqué than Olivine's, it is also made more dramatic through the use of lighting and a somewhat more elaborate costume which she removes piece by piece, until she is stripped to the bare minimum. More than just a striptease, however, her dance is an embodied performance of what Cooper refers to as the "fantastic un/dress code of the dancehall",[24] as well as a metaphorical expression of her own transformation within that space which has involved role play, shape-shifting, and the final revealing of her identity. Accorded greater nuance and symbolism, Marcia's performance relies less on raw eroticism for impact. This is reflected in the way it is viewed by the camera which tends to refrain from the explicit attention to the pelvic area and low angle close-ups, preferring to utilize instead, eye-level medium and long shots. In the second dancehall scene when Marcia becomes a participant in the revelry of the space and is seen in full dancehall fashion, she is not only excluded from patriarchal visual codes but also the more raunchy dancing that prevails. While several of the women engage in risqué acrobatic moves (or "skin out"), Marcia performs a comparatively modest dance and is framed in a medium shot as she dances; the single close-up focuses on her face. In another scene, when Marcia challenges Olivine on the dance floor at a club, this differential framing is apparent when her performance of (what seems to be) a particularly risqué dance move is edited so that it is not seen by the cinema spectator.

Marcia's relatively modest performances in some scenes might be explained by her status as newcomer to the dancehall, nevertheless, they serve to support her exemption from some of the more intense modes of patriarchal visual framing. This differential framing accorded the heroine, and her less risqué choreography, suggests a subtle hierarchy which values moderation and restraint in the erotic performance. Such restraint however, contradicts the aesthetic of flamboyance and the spectacular which, throughout, the film has associated with the dancehall. In effect, it suggests the subtle intrusion of a middle-class sensibility in this attempt to legitimize the cultural practices of the dancehall, and thus indicates yet another site of ideological tension.

Dancehall Queen is indeed a text that is defined by the friction of contesting meanings and ideologies that are held together by tension within the narrative. At the very centre of this tension and plurality is the image of the skimpily clad but fantastically clothed woman in the dancehall who dances joyously, as much for her own pleasure as she does to celebrate the pleasure that she brings to those who watch her. In its retention of mainstream cinematic codes to frame erotic performance, the film reflects the existence and influence of patriarchal values in the dancehall, but it also carefully articulates the idea that the dancehall constitutes a space for women, especially those who are poor and marginalized, where they may assume alternate identities and claim the pleasures and power of the body. At the very least, the film encourages the spectator to explore his or her own attitudes towards the dancehall and its controversial erotic female performance. The image of the joyously dancing woman and the pleasure it produces resists the censure of a puritanical ideology; it also resists containment within a traditional feminist reading that would rob the dancing subject of her own power. Still, Marcia's surrender of the dancehall queen trophy and her resumption of her everyday identity after the contest also suggest that the joyous dance, while empowering, is also fleeting; the challenges and concerns of the everyday world still wait to be confronted. As Marcia declares at the end of the film when she hands Olivene the trophy and acknowledges her as "Queen of the Dancehall": "There's a whole new world out there waiting and I'm going to get some."

7
REAL/REEL LIFE IN JUNGLE
Alienated Spaces in *Third World Cop* and *Ghett'a Life*

IN JAMAICA'S SMALL AND FRAGILE FILM SECTOR, Chris Browne has the somewhat unusual distinction of having directed two successful features. Both of these films are set in the depressed urban community Arnett Gardens, known as Concrete Jungle or simply Jungle or Dungle. Browne's first film, *Third World Cop* (1999), is a detective story about a policeman's attempt to expose a gun running racket located in the poor community that was once his home and in which his childhood friend is a central player. In *Ghett'a Life* (2011), Browne's second film, a young man's defiance of the neighbourhood don is played out against the background of violent partisan political rivalry in what is referred to in Jamaica as a garrison constituency: a "violently defended geographical power domain" in which "local political bosses control the streets and all forms of political life".[1]

Kingston's inner city is central to Browne's artistic vision and his work as a filmmaker. In an interview with the author, Browne asserted that while there may be stories to be told of uptown Jamaica, someone else will have to tell them; he is interested in stories of struggle in the inner city.[2] White and middle-class, Browne claims a close connection with downtown Kingston through his work in the commercial video sector, but, ironically, his description of the two worlds that he moves between seems to affirm the very social and spatial divisions that he claims to overcome. Speaking at his home in a Kingston suburb, Browne stated:

> I do music videos and we shoot them in the ghetto every day, so I'm in the ghetto all the time. At some points I used to be in there four days a week, in all

different ghettos, in all parts of Jamaica . . . So I see the people, I know what's going on; I hear what they have to say, I see what's going on. That world is [as much] a part of my world as this world is. This is where I sleep and eat and raise my family, and that is where I go to work. It's full of stories; it's full of tragedies, full of life, so I tell my stories.[3]

It is instructive that Browne refers to his films as *"my* stories" (my emphasis), rather than explicitly claim to be speaking on behalf of the marginalized. In doing so, he might be understood as expressing a consciousness of shaping life into art, that is, of imposing certain narrative conventions and a superstructure – ultimately, ideological formations – on his raw material. He affirms that he likes happy endings as well as stories with a moral, and says that he tries to adhere to what he sees as a social responsibility to make certain kinds of films.[4] Describing *Ghett'a Life* (which had not been released at the time of the interview) as "a fantasy" and "a film of hope" that is "supposed to make everybody come out [of the theatre] feeling good", Browne stated: "There are so many stories we do of the ghetto, where people pick up the gun, but how negative that is. Yeah, you can make money from them, but what are you teaching the kids?"[5]

Despite Browne's assertion of bringing to bear a very personal and subjective perspective or vision in his work, his films are popularly conceived as authentic representations of life in the inner city, and as such are seen as performing the important social function of providing persons who live outside the ghetto with an understanding of what life in these communities is really like. Conceptualizing *Third World Cop* as the proverbial "window to the real world", reviewer Andrew Clunis wrote:

Third World Cop is reality and it should be quite enlightening to those people who live in their secluded St. Andrew suburbs and don't understand the runnings of the inner city. What you see on the screen there is what happens within the city continuously. In fact, many of the action scenes are no different from the daily evening newscasts. The film should tug at the consciences of various people in the country, prompting them to address the social conditions under which hundreds of thousands of Jamaicans live.[6]

More than ten years later, Garth Rattray's review of *Ghett'a Life* would resonate with Clunis's comments:

> This is immeasurably more than a movie – it is a soul-spun presentation that begged for intervention from inside and outside the ghetto, from the rich and the poor, from the empowered and the disempowered, from the enchanted and the disenchanted, from home and abroad, from you and from me. . . . This is as close to ghetto life as most viewers will ever get. While remaining focused on the theme of the movie and the message in his film, Mr Browne delivered a gripping representation of everyday inner city life; the ridiculousness of entrenched politico-gang division, rivalry that destroys many lives (while benefiting only a few) and the easy availability of guns (destructive tools for the resolution of all conflicts/disagreements). There was just enough violence and expletives to make necessary points and move the plot forward while bestowing authenticity.[7]

As indicated by the reviewers, Browne's films are popularly regarded as texts which show non-residents what life in the inner city looks like and thus may be understood as participating in the process of "imagining the nation": they appear to offer viewers "strips of reality . . . out of which scripts can be formed of imagined lives".[8] In effect, the reviews affirm that Browne "shows us as we are", but Doreen Massey's insistence that "the identities of places are always unfixed, contested and multiple"[9] raises fundamental questions about the validity or even usefulness of using "authenticity" as a value in representing place, and it also troubles and problematizes the perceived social function the reviewers ascribe to the films, of speaking on behalf of the inner-city resident to those outside the ghetto.

My concern in this chapter is not to hold up Browne's films to some supposed objective definition of Kingston's inner-city areas to assess whether they are or are not "authentic" representations of a specific locality. Rather, I am concerned, as Massey urges us to be, with the politics of definition that operates within these texts, with questions about the nature of the criteria used to establish authenticity, as well as the extent to which these films' engagement with "ghetto life" can be understood as counter-hegemonic or, conversely, actually functions to reinforce the status quo. Thus, do these films "imagine the nation" in ways that support a "deep horizontal comradeship"[10] and contest social hierarchies by insisting on the equal standing of all citizens? Or do they reinforce relationships of subordination and domination that create and maintain pockets of privilege and notions of elitism?

This discussion must necessarily begin by considering the aesthetics of the film, as well as its mode of production. Produced by the same team that brought *Dancehall Queen* to the screen, *Third World Cop* was made using the same model that had been employed unsuccessfully with the earlier film, that is, a limited production budget was maintained in order to maximize profits. Chris Browne proved to be the right man for the job. He wrapped up shooting just three days outside of the twenty-day schedule and was able to make *Third World Cop* for about US$600,000 (compared to the US$1 million incurred by *Dancehall Queen*). Well known as a cinematographer and for his commercial work, Browne was brought on board to direct the film, but he says of the experience that he felt like "a hired gun" and was unable to implement many of his own ideas.[11] While the production context of *Third World Cop* suggests a more profit-driven process, in contrast, *Ghett'a Life* was a labour of love, a personal project in which Browne had full artistic control. He wrote and developed the script himself and then went about the difficult task of raising funds, mainly from local investors, to make the film, a process that took him several years. There are clear continuities between the two films, however, that speak perhaps to the genres in which Browne operates and also to dominant ways of thinking about the ghetto as place.

As "aesthetic commodities"[12] both films adopt a realist approach which, as Robert Stam points out in his survey of the historical use of the term, creates an illusion of the real even as it operates according to specific well-defined conventions. One of the definitions of realism that Stam provides is that it is "a constellation of stylistic conventions that, at a given moment in the history of an art, manage, through the fine-tuning of illusionistic technique, to crystallize a strong *feeling* of authenticity".[13]

In film, these stylistic conventions produce "a fictional world characterized by internal coherence, plausible causality, psychological realism, and the appearance of seamless spatial and temporal continuity".[14] It is the fictional world with these characteristics that the movie audience often responds to with what bell hooks describes as "a certain sense of magic, a certain sense that reality is being documented", and a reluctance to acknowledge that the movie is really about filmmakers "consciously knowing what kinds of images will produce a certain kind of impact".[15]

While realist film has traditionally been associated with the social democratization of narrative and the recognition that members of the lower classes are also worthy subjects of "problematic-existential representation",[16] the use of realism as a narrative and aesthetic mode in Caribbean films about such groups presents certain challenges. One has to do with the tendency of the realist film to support a singular perspective rather than alert the spectator to the possibility of multiple, coexisting valid perspectives. Another consideration, an old concern in critical debates about artistic expression in the Caribbean, has to do with both the aesthetic and political implications of using the language of the dominant power to express the experiences and reality of a subordinate group.

Wahneema Lubiano, in his discussion of the work of the African American filmmaker Spike Lee, warns of the dangers of the uncritical acceptance of realism as a mode of expression. He notes that realism poses a fundamental, long-standing challenge for counter-hegemonic discourse because it enforces an authoritative perspective: "Deployed as a narrative form dependent on recognition of reality, realism suggests disclosure of the truth (and then closure of the representation); realism invites readers/audience to accept what is offered as a slice of life because the narrative contains elements of 'fact'."[17]

Thus, as Lubiano implies, the realist film sustains a double fallacy: the illusion of the existence of a singular "Truth" that can be fully grasped and understood by the spectator, and the further illusion that "the truth" can be – and is – contained in the text. Lubiano affirms, however, that "truth" or "fact" is not an absolute value, but constitutes subjective claims. He states: "Telling the 'truth' demands that we consider the truth of something compared to something else. Who is speaking? Who is asking? And to what end?"[18] Kobena Mercer's critique of realist aesthetics in black filmmaking in Britain resonates here when he reminds us that "the selection of *who* is given the right to speak may also exclude others".[19] Such statements may lead us to look afresh at the claims for authenticity in Browne's films, as well as ponder what other "truths" about the ghetto might be silenced by the version of reality asserted by these films and by the hegemonic insistence, by those who have access to vehicles of public discourse, that these films are authentic representations of ghetto life.

As realist narratives, the seemingly unassailable element of "fact" upon which *Third World Cop* and *Ghett'a Life* rest is the assertion that crime and violence are mundane and inescapable facets of ghetto life in Jamaica. It is not my intention here to seek to either confirm or deny this notion; I merely wish to draw attention to its broad acceptance as truth and the way in which it has become naturalized as a fixed and primary characteristic of the Jamaican inner city in the two films discussed and in other media representations, including those that originate beyond Jamaican shores. The Kingston "ghetto" as a site for drugs, crime and violence has now become almost as closely associated with Jamaica in the popular imaginary as palm trees and white sand beaches. This commonplace association of violence and crime with a specific locality, however, rather than an indication of authenticity, can be understood as emerging from what Mercer describes as the existential dilemma of dependent expressivity. Confronted in literary debates around aesthetics and politics in the African, Caribbean and Afro-American novel of the 1940s and 1950s, Mercer states, dependent expressivity refers to the struggle of the colonized to express an authentic self in the language imposed by the imperial power of the colonizer.[20]

This old argument raises new and urgent questions in films about violence and urban life in which the imitative and uncritical use of cinematic language and genre codes and conventions tends to reproduce problematic representations of Caribbean life. Craig A. Smith refers to this issue in an essay on *Shottas* (2002), a film that delves into much the same terrain that *Third World Cop* and *Ghett'a Life* are concerned with, that is, male violence and urban life in Jamaica. Smith states that stylistic and ideological mimicry of certain American films has resulted in representations of masculinity predicated on violence and a code of silence: "Despite all the claims to *Shottas*' rootedness in the Jamaican experience, it is a film that has been seen many times before, but this time it is set to a reggae beat and the rhythm of Jamaican patois. Even more disturbing, this film simply recapitulates many of the very same dangerous tropes found in black oriented films from the US."[21]

In contrast, some of the earlier Jamaican films about men in ghetto spaces are also predominantly realist, but they do make use of other aesthetic conventions, thus relieving the total involvement with dominant cinematic codes and genre conventions that occurs in films like *Shottas*, *Third World Cop* and *Ghett'a Life*. In *Rockers*, self-reflexivity, including direct address to the camera, cinematography and editing reminiscent of cinéma-vérité and a persistent disregard for tight cause and effect relations in narrative structure contribute to a perspective of ghetto life that is both complex and optimistic. In *The Harder They Come*, Henzell's dense use of symbolism in the mise en scène provides a sense of the multiple identities of place, while self-reflexivity complicates the portrait of Ivan and provides the potential for multiple interpretations of his final actions. Ivan certainly transforms himself, in part, through referencing of certain tropes in popular gun films, but Henzell also exposes and critically comments on the role that popular cinema plays in identity formation.

The aesthetic choices made in these two earlier films reflect an intention to challenge and move beyond generic codes, what Steve Neale describes as "an aesthetic regime based on regulated difference, contained variety, [and] pre-sold expectations" that is maintained in the film industry in order to maximize profits.[22] What characterises *Third World Cop* and *Ghetta' Life*, then, is the willingness to remain within that regime; a tendency to adhere to, rather than challenge, dominant conventions of film narrative and, in particular, genre codes that have tended to reproduce harmful stereotypes about black men, violence and poverty. From this point of view, claims for the authenticity of the two films are ironic, for what these films reference is not merely real life, but *reel* life: in effect, a range of Hollywood generic conventions that result in highly stylized enactments of violence and representations of masculinity.

It would appear that the narrative conventions and codes of certain Hollywood genres may be so well known that they seem to create a sense of actuality for the viewer who is familiar with in them, rather than proclaim that mediation is at work. As Neale points out, the boundaries between generic regimes of verisimilitude (the rules or conventions of the genre) and public opinion or cultural regimes of verisimilitude (that which the audience believes to be real) are often blurred. Further, he states, this blurring of boundaries does not only occur in films and other genres, as "the two regimes merge also in public discourse, generic knowledge becoming a form of cultural knowledge, a component of 'public opinion'".[23] Thus,

Neale speaks to a circular and self-fulfilling process that certainly seems to be at play in the popular response to Browne's films. In this regard, Neale points out that one needs to be mindful of the distinction between *authenticity*, that which relates to fact, and *verisimilitude*, that which is probable or has the appearance of being real or true. Browne's films are described as authentic not because they reflect fact or what is true, but because they reflect or coincide with public opinion: that which people believe to be true.

I want to identify two scenes in *Third World Cop* in which there is a provocative blurring of cultural and generic regimes. The opening scene of the film introduces the protagonist, a policeman ironically known as Capone (Paul Campbell). The film begins with shots of Capone making love to a woman that alternate with a series of images that identify him as a policeman. The couple's lovemaking is interrupted when two men holding Capone's partner hostage gain entry to the room. Although he is taken by surprise and outnumbered, Capone is prepared for all eventualities and, slipping a gun from beneath his pillow, he shoots the two intruders. Standing over one of his wounded would-be assassins, Capone pronounces, "Ah go send you home, guilty as charged", and shoots again, not in self-defence this time, but in cold blood. Dominance supported by the gun is again dramatically enacted when Ratty (Mark Danvers), Capone's childhood friend who is involved in a gun importation ring, carries out a highly stylized execution of Deportee (Desmond Ballentine), a former ally who betrays him. In this scene, Ratty sits at a table and slowly and very deliberately tears a page from the Bible and uses it to roll a spliff (a cigarette made from marijuana). Standing with arms outstretched and gun in one hand, he recites (and literally smokes) Psalm 23 as a prelude to the killing. Ratty declares: "Yea, though I walk through the valley of the shadow of death, I will fear no evil: for thou art with me; Thy rod and thy staff, they comfort me." Ratty then shoots Deportee in the chest.

In both scenes, Capone and Ratty's high-ranking status as men in the ghetto community is constructed through their ability to wreak violence on the bodies of other men who challenge their authority. Both scenes also provocatively, and I think unintentionally, equate this with sexual performance, although less explicitly so in the latter scene. The association of masculinity with dominance, the ability to use force to subdue others and sexual performance certainly resonates with traditional assumptions about masculinity in Jamaica, but the highly dramatic way in which the film enacts these cultural values is modelled on *reel life* rather than *real life*. Certainly, Ratty's Bible-quoting execution of Deportee is reminiscent of hitman Jules (Samuel Jackson) in Quentin Tarantino's *Pulp Fiction* (1994), who recites verses from the Bible before killing his victims. Capone, on the other hand, is modelled on the Harry Callahan character (played by Clint Eastwood) in *Dirty Harry* (1971) and its subsequent sequels. Like Harry, Capone is a no-nonsense, stoic cop who always maintains tight-lipped control of his emotions and has no problem with taking the law into his own hands.

Indeed, although Browne said that a senior member of the Jamaica Constabulary Force provided them with material for the film, he describes *Third World Cop* as "kind of like a Clint Eastwood movie".[24] Importantly, like *Dirty Harry* and other cop films, *Third World Cop* affirms the need for the police to use excessive force in order to contain criminal threat. Indeed, Timothy O. Lenz describes *Dirty Harry* as a film which challenges the liberal orthodoxy that violence is an atavistic impulse which needs to be controlled by law and instead advocates the justice and social utility of violence.[25] In *Third World Cop*, the opening scene affirms this premise. The two men who ambush Capone had been brought before the court for murder, but their charges had been dismissed. Thus, the narrative justifies Capone's illegal execution of his wounded assailant on the grounds of a dysfunctional judicial system and an uncontrolled, brazen criminal class.

The final image of the scene rescues the sequence from full-blown mimicry. In the final shot, the camera revisits a photograph that was seen earlier, showing Capone as a young man proudly dressed in an immaculate policeman's uniform. When we see the image for the second time at the end of the sequence, the photograph is splattered with blood (presumably that of the man Capone has just killed). Transformed into a symbol of lost innocence that troubles the appropriateness of Capone's summary execution of his intruder, the photograph deftly introduces a note of irony and social commentary. In *Shottas*, Smith identifies "a complex tension within the text" that is produced by the film's attempt to both problematize *and* sanction the misguided patriarchal ideologies that create the shotta.[26] A similar tension occurs in *Third World Cop* in the film's ambivalent treatment of violence. In the Deportee execution scene, for example, the act of violence is defined as transgressive but, paradoxically, is also manipulated in order to create pleasurable feelings of tension and excitement for the spectator. In the film's opening scene, the pointed association of male sexual potency and violence, followed by the cautionary image of Capone's blood-spattered photograph, also speaks to this tension and ambivalence. At one level, therefore, *Third World Cop* aims to critique the prevalence of violence in the Jamaican inner city and the way it functions within the culture to support oppressive patriarchal structures and criminal networks among the marginalized. However, the film also exploits acts of violence in order to provide sensation and spectacle for the entertainment of the spectator. In *Third World Cop*, this deep-seated tension and ambivalence may be related (as Smith asserts is the case in *Shottas*) to the text's representation of certain forms of masculinity. It is also, however, an important corollary of Browne's intensive referencing of genre conventions, which in turn has significant implications for the film's representation of place.

Robert Warshow asserts, "Really, it is not violence at all which is the 'point' of the Western movie, but a certain image of man, a style, which expresses itself most clearly in violence."[27] Thus the genre's emphasis on the performance of masculinity has made it a popular, frequently imitated model for manhood in the Caribbean, a society where, as Chevannes points out, the public space of the street, not the home, is considered the domain of the male as well as the site where the final stages of his socialization take place.[28] The work of a number of Caribbean writers testifies to the tendency of earlier generations of young Caribbean men to resort to mimicry of the Western to demonstrate masculinity.[29] Laurie Gunst locates Hollywood's influence more specifically in the criminal activity of the Kingston inner city, citing the example of posses who adopted "the gunslinger ethos of American movies":[30]

> They are a Caribbean cultural hybrid: tropical bad guys acting out fantasies from the spaghetti westerns, kung fu kill flicks, Rambo sequels, and Godfather spin-offs that play nightly in Kingston's funky movie palaces and flicker constantly behind young men's eyes. The posse men see themselves as Clint Eastwood in *Dirty Harry*, Al Pacino in *Scarface*, or – if they're old enough

to remember the 1960s – the rampaging misfits of Sam Peckinpah's *Wild Bunch*.[31]

This cultural trope is reflected in *Third World Cop* in the measure of celebrity accorded to Capone because of his gun skills. Even the men in the community, one of whom becomes a casualty of Capone's gun, express admiration for Capone's aggressive policing methods and hail him as a "star shotta". This is not to say that the film does not also attempt to critique hegemonic masculinity. Capone does experience brief moments of emotional vulnerability, even though they are experienced in private within a domestic space and are witnessed by a woman rather than by other men. More often, however, the film affirms problematic expressions of masculinity that valorize the use of force and skill with the gun, the cool pose and the tough exterior displayed by the hero of the Western.

In *Third World Cop*, the ambivalent treatment of violence is also implicated in the formation of the identity of place. The title of the film declares Browne's concern with place but the term "Third World", stripped here of any association with a politics of resistance, has derogatory connotations and functions to evoke a sense of place that draws on colonialist and racist associations with tropical and non-European cultures and environments. Jamaica is depicted as a rundown, barely functioning society where very little works as it should. This is particularly apparent in the police force, where there is an abundance of incompetence. "Third World" also denotes the Jamaican inner city as a site that is governed not by the codes and conventions of the so-called, presumably more civilized First World, but by the savagery of a particularly ruthless criminal class. Such associations are supported by a number of gruesome images of violence in the film. Deportee's dead body is one such image; another is that of a severed finger, incongruously nestled in a bed of cotton wool in a heart-shaped chocolate box that is carried around by a young man in remembrance of his murdered brother.

The film's construction of place is central to the justification of the excessive use of violence by the police. Such force, the narrative asserts, is necessary in order to contain and control the Kingston inner city's extraordinarily violent and daring criminal population and ensure that it does not affect (or infect) other places in Jamaica. The cowardice of Floyd (Winston "Bello"

Bell), Capone's partner, who is bumbling and ineffective, underscores the need in this environment for a tough, fearless policeman who is not reluctant to act boldly and take matters into his own hands when necessary, even if it means breaking the law. One of Capone's antagonists, Not Nice (Lenford Salmon), a policeman who is on the take from the don, Onie (Carl Bradshaw), also operates in the narrative to support Capone's legitimacy as he is even more ruthless than Capone. Capone's propensity for violence, therefore, is constructed as a necessary characteristic of the effective policeman in the "Third World" environment.

Unlike *The Harder They Come* and *Rockers*, violence does not function in *Third World Cop* in the Fanonian sense as a potential tool for the liberation of the oppressed. Rather, it is the means through which the state maintains control not only of a criminal population but also, it is inferred, of a particular social class. For in *Third World Cop*, the taint of criminality encompasses the entire community of Jungle. Even the pastor who Capone approaches for information is touched by corruption as Capone must purchase tickets for a church function before he will cooperate with the policeman. Few people in the ghetto are shown gainfully employed. With the exception of Rita (Audrey Reid), Capone's nascent love interest, all of Capone's childhood friends earn their livelihood through illegal means. On his first day on the job in Kingston, Capone becomes suspicious of two men purely on the basis of their appearance and demeanour: the dancehall music that blasts from their car and their equally loud "ghetto" fashion define them in the film as lower class. Indeed, they turn out to be part of the illegal gun importation operation run by the don of Jungle, Onie. Thus "ghetto" becomes a metonym for "criminal" and the ghetto resident is constructed in the film as other, defined by moral and ethical codes which are markedly different from those of the absent but invoked residents of uptown.

While the film affirms the dysfunction and pathology of the inner-city community, the middle class and elites on whose behalf Capone polices the ghetto are largely absent, although their existence is inferred, particularly in Ratty's poignant declaration of his desire to escape the ghetto. Elided from the narrative, the middle class and elite groups, as well as the means by which they maintain their status or dominance in a society marked by economic disparity, are not made available for the scrutiny of the spectator.

The relationship between Capone and Ratty is central to the film's naturalizing of certain dominant attitudes and beliefs about the inner city and the people who live there. Like Ratty, Capone's origins are in Jungle but as he has become a policeman, he is positioned in an oppositional relationship to the inner-city community by virtue of its construction in the film as a site of deviance and criminal activity. Capone's alienation from his origins is concretized in the tension and conflict of his relationships and interaction with ghetto residents, primarily with Ratty. The divergent paths of these two characters emphasizes the importance of individual action in the struggle to emerge from poverty by showing how two men with the same origins end up in very different positions because of the choices they make in life. Capone's choice of a career in law enforcement provides social mobility, allowing him to move to the lower-middle-class community of Portmore, which he refers to as "the city of the future". Ratty also yearns to get out of the ghetto, but he chooses to do so by engaging in illegal activity. When the two men go fishing, re-enacting an old childhood practice, Ratty stares at the large container ships traversing the harbour and tells Capone: "You remember di days when wi use to look pon dem ship dey an wonder a which foreign country dem a go? Mi always dream about getting out a dis bumboclaat ghetto dungle, build a larger life. You do it. . . . Bwai, mi nuh reach dey yet. One day, one day, by the hook, by the crook", the last sentence said with slow and deliberate emphasis. (You remember the days when we used to look at those ships and wonder which foreign country they were going to? I always dream about getting out of this bumboclaat ghetto jungle, build a larger life. You did it. . . . Boy, I haven't reached there yet. One day, one day, by the hook, by the crook.)

Ratty's words are loaded with irony, for unknown to Capone at that point, he has already acted on his intentions to escape the ghetto "by the crook" (that is, by illegal means). The film ends by emphasizing that it is precisely Ratty's choices which lead to his destruction. Out of expediency he agrees to cooperate with Capone and give evidence against Onie, but ultimately reneges on his promise, turns on Capone and tries to shoot him. Capone is the faster draw and kills Ratty. Eulogizing over his body, Capone states: "You is a fool Ratty. You coulda had a life but you choose to die." (You are a fool Ratty. You could have had a life but you chose to die.)

The didactic intention of the film's ending is overt and tends to obscure and mitigate the narrative's feeble allusions to the broader socioeconomic causes of poverty and crime in the inner city. When Capone tells Ratty that he will be sent to Antigua as part of a witness protection programme, Ratty's puzzled response, "Antigua? Ah weh dat dey, inna Portland?"[32] (Antigua? Where is that? In Portland?), might be understood as a reflection of the state's failure to educate and develop the minds of its poorest citizens. Ratty also eloquently testifies to the deliberate marginalization of the ghetto resident, suggesting that class prejudice and neglect by the state have operated to bar the urban poor from participation in the country's economic life. He states, "It look like any bloodclaat body care bout mi? Investors nuh come down ya so, yu nuh. Govament no care fi wi. Cyan get no real job cause a mi bloodclaat address." (Does it look like any bloodclaat body cares about me? Investors don't come down here, you know. The government doesn't care about us. Can't get any real job because of my bloodclaat address.) Here Ratty echoes an often heard complaint that inner-city residents are regularly denied certain types of employment because of where they live, but this is the only instance in which Ratty, or any other character, refers to the external factors that contribute to the maintenance of urban poverty. Further, despite his protest of limited opportunities for the ghetto resident, the narrative assures us that Ratty certainly has other options. He shows considerable talent for event organization and artist management and Capone urges him, in vain, to develop these skills in ways that would allow him to quit the ghetto through means that are legal and productive, both for himself and the wider community.

Ratty's death, therefore, is constructed within the context of his adherence to what the narrative implies is the criminalized and deviant culture of the ghetto. Towards the end of the film, this choice and this culture are concretized in Ratty's endorsement of a code of silence – identified by the much-bandied phrase "informer fi dead" (informers should be killed). This code of silence is often blamed for the reluctance of ghetto residents to cooperate with the police and thus is seen as supporting the prevalence of crime in ghetto communities. In the final scene when Capone reminds him of his promise to give state's evidence, Ratty replies, "Yu really tink seh mi a be turncoat. If mi inform on my people den mi cyan go back to dem. Watcha!

Mi a go tek di new identity weh yu a give mi, seen? Chill out for a while and mi come back home as a bigger hero." (You really think that I would become a turncoat? If I inform on my people then I can't go back to them. Watch this! I will take the new identity that you give me, understand? Chill out for a while and [then] I will come back home as a bigger hero.)

Ratty's statement echoes Ivan's desire to be a star bwai: a "smaddy", or *somebody* in a materialistic society that dehumanizes the poor and renders them faceless and anonymous. The film, however, does not explicitly locate Ratty's statement and actions within a broader social context where his need to be regarded as a hero and leader in his community might be more explicitly understood as an expression of a desire to participate, like Capone, in a brand of patriarchal masculinity that the film itself valorizes and defines as important in a Jamaican social context. Rather, Ratty's actions are narrowly conceived as the result of a moral flaw and the adherence to undesirable cultural values.

As with *Third World Cop*, Browne's later film, *Ghett'a Life*, also identifies individual agency rather than broad-based public sector intervention or state supported action and involvement as the mechanism for social change in the inner city. Revisiting the lower income community of Jungle more than a decade after *Third World Cop* was made, Browne does not respond to Ratty's cry that "govament no care bout mi" by insisting on or encouraging involvement from outside the ghetto. Rather, *Ghett'a Life* affirms that the impetus for change must come from within, that is, through the psychological transformation and efforts of those who reside in ghetto spaces. While there is certainly some element of truth in this assertion, it essentially places the burden of social transformation on the shoulders of those who are most vulnerable and have the least resources, and relieves those outside the ghetto of the sense that they share responsibility for helping to alleviate the problems faced within.

This way of thinking about change reinforces traditional notions of the ghetto as cut off from the social relations and networks that operate in other places in Jamaica. The garrison community is particularly prone to such notions of isolation and alienation as, particularly during periods of political instability, its geographical boundaries may be intensely policed to bar non-residents and opposing political supporters from entering, as occurs in *Ghett'a Life*. However, as both Carl Stone and Obika Gray point out,[33] the distinctive (and dysfunctional) features of the garrison community – crime, violence, restrictions on mobility, donmanship and the universal public support for one political party – are not "natural", and are not the simple and unavoidable result of poverty. Rather, they are a direct outcome of the garrison's critical location within the struggle for national political power, and represent the political elites' manipulation and exploitation of poor, urban communities and social groups in the attempt to gain political power.

Massey proposes a sense of place that is "extroverted", that is, it involves a consciousness of a locality's links with the wider world. She points out that "the particular mix of social relations which are thus part of what defines the uniqueness of any place is by no means all included within that place itself". It may include, she states, "relations which stretch beyond – the global as part of what constitutes the local, the outside as part of the inside".[34] Thinking of place from this perspective, the garrison community can be understood as not only integrally connected to national structures of political power but also as a manifestation and expression of deeply entrenched cultural and political values that are pervasive in Jamaica.

Carl Stone's use of the term "geographical power domain", rather than "garrison", underscores and more accurately reflects how such communities exist as part of the network of social and historical interrelations that constitute political power in Jamaica.[35] Stone describes the geographical power domain as developing out of a political system of patron-clientelism in Jamaica, in which economic and social favours to a poor and socially fragmented population are exchanged in return for party support. He explains that garrison communities were formed when political leaders attempted to assert personal hegemony over local power domains by using the violent and emotional support of the party hardcore to keep their political territories free of contenders' challenges or independent political initiatives. One of the methods used to create garrisons in downtown Kingston and lower St Andrew was the strategic and deliberate placement of party supporters in state-owned housing schemes by successive political administrations. As much as the term "garrison" infers enclosure, separateness and alienation from other parts of Jamaica, therefore, such communities are more properly conceptualized as historically formed and engineered by forces that extend beyond their geographical boundaries.

The film's reliance on the conventions of classical narrative cinema – a character-led plot, carefully delineated structure of order/disorder/order-restored and a narrative that unfolds through a chain of events that are causally linked – ensures that the exploration of the phenomenon of garrison politics and its deleterious effects on individuals and community development remains narrowly located within the sphere of personal experience rather than venturing into the broader sociological or historical causes to which Stone refers. These narrative elements contribute to what Lubiano refers to as the realist text's suggestion of disclosure of the truth and then closure of the representation.[36] In effect, Browne uses techniques or conventions that encourage spectators to feel that they are looking at *real life*, but then provides, not only a *reel life* explanation of garrison politics but also a *reel life* resolution of the problem.

In her discussion of classical narrative cinema, Susan Hayward comments, "The name of the game is verisimilitude, 'reality'", but she points out that "an examination of what gets put up on the screen in the name of reality makes clear how contrived and limited it is and yet how ideologically useful that reality none the less remains".[37] Hayward notes that in the character-led or psychologically motivated narrative, the initial event is often left unexplained if it is not psychologically motivated. Thus, she points out that in *Gone with the Wind* (1939), the American Civil War, which is the backdrop for the story's action, is represented as a clash between the southern states' traditions and the northern states' ideological conviction that slavery must be abolished. In this respect, Hayward states, "history becomes ahistorical (events have no past, no explanation, no cause). As such history is eternally fixed, naturalized."[38]

A similar process can be observed in *Ghett'a Life*, in which the historical formation of the garrison constituency, as well as the emergence of a violent electoral process, is elided from the narrative. Emphasis is certainly accorded the discordant and dysfunctional features of garrison life and Browne successfully conveys the challenges faced by residents living in an inner-city community affected by divisive partisan politics. But in his exploration of these challenges, rather than clearly and explicitly defining them – including the dominance of the don – as a consequence of the political parties' historical struggle for power, Browne infers that the conditions which prevail in Jungle are largely the result of the actions of an individual, the don, Sin (Chris McFarlane). This logic is faulty but it is key to the film's ideological assertions, for it functions to conceal the ways in which the garrison, far from being isolated and alienated from the network of social relations in the nation, is undoubtedly enmeshed in the postcolonial political elites' struggle to obtain and preserve their dominance. In other words, using Massey's perspective of place, *Ghett'a Life* obscures how the network of social relations that defines the garrison community can be traced out of the ghetto to the country's two political parties, and beyond that, to the House of Parliament, Gordon House, that august symbol of Jamaica's independence and nationhood, where sit the members of parliament who represent the garrison constituencies, and who engage in and benefit from garrison politics.

The film achieves the exclusion of the garrison community from the mix of social relations "which stretch beyond"[39] by subtly positioning the don, Sin, rather than the member of parliament, Hewlitt (Lenford Salmon), at the nexus of power in the community. Browne claims that in *Ghett'a Life* he foregoes the generic story of the black ghetto youth who takes up the gun; in fact, this trajectory is merely shifted to the black villain. The film opens with a sequence which emphasizes Sin's brutality and disregard for human life. As he beats a man with a cutlass and then orders his henchmen to kill him, we are made cognisant of the absolute authority he exercises in Jungle. This scene is followed by an image of a helicopter flying over an inner-city community as a news report informs us of an impending general election and a "recent upsurge in violence" in Jungle that continues unabated, "despite the intervention of the church and representatives from the two major political parties". In contrast to the national security forces helicopter which surveys the garrison from above, Sin is positioned inside the community and is often seen driving through the streets of Jungle. Importantly, while the juxtaposition of these two scenes establishes the election as the backdrop for the violence we have just witnessed, it is clear that the beating is not politically motivated: Sin beats the man and orders his death as punishment for stealing his money. In another scene, an elderly resident of the community bypasses Hewlitt, the member of Parliament, and appeals to Sin for financial assistance. Sin gives her money to the approbation of other residents and is hailed as "Papa Sin", a benefactor to the community.

Hewlitt not only plays a subordinate role to Sin in the community, but he is also marginal to the plot. *Ghett'a Life* is a coming-of-age story which focuses on the struggle of the young, male protagonist, Derrick (Kevoy Burton), to achieve his dream of representing his country in the boxing ring. In his quest for autonomy, Derrick must contend with the objections of his father, Lenford (Carl Davis), but more critically, he must confront Sin's opposition. The boxing gym is off limits for Derrick because it is located in an area controlled by the opposing don who is loyal to the opposition or "green party". Sin's allegiance is with the party in power, the "orange party", and in keeping with the culture of political divisiveness in the garrison, he enforces a strict policy of segregation.[40] Residents of the community are not allowed to fraternize with those who support "the other side" nor are they supposed to enter "enemy" territory. Derrick, therefore, risks his life and endangers his family when he defies Sin. Importantly, however, Sin opposes Derrick because the young man's independence and willingness to think outside of the garrison code threatens Sin's authority; Derrick's actions have no direct implications for the contest of the national elections, nor does he have any political ambitions. Sin acts out of self-interest, telling Derrick: "Have to bun you before [you] make a big epidemic." (I have to burn [destroy] you before you cause a big epidemic.) Derrick threatens Sin's attempts to control the minds and bodies of the residents of Jungle.

In contrast to Sin's centrality in the narrative, Hewlitt is a shadowy figure about whom not much is known. While it is clear that Hewlitt is aware of Sin's nefarious activities, and even instructs him to kill the opposing don, Ratchet, Browne forgoes the opportunity to fully develop Hewlitt in ways that would more explicitly expose the sordid link between national politics and garrison violence in Jamaica. As with the history of the garrison's origins, what is important here is what is excluded from the narrative and the impact that the inclusion of that material might have on the way the spectator understands the social and political issues with which the film is concerned. What position does Hewlitt occupy in the hierarchy of the political party to which he belongs? What is the nature of his relationship with the party leadership? To what extent is the party leadership aware of Hewlitt's connection with Sin and does it condone the use of violence as a tool to maintain power? This is terrain with which the narrative is not concerned. Instead, the film's emphasis on the don as the causal agent of the garrison's dysfunction supports the myth, maintained by politicians, that the garrison is a contained microcosm only tenuously connected to the larger structures of political power. Indeed, rather than more explicitly develop the link between violence in the ghetto and high-ranking, national political figures, *Ghett'a Life* vilifies Sin, whose dark complexion and speech infer lower-class origins. Thus, the film ensures that violence in the garrison constituency remains contained and disconnected from so-called polite society uptown that participated in its formation.

Both *Ghett'a Life* and *Third World Cop* reflect post-1980 changes in the internal political structure of garrison communities when the locus of power shifted, with dons gaining more autonomy and becoming increasingly independent of political leaders. Amanda Sives notes that as gangs became more active in the drug trade and less reliant on the political parties for guns and funds, the politicians' power over the gangs in their constituencies weakened.[41] Brian Meeks points out that it is during this period of greater economic independence that dons began to be perceived by many citizens "not as selfish, self-interested drug lords but as protectors of the community".[42] It is difficult, however, to precisely fix *Ghett'a Life* on a historical timeline. A national election forms the background to the film's action, but the film is not specific about which election this might be. The emphasis on the extreme political segregation of the community is reminiscent of the period prior to 1980, but the presence in the narrative of more modern technology, such as the cell phone, suggests a later period. The use of actual news reports and cameo appearances by journalists contributes to the film's sense of realism, but this also obscures the film's temporal orientation as images of journalists from different eras are used to represent the same period. Regardless of the period which the film intends to portray, however, the erasure of the history of the origins of the garrison is a deliberate choice that has important ideological and political implications.

An important corollary of the film's separation of the garrison community from the history of its formation and from the power struggle of the elites is the narrative's investment in the ideological construct that the individual has the power to transform his destiny regardless of the socio-economic conditions or environment in which he is placed. As in other stories in which a quest is the central motif, the narrative hinges on the choices made by the protagonist, that is, his response to the challenges with which he is presented and thus on the question of character. By privileging the dyad of plot development and characterization over the examination of social causes, the narrative advances the myth that strength of character is the primary prerequisite for social change.

An early sequence in the film illustrates this logic. One of the ways in which the film asserts a sense of realism is through the use of actual television newscasts and cameo roles featuring public figures rather than actors. In one scene, an interview with a well-known Jamaican human rights activist plays on the television in a shop where Derrick and his friend, Big-Toe (O'Daine Clarke), are buying groceries. In the interview the activist states, "[That] so many political leaders have found it necessary to get into bed with the dons suggests where the real influence and power within the community lie." This interview is followed by another in which boxing champion, Lennox Lewis, playing himself, declares, "When I started out there were a lot of obstacles and if I didn't believe in myself and make that first step . . . I wouldn't get anywhere. So the main thing is that you have to persevere and persevere and believe in yourself."

The juxtaposition of these two interviews, which carry the illusive weight of "real" or actual social commentary in the first instance and "real" or actual personal testimony in the second, is critical to the film's ideological assertions. In the first interview, the comments of the human rights activist function to obscure the historical role that politicians have played in elevating dons in ghetto communities and facilitating their rise to positions of power. Against the background of the activist's assertion of the dominance of the don, the second interview affirms the power of the individual to overcome obstacles and assures the spectator that success is always possible so long as one does not give up.

This is the virtue that informs Derrick's struggle and which, it is implied, is necessary – and indeed, all that is needed – to ensure success. Derrick achieves his objective of boxing for the country through perseverance, and perseverance is also at the root of his ability to overcome the challenge of the don's opposition to his goal. This is a comforting illusion, and it is probably not even necessary to point out that the idea that perseverance always yields success, particularly in the case of overcoming the violent threats of a don, belongs to the realm of *reel* life, rather than *real* life. As the narrative plays out the drama of Derrick's pursuit of his goal, it reproduces a Jamaican ghetto version of the American dream. But the corollary of the myth that Everyman can pull himself up and out of whatever conditions he may have been born into, is that the inability to do so is the result of a failure of will, lack of character or a flaw in character. Thus, the film affirms that the residents of the garrison play an important role in their own oppression. Some regard "Papa Sin" as a benefactor who provides resources to members of the community, while Derrick's father, Lenford, and his friend Big-Toe accept Sin as a necessary evil because they mistakenly believe he protects the community from attack from the other side. Lenford, in particular, on the threshold of participation in representational politics, turns a blind eye to Sin's nefarious activities, refusing to acknowledge his involvement in murder until he is faced with irrefutable evidence that Sin was responsible for the death of his older son. The film suggests, therefore, that Sin's authority in the community is not only enforced through violence and threat, but is also willingly supported by the residents, who are complicit in maintaining the rule of the don.

Browne conveys the emotional intensity of the garrison residents' convictions through the use of religious metaphor. In an interview, he stated that in other parts of the world people kill each other over religion, but "in Jamaica, what we kill one another over is politics".[43] Thus, in Jungle, loyalty to party carries greater weight and importance than religious affiliation. Lenford repeatedly refers to the supporters of the opposing party as "the devil", stating, "We is Jesus and dem is the devil; and the devil can never beat Jesus!" Sin refers to himself as a shepherd who must endure the travails of keeping the flock together, but the profanity of his language reveals his subversive use of the simile. In a pronouncement that echoes the jealousy of the Old Testament God who demands loyalty and obeisance from his followers, Sin declares to Derrick: "As a shepherd it's not always easy to keep the flock together because there's always that one little fassy that just stray away from the flock. Why you tink seh you can just fuck off and join another flock and come dis shepherd yah."[44]

As occurs in Deportee's execution scene in *Third World Cop*, Browne uses profanity to convey the malevolence of the badman. Declaring his inviolable power in the community, Sin claims to exceed all other authority, including that of God: "There is nowhere to run in this community, not from me. I run this community, not yu mother, not yu father, not the MP, not you! And if Jesus Christ want to crucify bout ya, God have to ask me permission." The declaraton suggests that rather than serving as the people's saviour, "Papa Sin" is an Antichrist figure, leading the people towards negation of self.

Unlike what occurs with other cinematic badmen – Ivan, Ratty, police shotta Capone – the narrative does not encourage identification with Sin. Rather, the film's representation of the don as an unequivocal figure of evil provides a scapegoat for the dysfunction of the garrison and in turn supports a simple but unrealistic resolution of the community's problems that hinges on Sin's death. Hayward notes that classic narrative cinema must have closure and that "whatever form the closure takes, almost without exception it will offer or enunciate a message that is central to dominant ideology".[45] This is true of *Ghett'a Life*: Sin's death leaves Derrick free to pursue a career in boxing; his father acknowledges and rejects the evils of garrison politics; the girlfriend of Derrick's murdered brother appears with a son and now feels free to become integrated into the family; a large mural in the community, featured at the beginning of the film and which proclaimed Sin's dominance, is painted over by a group of young people, led by Big-Toe; a news report announces that Sin's funeral was poorly attended, signifying the community's lack of respect for and rejection of the don. In short, order is restored with Sin's death as the narrative assures the spectator that the elimination of "the bad guy" will bring an end to the violence in the community. Thus the film's closure, reiterating the idea of individual cause, exonerates the postcolonial political elite from its role in creating and maintaining a politics of violence and exploitation.

Ghett'a Life is a story of triumph despite overwhelming odds and may well be an inspiring film for persons in difficult situations. It denounces the tyranny of donmanship, the political divisiveness of the garrison community and affirms, contrary to popular middle-class sentiment, that something good can indeed come out of the ghetto. As with *Third World Cop*, however, Browne's emphasis on the importance of individual choice and motivation leaves the structures of power that maintain the rule of the don, crime, violence and poverty in the inner city unchallenged. If these films speak to the uptown Jamaican on behalf of the inner-city resident, they convincingly convey a sense of the harshness that poverty imposes, but they also reassure the spectator that social transformation is a matter of will and character, and that those who do not make it out of the ghetto only have themselves to blame. Despite the work that these films do to expose the challenges faced by the urban poor, both *Third World Cop* and *Ghett'a Life* conform to dominant, class-bound perspectives of "ghetto life". Such views coincide with public opinion and leave the status quo intact. Browne's work, therefore, points to the need for greater participation in the Jamaican film industry by persons from a broad spectrum of socioeconomic groups.

8
DREAMING HISTORY AND THE NIGHTMARE WORLD OF JAMAICAN POLITICS IN *BETTER MUS' COME*

IN AUGUST 1981 I ARRIVED IN KINGSTON, Jamaica, to begin undergraduate studies at the University of the West Indies, Mona campus. It was almost a year since the disruptive general election of October 1980, yet everywhere I went I was reminded of the trauma Jamaicans had recently suffered. Prior to arriving in Jamaica, I had worked as a junior reporter at the *Barbados Advocate* newspaper, where I had watched stories spew out of the newsroom telex machine, grimly charting the course of that election campaign and keeping count of the growing number of persons killed in the unprecedented violence of the long run-up to the election. In my early years in Jamaica, I was abruptly confronted with the human expression of those statistics: in numerous conversations, Jamaicans inevitably told stories about their experiences as they tried to convey to me, the newcomer, what that tumultuous period had meant to them.

The period that Jamaicans now loosely refer to as "the Seventies", but which really encompassed the mid-1970s to 1980, marks a rupture in Jamaican society in which the ugly struggle for parliamentary power erupted into blatant partisan political violence, social disruption and chaos. The independence promise of national unity and a harmonious society was revealed as little more than a flimsy illusion. Jamaicans' stories of the experiences of the 1970s can be understood within the context of what Teshome Gabriel describes as popular memory, "the oral historiography of the Third World",[1] which, he states, functions like folklore to pass memories from generation to generation. Gabriel proposes that popular memory and folkloric traditions attempt to conserve what official histories insist on erasing, and thus, "wage a battle against false consciousness and against the official versions of history that legitimate and glorify it".[2] The stories I heard about the 1970s constitute an expression of popular memory: a kind of urban folklore that registered accounts of "minor" events that often never made the news and which also expressed the multiple perspectives that were never recorded by official history. In this chapter, I discuss Storm Saulter's debut feature film, *Better Mus' Come* (2010), within the framework of Gabriel's notion of popular memory. Inspired by events that took place at Green Bay, Jamaica in 1978, the film is a representation of a particular moment in modern Jamaican history and functions, like individuals' stories of "the Seventies", to document and preserve that which official history has neglected or omitted.

Talking to Emiel Martens about the making of his film, Saulter recalls growing up hearing his parents and their friends tell stories about the 1970s that painted it as "such a wild and violent period on the island that everybody now [wanted] to forget about it".[3] Rather than allowing us to forget, however, Saulter seems intent on reminding us of the horrors of this turbulent period by exploring the complex and disturbing connections between poverty, violence and the struggle for political power. By using the medium of dramatic film to tell this particular story, Saulter shows (rather than tells) the history of an actual or real event in ways that make it accessible to a broad audience. He transports the story of Green Bay beyond the realm of newspaper archives, academic discourse and historical commentary, and makes it visible to persons who continue to exist in the nexus of politics, poverty and exploitation that the film explores and decries. This is an act of remarkable importance for, as Arthur Marwick states, "It is only through a sense of history that communities establish their identity, orientate themselves, understand their relationship to the past and to other communities and societies."[4]

In his discussion of how film contributes to our understanding of the past, Robert A. Rosenstone defines the history film as a "dramatic motion picture that focuses on verifiable people, events and movements set in the past".[5] Refuting the widely held view that dramatic films (in comparison to written history) "destroy the past rather than allow us to see it",[6] Rosenstone affirms that "filmmakers animate the past", permitting us to "glimpse moments of our history", not "the soundless and colourless world" that is presented on paper, but a "world filled with colour, sound, dialogue and action".[7] As a filmmaker, Saulter shows history in a way that is appealing and compelling in an age when images have "become more important to society than words".[8] He employs a medium that facilitates, as Rosenstone points out, a "visceral experience" that allows us to identify with and relate to people and events of the past on a more intimate level than do books.[9] While Rosenstone affirms that the dramatic film will never be a good medium for getting across reams of accurate data, he also insists that history "is not just a recitation of the facts of the past, but a story full of whatever meaning we impose upon the traces of the past".[10] This chapter, then, seeks to explore the meanings which Saulter has imposed on the events that took place in 1978 at Green Bay, St Catherine, and in doing so considers what the film contributes to our understanding of a traumatic and divisive period in modern Jamaican history and how this glimpse of the past informs our sense of identity as a national community.

In the film, the 1970s are depicted as a period in which notions of national unity were severely tested as the political elites' desire for power divided poor urban communities, turning them into nightmare spaces marked by violence and terror. The film's reflection on the past functions as a critique of the post-independence political process as it exposes the subversion of that process by political elites who, by creating new hierarchies based on party affiliation, attempted to ensure their continued dominance in the new postcolonial society. Saulter's referencing of the past is complex: he draws on both historical events and the 1972 film *The Harder They Come* (which also references past events) to explore the iconic cultural figure of the badman, which arguably achieves one of its most horrendous expressions in the political conflict of the 1970s. Exploring difficult questions about the identity of self and nation within the context of the trauma of that period, Saulter creates a haunting portrait of a man who is a gunman and political thug, but also a lover, a poet and philosopher, a caring and attentive father. "Top-ranking" Ricky (Sheldon Shepherd) struggles to put his gun aside, but, caught up in the nightmare conflict and carnage of one of the bloodiest periods of modern Jamaica, he repeatedly resorts to the gun as the means through which he attempts to assert some measure of control and authority in an environment defined by turmoil, violence and loss.

Set in 1978 and inspired by real events, the film's specificity is not at the expense of retaining an openness of perspective. Saulter does not attempt, as Gabriel states of official, scribal history, to "arrest the future by means of the past" by claiming "a 'centre' which continuously marginalizes others" and inhibits them "from constructing their own history or histories".[11] The mode of inquiry adopted by "official history" or Western historical discourses necessitates what Hayden White refers to as the "disciplining of the imagination",[12] in which certain forms of knowledge are rejected and limits are imposed on what can be thought of as a specifically historical event and thus a specifically historical fact. White points out that for the historian, "the imagination is disciplined by its subordination to the rules of evidence which require that whatever is imagined be consistent with what the evidence permits one to assert as a 'matter of fact'".[13] In contrast to this approach, in his representation of a specific historical event, Saulter does not appear overly concerned with the possible distinctions that can be made between fact and fiction. Rather, his priority appears to be creating a story that places the spectator in a particular time and place in ways that create openness to other kinds of truths that are not necessarily conveyed by statistics and facts. Saulter, therefore, is primarily concerned with the "discipline" imposed by the process of story-making and thus actively *uses* the imagination to recreate the past and lay bare the trauma Jamaicans experienced in the 1970s. His intention is not the production of an inviolable, authoritative narrative of past events, nor the creation of a supposedly stable, factual and unproblematic account of the past that is equated with "truth". Saulter does not claim what is often presumed to be the prerogative of the documentary. Instead, what seems to be in operation in the film is a way of looking back that suggests there may be critical lacunae in formal historical narratives which imagination can attempt to redeem in order to produce new perspectives, new knowledge and thus open up vistas of alternative truths, which in turn lead to new ways of understanding the past and our relationship to it.

An intertitle at the beginning of the film which informs the spectator that *Better Mus' Come* is inspired by real events is, therefore, most instructive. The word "inspired" indicates that the historical event is but a starting point, a place of beginning, the raw material that then becomes subject to imagination, creativity and the demands of narrative. In order to respond to the lacunae, contradictions and ellipses of formal, scribal "History",

Saulter's imagination ranges beyond not only that which can be categorized as verifiable facts, but also outside the borders of political correctness and so-called objectivity that often prevail in official accounts of political conflict in Jamaica and which shrink from the outright condemnation of acts by one or other of the political parties. Saulter does not disregard formal historical accounts. He has stated on several occasions that the film is the result of extensive research, and this is evident in many of the details of the narrative. What emerges, however, is a sense that what is contained within the formal historical record is insufficient and unsatisfying and, where history is silent, the filmmaker has called on imagination to fill the void. Thus, the boundaries in the narrative between actuality and imagination and fact, fancy and memory are blurred as the past becomes subject to a declared process of interpretation rather than a process of recounting that ultimately makes (false) claims of objectivity. In this sense, Saulter's retelling of the past resonates with Gabriel's description of popular memory, which he affirms "is neither a retreat to some great tradition nor a flight to some imagined 'ivory tower', neither a self-indulgent escapism nor a desire for the actual 'experience' or 'content' of the past for its own sake. Rather, it is a 'look back to the future', necessarily dissident and partisan, wedded to constant change."[14]

Gabriel's idea of "looking back to the future" – in effect, drawing on the past to inform a critical understanding of what exists and how best to navigate what is to come – underlies my use of the metaphor of the dream to describe Saulter's mode of inquiry into the past. I draw on Freud's notion of dreams as a means of revisiting past trauma and the meaning of which, if unlocked, can lead to a deeper understanding of the self. The metaphor of the dream is used, then, to draw attention to the ways in which the film makes use of alternative modes of knowing and understanding the past that depart from the traditional methods employed by formal historical enquiry. Thus, in *Better Mus' Come*, the use of the imagination and creativity in shaping a narrative of the past represents not an ultimately useless flight of fancy or fantasy but rather a form of critical enquiry.

Gabriel locates his discussion of popular memory within the framework of the alternative practices of Third Cinema, so called to distinguish this oppositional film practice or counter-cinema emerging from Third World countries in the late 1960s from First Cinema (Hollywood and other commercial cinemas) and Second Cinema (European art cinema and auteur film). My concern is not to make a claim for *Better Mus' Come* as Third Cinema, either within the conceptual framework that Gabriel describes or those provided by other theorists, such as Fernando Solanas and Octavio Getino.[15] In fact, *Better Mus' Come* does not conform to some of the narrative strategies that Gabriel associates with Third Cinema, such as lack of closure and the use of multiple points of view rather than an emphasis on the hero.[16] I do want to maintain, however, that even as he draws on some of the approaches to narrative that are dominant in commercial cinema, Saulter encourages a critical response, in part by alerting the spectator to his method – his reliance on fiction – by quite explicitly evoking the form of the dream, and also by avoiding romanticizing his hero.

There are a number of sequences in the film which introduce the idea of the dream as an alternative state of perception or awareness. These sequences propose a state of altered consciousness: a reflective or dreamlike state which lies somewhere between fantasy and actuality, reality and the imagined, and which constitutes an alternative ontological state. This, in turn, proposes an alternative epistemology: another way of knowing, understanding and making sense of self and the world. These "dream" sequences also function as a metaphor for what Saulter attempts to do with this film: by imaginatively binding together historical sources and personal stories, factual and fictional elements, personal and public perspectives, he creates another way of looking back at the past, making sense of it and suggesting meaning.

In the first of these sequences, Ricky looks at a photograph of his baby-mother and then appears to recall her murder by gunmen. The use of slow motion and muted colours and the absence of diegetic sound render the murder scene dreamlike and distinguish the action from present time in the narrative. The scene is framed as a memory, but Ricky does not appear to have been present at the shooting. The scene must, then, be Ricky's imaginative reconstruction of events that he did not actually witness, that is, it is his piecing together of what must have been the accounts of others. At a critical point in the narrative, Ricky's "memory" of this killing will function to propel him towards a specific course of action, and he will seek retaliation for the murder of a respected teacher. In that instance, the replaying of this painful "memory" of loss will function to convey the complexity of his emotions and help explain why he makes specific choices.

Another dream sequence creates a sharp contrast between the idyllic dream world of the imagination and the nightmare of chaos and terror that is Ricky's waking reality. In this sequence we see images of Ricky's girlfriend, Kimala (Sky Nicole Grey), dancing around sheets hung on a clothes line as we hear Ricky's voice reciting a poem:

> Yesterday I hid and watched a lady as she danced.
> She was dancing to a song,
> That of African origin.
> And the sound of playing drums were prominent throughout the dance.
> She mimed her way to the music
> Hips pulsating
> Her posture was flexible and yet rigid
> She danced and she danced and she danced and she danced

The sense of spatial and temporal dislocation is even more intense in this later scene for it immediately follows a sequence which chronicles a severe outbreak of violence in the community that leads Ricky to send Kimala and his son out of the city in order to ensure their safety. The spectator understands, therefore, that the poem sequence marks a break in the continuity of the narrative. Again, the sequence begins with an image of Ricky lost in contemplation, and the slow motion, extra-diegetic music and sound further convey that the action is not occurring in present time. In fact, as Ricky is awakened by loud knocking on his door, we realize that he has literally been dreaming about Kimala. It is a complicated dream, for in the sequence Ricky not only recites the poem, we also see him writing it, an image that, in turn, recalls an earlier scene when he abandoned an attempt to write the poem. In his dream, Ricky is able to complete this poem about love and belonging that he could not write in his waking hours. Thus, the dream functions as an idyllic space in which Ricky realizes desires that elude him in his waking moments, that is, his deep yearning for something fine and beautiful that will transcend the horror of the nightmare in which he lives and which he expresses in both the desire for a relationship with Kimala and the realization of his creative self. This dream sequence ends when Ricky is awakened by the members of his gang to attend the meeting that will lead to his ghastly death; thus he wakes from his idyllic dream into a reality that is a nightmare.

Better Mus' Come is not a horror film, but it is full of horror. The sense that Ricky exists in a terrible waking dream from which he cannot escape is conveyed through the film's use of iconography and motifs that impart a Gothic resonance to the representation of the partisan conflict of the 1970s. One such motif, repetition, is developed by the circular structure of the narrative and also supports the idea of reflecting on and making sense of the past. The opening sequence of the film shows Ricky and the members of his gang driving out of their Gold Street community, which is heavily patrolled by police, to a distant location near the sea, that we later learn is Green Bay. The mood of the men huddled in the van is sombre, tense and, for Ricky, reflective. As the van drives, we hear an extra-diegetic voice which, through editing, we identify as Ricky's, reciting a poem:

> Shadows stand upright in the streets of the town.
> The orders of the soldier come straight from the crown
> The rebellion in my nature
> Is hard like a fist.
> But why?
> Against whom does my rebellion exist?
> My son?
> My brother?
> My father?
> My friend?
> Why does the good man die in the end?

As the van reaches its destination, the screen fades to black and the final lines of the poem are heard over the black screen, giving the poem added emphasis and, as we will discover, prophetic resonance. At this point, the narrative goes back in time to give an account of the events that led to this moment. Towards the end of the film, the opening sequence is revisited: Ricky wakes from his dream of Kimala to set out on the journey to Green Bay. When the sequence is repeated, however, the significance of that journey to the coast has been revealed and the identities of the men in the van are now known. Ricky's poem about death and rebellion is not heard in the second playing of the scene, but as we watch images that have been rendered familiar because of the repetitive structure of the narrative, the poem acquires added significance. We have learned that the men in the van are gunmen for the JLP, that their lives are steeped in blood and violence, and that they may be going to meet their deaths. When the van reaches its destination, the men discover that, as Ricky had feared, they have been tricked. Hired to do illegal security work, they learn that the offer of employment was a ploy to lure them to the isolated area and kill them. Most of the men are gunned down on the spot, but one man, Flames, escapes. Ricky tries to flee but is shot dead.

The repetition of the sequence which chronicles the journey to Green Bay emphasizes the significance to the narrative of the actual events that have come to be referred to publicly as the "Green Bay Massacre", or, in more neutral terms, simply "Green Bay". These events take up very little running time in the film, but as Saulter explains in the interview with Martens, the story of Green Bay was critical to his structuring of the narrative and the meaning which the film assigns to the period of the 1970s:

> That dramatic event helped me to anchor my story. I pieced together snippets of information and loosely reconstructed the lives of the people who ended up at Green Bay. This moment really showed the circle of tricking people, using people, and finally getting rid of people once they act up. So the Green Bay Massacre became the endpoint of my story which I then built backwards into a journey of one character in particular. I focused on a guy in the lower ranks of society and the decisions he has to make as a consequence of the communally segregated political parties of the 1970s.[17]

Indeed, in some circles in Jamaica, Green Bay functions as a kind of synonym for the political excesses of the 1970s and in particular, the state's incursion on human rights as the struggle for national power intensified and devolved into extreme acts of violence on both sides of the political divide. It is one of a number of controversial events that occurred during the period that reflect an increasingly divided nation, the corruption of state institutions and the possible abuse of state power. At the centre of Green Bay lies the issue of disputed accounts of what occurred at that isolated shooting range in St Catherine and what the incident has come to mean to Jamaicans. Members of the Military Intelligence Unit in the Jamaica Defence Force claimed that on 5 January 1978, they discovered fourteen men at the military firing range at Green Bay and returned fire when they were fired upon. However, two of the men who survived the shooting and managed to make their way back to their community said that they had been lured to the range with promises of employment doing security work. They stated that on reaching the range they were told to stand in a group and were then fired upon. The survivors' accounts of the events at Green Bay constitute a chorus of dissenting voices that identifies agents of the state as the instigators of a criminal act against citizens and demonstrates the lengths to which the political elite is willing to go to maintain power.

From the point of view of the film's engagement with popular history, the existence of contesting accounts is pertinent, as is the way in which the alternative version of the Green Bay events emerged and entered public discourse. Looking back at reports in the *Daily Gleaner*, it would seem that the alternative version to the official report emerged gradually, as information from sources within the communities in downtown Kingston, where the survivors lived, trickled out, and also as citizens identified and mulled over inconsistencies in the official statement. On 6 January 1978, the *Daily Gleaner* broke news of the incident. The front-page story affirmed, that according to a report from the Police Information Centre,

> about 14 suspicious-looking men in civilian dress were seen going into the hills toward the Jamaica Defence Force base and firing range at Green Bay. . . . The Security Forces mounted a Police/Military ambush in the area and later surprised the 14 men who were conducting target practice on the military firing range. Challenged by the Security Forces personnel, the men turned their fire on them and during the exchange of gunfire that ensued, five were killed on the spot. During the shoot-out the other nine men scattered and escaped into the rugged terrain of the Port Henderson Hills.[18]

This version of the events was publicly challenged in the *Daily Gleaner* when, in its front-page coverage of a "peace treaty" that had spontaneously emerged between rival political gangs in Western Kingston, an accompanying story queried whether the peace initiative was a response to Green Bay. Under the headline "Did Green Bay Spark the Truce?", writer Neville Toyloy quotes a "youth" who was on the street celebrating the peace agreement with hundreds of other residents as saying, "Uptown man don't know about it but ask anybody downtown, go Southside [Central Kingston] and you will hear the full story."[19] Toyloy does not give "the full story", but the report does introduce, however tentatively, into public discourse, the idea that the official version of events was false. The youth's comment is itself instructive as it draws attention to a distinction between the knowledge systems of "uptown" and those that operate "downtown", and infers that for certain citizens, the lived experience in marginalized communities counters the hegemonic influence of official discourses.

After Toyloy's front-page story, the question of what actually happened at Green Bay became a recurring theme in the newspaper.[20] Eventually, on January 26, the *Daily Gleaner* would not only show the human cost of the events, publishing a photograph of the babymothers and some of the children of the five dead men, but in a story headlined "Killings remain a mystery", the newspaper provided an alternative version of the events. "The story of those who lived and returned to 'southside'", culled together from interviews with three of the dead men's partners "and others", related how the fourteen men had been recruited to do "bodyguard work" and were then ambushed by security forces at Green Bay and shot at. The *Daily Gleaner* report also identifies an undercurrent of dissent in response to the official reports, even beyond the borders of Southside and other downtown communities. The newspaper comments that the incident caused a stir, as "the talk on the street corners and homes and places of relaxation was that a lot of questions were left unanswered 'especially as no guns were found'" (that is, by the police or Jamaica Defence Force).[21]

Even though all the Military Intelligence Unit soldiers were acquitted at the trial held in 1982, it is safe to say that the majority of Jamaicans accept the unofficial account of events that defines the soldiers as murderers. The more contentious question is whether the PNP administration had prior knowledge of the plot or whether the soldiers were acting of their own accord. The men killed were loyal to the opposition and lived in a JLP enclave in the constituency of then prime minister Michael Manley. Thus, the issue of PNP involvement potentially threatened to link the abuse of state power with the highest levels of the political administration. In the aftermath of the incident, the now infamous statement by Minister of Security Dudley Thompson that no angels died at Green Bay fuelled speculation that the PNP was involved in the incident. Political scientist Amanda Sives states, however, that the available evidence suggests the shooting was not sanctioned by the PNP government. The most plausible account, she states, "is that the actions were carried out by senior officers in the JDF [Jamaica Defence Force] without official approval".[22] In contrast, writing in his memoir published in 2009, Edward Seaga refers to "the Green Bay massacre" as "a diabolical plot by corrupt members of the JDF and highly placed members of the ruling party".[23] Seaga states: "The PNP government used corrupt members of the security forces to entrap JLP community leaders in Southside, an area in the West Central Kingston constituency of Michael Manley, and lead them to their death. The purpose behind the elaborate deception was to demoralize Southside and to provide fabricated evidence to show that the JLP had a hand in the illegal importation of guns."[24]

Seaga's take on Green Bay is hardly surprising: a former prime minister, he was leader of the opposition in 1978 when Green Bay occurred. He is also a controversial figure whose own involvement in the violence of the 1970s has been debated. But his insistent tone and inflammatory language, some thirty years after the event, convey a sense of the volatile mood of the country during the 1970s and show how certain incidents, such as Green Bay, continue to function as critical signifiers of the upheaval and political divisiveness that marked the period.

Saulter's decision to use Green Bay as the anchor for the narrative has a particular resonance for Jamaican audiences; for them, it likely raises issues of history, power and truth. And yet, *Better Mus' Come* is not an attempt to arbitrate the conflicting accounts of what happened at the firing range. In Saulter's representation of events, Green Bay is portrayed as a plot masterminded by the Military Intelligence Unit in order to ruthlessly dispose of JLP gunmen. Nor does the film delve into the more controversial question of whether members of the PNP government had knowledge of the plot. Instead, Saulter adopts an existentialist approach: starting with the early morning drive to the firing range – a historically determined fact – the narrative goes back in time to recreate a chronology of the complex forces and events that caused the men from Southside to be in that place at that time.

In this sense, the film can also be understood as a response to the outrageous assertion of a PNP government minister, that no angels were killed at Green Bay, for the lacuna that Saulter addresses is the lack of information about the realities of the victims' lives, a narrative that official history has chosen to ignore or forget. Saulter calls on imagination to recreate a story about who these men were, what their lives may have meant and what desperate circumstances might have brought them to a particular moment in history. A critical element of that story is the question of how citizens' lives could be deemed expendable by agents of the state, and what the film reveals is a nefarious system of politics at work that feeds off the desperation of the poor. To be sure, the film is not a plea for the victims' innocence; the Southside men were alleged to be gunmen for the JLP and Saulter does not attempt to sanitize their reputations. However, particularly through the representation of the protagonist, Ricky, Saulter asserts that this is not all they were and that the human being's worth is more than simply the sum total of his actions.

This assertion of the value – and complexity – of human life and experience is directly tied to the film's concern with the badman, cultural attitudes towards this figure and the film's location of this figure within a critique of the ruthless contest for national power by the political elite in Jamaica in the 1970s. In his impressive treatise on the Jamaican urban poor and their relation to state power, Obika Gray identifies a cultural style of "badness-honour" as one of the strategies employed by the rebellious poor (and others, including their political leaders) "to affirm their right to an honour contested or denied".[25] Gray suggests that this cultural style, a stylized outlawry also known as "badness" or "badmanism",[26] did not emerge in the 1970s but intensified and became more prevalent during that period. He describes badness-honour as "a repertoire" of behaviours employed by proponents to intimidate others that can range from "language, facial gesture, bodily poses and an assertive mien" to "the aggressive display of unpredictable and ominous corporeal power".[27]

Within the context of Gray's concept of badness-honour as encompassing a repertoire of behaviours and responses, Ricky can be thought of as an extreme expression of the phenomenon: an example of *ominous* corporeal power. Ricky is not merely a badman – he is a political gunman. The distinction is an important one, for the latter term implies an extreme position along the continuum of "oral-kinetic practice[s]"[28] that Gray identifies as constituting the repertoire of badness. In Jamaican parlance, Ricky is a *real* badman. While Gray notes that "ominous threat rather than actual violence is the stock-in-trade of those exhibiting badness-honour",[29] the word "gunman" conveys not merely the *threat* of violence but also the willingness to use a gun and, arguably, evokes less the sense of a cultural pose, performance or "dramaturgy"[30] and more the real and actual use of a deadly weapon. As a result, while the political gunman may be treated with respect and regarded as a hero within the narrow confines of the community which he claims to defend and protect from the violent actions of the opposing party and their gunmen, more often than not, beyond those borders, he is regarded as a figure of repulsion: an abject figure in the culture on to which society displaces notions of man's capacity for evil and terror and, in particular, the enactment of violence against his fellow man. It is Flames, one of Ricky's men, rather than Ricky himself, however, who comes closest to resembling this extreme expression of the badman. A habitual user of cocaine, Flames offers the drug to another member of the gang so that he can "kill like superman". In another scene he becomes the embodiment of every Jamaican householder's nightmare when he breaks into a house in the middle of the night, demands money from the occupants, and eventually shoots and kills them. The more heinous acts of violence are displaced onto Flames, but as a hired gun for the JLP, Ricky still takes on a sinister identity, particularly for members of the Jamaican audience who have greater economic opportunities and exist outside of the nexus of politics, poverty and political exploitation that persists in marginal communities.

In chapter 2 of this book, I argue that the 1972 film, *The Harder They Come*, transforms the badman figure from the common criminal of the newspaper accounts to a postcolonial rebel who refuses to be defined and dehumanized by the society's persistent colonial elements and values. That iconic film is key to Saulter's treatment of the gunman in *Better Mus' Come*. Both films are involved in the project of recuperating the past. *The Harder They Come* takes as its inspiration events in 1948 when Ivanhoe Martin's killing of two policemen and subsequent evasion of police capture held the nation in suspense for some six weeks. In its interlocution with history, *The*

Harder They Come situates its protagonist, Ivan, in a society marked by postcolonial tensions of wealth and poverty, power and powerlessness. Set in the latter part of the same decade in which *The Harder They Come* was released, *Better Mus' Come*, also inspired by real events, is similarly concerned with the unequal distribution of wealth and power in the postcolonial society. Saulter, however, explores this social imbalance very specifically within the context of the struggle for power by members of a political elite.

Both films attempt to humanize the gunman figure by insisting on a complex identity that resists the untextured superficiality of stereotypes. But whereas Ivan's quest for self-identity is informed by the very forces that seek to marginalize him and culminates in the achievement of a questionable form of celebrity, Ricky's humanity is affirmed by an insistence on his ordinariness and the many ways in which he demonstrates his inclusion in the flow of everyday life. Society's denigration of the political gunman, then, is challenged in *Better Mus' Come* by Saulter's ability to make the spectator care about and identify with this character because we recognize him as one of us, a man whose ambitions are inherently familiar. He is a caring parent and an ardent lover, a man longing for love and harmony and struggling to make a life for himself and those he loves.

It is specifically through Ricky, therefore, that *Better Mus' Come* challenges a popular conception of the political gunman as a cold-blooded figure of unrelenting evil, such as is seen in the character Sin in *Ghett'a Life*, whose very name infers that he is beyond redemption. While Saulter discredits the political ideology Ricky espouses, exposing it as a means through which the political elites use the poor to further their own selfserving agenda, Ricky nonetheless sees himself in the role of warrior. As Sives reminds us, for many in Jamaica's inner cities, the political party is not merely a source of economic benefits, it also bestows "status and identity within an emerging political order",[31] so that political violence is imbricated with issues of identity and belonging as "the party, and particular party figures, provided a core around which a political and communal identity was created".[32] Sives further states that the historical social alienation and exclusion of the urban poor, as well as the breakdown of rural bonds and forms of livelihood through urbanization, help to explain why the desire for a political identity resonates so intensely in poor urban communities in Jamaica. "It is the protection of this partisan identity which is one of the factors explaining the violence",[33] Sives states. As a warrior, Ricky is entrusted with the critical task of defending his community, a JLP enclave in a PNP constituency, against the violent actions of the rival PNP gang which periodically invades Southside and which was responsible for the death of his son's mother. On a larger stage, he also fights against the introduction of communism in Jamaica and closer ties with Cuba which, in his view and in the view of other Labourites (JLP supporters), will be the outcome if the PNP wins the next election. Saulter, therefore, carefully inserts Ricky into a specific historical moment that is defined by local conflict but which is also contextualized within the play of the larger global antagonisms of the cold war. Ricky is, to a large extent, caught in the grip of forces that are beyond his control.

In a scene that references *The Harder They Come*, Saulter demonstrates how critical political identity and loyalty were in the latter part of the 1970s. In a repeat of Ivan's experience in the earlier film, one of the members of Ricky's gang, Shorty (Everaldo Creary), goes to a construction site and begs the foreman for work. He is turned away, not because of his lack of skill or the lack of vacancies at the site (as occurred with Ivan), but because he is known to be a Labourite. When Shorty leaves the construction site, he is set upon by members of a PNP gang who attack and severely wound him. If we see this scene as being in dialogue with Henzell's earlier framing of unemployment and the lack of opportunities for the poor in the post-independence state, *Better Mus' Come* can be understood as directing our attention to the creation of a new postcolonial hierarchy based – not on colour or class – but on allegiance to one or the other of the two main political parties. The scene does not merely reflect the well-known connection between party allegiance, access to economic benefits for the poor and pressing issues of survival. It also, in the denial of Shorty's pleas for work and an opportunity to make an honest living, proposes the inherent injustice of this new hierarchical order in which one's rights as a citizen are curtailed on the basis of party loyalty and membership. In *Better Mus' Come*, therefore, as occurs in the earlier film, the turn to violence is critically tied to issues of identity, justice and rebellion against oppressive authority.

Ricky ponders these causal relationships in the poem we hear at the beginning of the film. This is an act of reflection that defines him, not as political gunman, but as creative thinker: a philosopher poet who critically examines his life. The persona in the poem (quoted earlier) conceptualizes the postcolonial nation as a reproduction of oppressive colonial structures, but also questions the use of violence as a form of resistance. The placing of the poem in the initial scene of the film is critical. It is heard as the men drive towards what they think is a rendezvous with someone who will give them "security work", a euphemism for access to illegal guns and an offer that has been made on the basis of their known identity as criminal elements in the community. As stated earlier, the poem foreshadows Ricky's death and prefaces the narrative focus on political violence. Ironically, it also locates Ricky within a critical perspective towards the use of violence at the very moment when he goes to meet a death that has been engineered because of his involvement in violent politics.

Like Ivan's music in the earlier film, Ricky's poetry functions as a vehicle for expressing his innermost thoughts and feelings. The two poems that he composes might be seen as expressing the seemingly contradictory elements that constitute the individual: the impulse towards violent rebellion on the one hand and the desire for harmony, beauty and love on the other. In this sense, Ricky's poetry emphasizes his humanness: he is not simply one thing, that is, a gunman, but a complex combination of often conflicting desires and impulses.

The connections and linkages that *Better Mus' Come* forges with *The Harder They Come* amplify the irony of Saulter's title. Taken from a song that the PNP used in its 1972 election campaign, the slogan "Better Must Come" imparts a sense of irrepressible hope and insistence on progress, phrasing change as inevitable, a moral imperative, rather than just another electoral promise: better *must* come. Within the context of the events of the film, however, the phrase resonates with irony. The title is first seen by the spectator after the dramatic firebombing of a PNP rally by Ricky and his men. In the scene, the JLP gunmen are defined as subversive and reactionary; associated with violence, subterfuge and outlawry, the gunmen offer a sharp contrast to the celebratory tone and progressive rhetoric of the PNP rally. As the jubilant crowd of PNP supporters chant "Better must come!", the Michael Manley character (Roger Guenveur Smith), speaking from the platform, exhorts: "Why should a child uptown have a better opportunity than a child from this community? Are we not the same people? Are we not the same blood? Then come together Jamaica because the word is love."

Ricky and two of his men, Flames and Shorty, disrupt the rally, throwing crude, home-made bombs at the platform, cutting short Manley's positive message of unity and equality and leaving fear, death and destruction in their wake. As the plot develops, however, Manley's rhetoric is itself brought into critical perspective. In a later sequence, cross-cutting juxtaposes images of the Manley character addressing a crowd of supporters with images of violent partisan rivalry, as well as images of the brutal response of the state security agencies. As the narrative shows the bloody conflict being played out on the streets of poor Kingston communities, Manley's speech is heard as a continuous soundtrack over the cross-cutting between various locations. The politician's rhetoric then becomes the site of dialogic interplay as image offers an ironic counterpoint to words. The Manley character's declaration that, "This is a revolution motivated by love! This is a revolution motivated by truth!", and his affirmation of solidarity with the people of Cuba "who are sending their blood . . . to liberate African people", is mocked by images of the shedding of Jamaican blood on Jamaican streets. The sequence creates an ironic perspective on the insistence that "better must come", chanted by Manley's supporters as he addresses them. It also brings into sharp relief the ambivalent positioning of the figure of the politician in the postcolonial society as the spectator is confronted with the gaping discrepancy between the rhetoric and promises of members of the political elite, in this case the prime minister, and their actual achievements.

The title of the film takes on its most ironic – and poignant – resonance within the context of the narrative's construction of the frustrated quest by the political gunman for a better life for himself and his son. Essentially existential in its framing of this quest, the narrative situates Ricky at a series of junctures where he makes critical decisions that lead him on an increasingly inexorable path towards death. Paradoxically, even as it suggests that Ricky arrives at a particular place in time – Green Bay in the early hours of that fateful morning – because of the conscious choices he makes, the narrative also conveys that Ricky is contained and governed by forces which he does not fully understand and over which he exercises little control. The film does not condone Ricky's choices, but by situating the gunman figure within a specific cultural, social and historical context, it attempts to impress on the spectator the difficulties the individual faces in attempting to initiate change within the nexus of poverty, chaos and violence that defines Kingston's poor urban communities, and which had reached unprecedented intensity during the 1970s.

Mobility is an important motif in the development of Ricky's quest for a better life. In a journey that reverses Ivan's iconic move from country to town, Ricky travels from the crowded city to the countryside to participate in a *binghi* and reason with the Rastafari elders. The journey takes Ricky and Kimala far outside the ghetto community to a rural location and introduces the possibility of change, not merely in terms of external and material conditions, but also within the context of Ricky's spirituality and the values that determine what is important in his life. As the accompanying song states, they are "stepping out of Babylon . . . into Mount Zion". The Rastafari elder with whom he reasons tells Ricky that two roads are before him and he must choose: "If is yourself is a murderer, then go and murder. And if righteousness is your calling, then become righteous." The Rastafari, therefore, is constructed as a symbol of self-determination that functions in opposition to the divisive partisan politics, the violence that it breeds and the exploitation and manipulation of the poor that it supports. Towards the end of the film, this symbol is revisited when Ricky is shot by one of the soldiers; the screen fades to black and then we see an image of Ricky swimming underwater, transformed into a Rastaman with long, flowing locks.

Indeed, at the binghi Ricky embraces peace. But a spate of violence in the community and the resulting series of events conspire to lure him away from the path of righteousness and towards the path of murder. Kimala begs him not to seek revenge for the death of the Rastafari teacher who was needlessly shot in cold blood by the rival PNP gang, to resist "killing people for slave master's promises", but caught up in the anger, frustration and outrage of the moment, Ricky ignores her pleas and takes up the mantle of warrior once again. Later, after getting injured and saving Kimala from rape by the PNP gang leader, he sends her out of the city with his son, but at the last minute he decides to stay. And finally, when he is roused from his dream of Kimala by members of his gang, he pauses a long minute, as if considering his actions, but decides to join the men for the meeting at Green Bay. In the scenes depicting Ricky's movement around the community as tension builds after the killing of the Rastafari teacher, the motif of mobility takes on a Gothic resonance: as the violence escalates, Ricky's negotiation of the myriad narrow, twisting lanes and walkways that traverse the community conveys a sense of the maze-like interiority of the archaic Gothic castle and suggests that he is trapped, not only within the physical boundaries of the ghetto but also psychologically, within a certain prescribed way of thinking that locks him into an easily imagined destiny.

The narrative also conveys, however, the complexity and difficulty of the choices Ricky faces. While he is wary of the offer of security work and his intuitive response is to refuse, his men urge him to accept so that they can earn some money. Ricky is responsible for providing a livelihood for the men in the gang; as Shorty, one of his men, states: "The men dem look to you fi leadership, yu know. . . . If yu nah mek sense, we have to go look to a next man" (The men look to you for leadership. If you don't make sense, then we will have to look to another man.) What is at stake is not simply Ricky's position of leadership in the gang and by extension the privileges that accrue to that status; in the nightmare world that Ricky inhabits, if his authority is challenged by another man, it is a contest that will most likely end in death. Ricky postpones a final decision on the crucial question of accepting the security work as long as he can, but with the eruption of violence in the community, the gang's need for weapons and money intensifies. Alas, the turn away from the path of his old values requires a degree of strength, foresight and conviction that Ricky does not possess and which, possibly, few of us can claim. Waking him from the dream of Kimala, Ricky's men press him with the demand to attend the meeting at Green Bay. It is at this point that the replay of the opening scene occurs and the final events leading to Ricky's death are fully played out. Thus, the repetitive structure of the film underscores the sense of futility and inevitability. Here, mobility – now associated with repetition and the journey to the firing range at Green Bay – again conveys a sense of entrapment as we watch Ricky and his men drive to what we now suspect will be their death.

Ironically, it is Flames, the gang member that most insistently urged

Ricky to accept the offer of security work, who survives the attack by the soldiers. He manages to get to the beach and swims out to sea, where he is picked up by a passing fishing boat. Ricky also flees to the beach but is shot down by one of the soldiers. As alluded to earlier, Ricky's death is the final scene in which a shift in consciousness and an alternative ontological state is suggested. As the soldier shoots, Ricky dives under the water and is transformed into a Rastaman, while inserted images of Kimala and Ricky's son convey the sense of the final thoughts or memories of the dying man and confirm that it is love, not power and politics, which is the most important facet of human existence. We are tempted by these images to hope that somehow, like Charles Kingsley's water babies, Ricky lives again under the sea.[34] The film possibly means to suggest another dimension to human existence: an afterlife in which Ricky, unfettered by the demands of the material world, is finally able to assume an identity of his own choosing. But the final image of the film counters such optimism and, instead, speaks eloquently of the terrible futility of the gunman's life and even challenges the very idea of spiritual change and transformation through death. This final image, a high angle shot which shows Ricky floating face down in a sea coloured red by his own blood, his gun discarded on the sea floor, is one of dread and horror that leaves us with a sense of pathos. There is no satisfaction in seeing this shotta shot down. Instead, we mourn his death because the film has shown us the value and potential of the human being.

The final sequences of the film maintain the existential focus of the narrative as well as its social commentary. Lying face down in the sea, Ricky's pose is reminiscent of the Christ figure, but the gun, now useless (and barely noticeable), that lies just beyond his reach amplifies the notion that Ricky has sacrificed his life for an empty cause, leaving his loved ones, Kimala and his young son, alone to fend for themselves in a hostile environment. The image of Ricky's body in a sea of blood is an awful reminder of the bloodshed and horror of the 1970s and the consequences of a form of partisan politics that blindly pursued power and divided the nation. This image then, and indeed the film, functions as what Gabriel describes as a "memory deferred by official history"[35] and forces us to recall that which powerful elites would prefer we forget.

EPILOGUE
Expanding Narratives of Identity in Jamaican Film

A national culture is the whole body of efforts made by a people in the sphere of thought to describe, justify and praise the action through which that people has created itself and keeps itself in existence. A national culture in underdeveloped countries should therefore take its place at the very heart of the struggle for freedom which these countries are carrying on.[1]
—Frantz Fanon

INCREASINGLY IN JAMAICA, THE EXPRESSION OF cultural narratives, myths and other stories that help explain and interpret the world around us is taking place on a screen, and the recognition of film as an important facet of national culture is growing. In the preceding chapters, I attempted to show how Jamaican films expand our understanding of Jamaica as place and nation by putting on the screen expressions and formations of identity that are seldom officially claimed as part of the fabric of national culture, and perspectives of Jamaica that are frequently suppressed in favour of more pleasing and agreeable versions or representations. This is one of the ways in which Jamaican films perform the role that Fanon identifies as appropriate for a national culture. Hall proposes, however, that the cinema is not merely a "second-order mirror held up to reflect what already exists" but a "form of representation which is also able to constitute us as new kinds of subjects and therefore enable us to discover who we are".[2] The films discussed in this book function in this capacity as well: they show us who we are in the sense of reflecting identities formed out of the experiences of the past, but they also show us, as Hall would say, who we are in the process of becoming. These films' continuing relevance to critical issues of identity in Jamaican society is demonstrated in multiple ways: in the farsightedness of *Smile Orange* in its anticipation of the social and psychological consequences of the dependence on tourism, issues which are now in the forefront of scholarly discourse on the industry; in *Dancehall Queen*'s prophetic claiming of the erotic performance of the dancehall as a complex, vital and dynamic cultural space and expression of national culture; in the attention paid to narratives of nation that pivot on the schisms and transformations of the critical period of the 1970s; and in the recurring narratives of badness that help us understand ambivalent responses to configurations of power in poor urban communities and the brutal responses of state authorities when these structures of power threaten to spill out beyond the boundaries of ghetto spaces.

As products situated within the modern, technologically driven global marketplace, however, films are, as Maryse Condé points out, "developed with money and for money";[3] they are, Randal Johnson states, "both symbolic goods and economic commodities".[4] In any film industry, therefore, questions of aesthetics, ideological intention and social function are necessarily entangled with considerations of market value and appeal. The relationship between these factors tends to be particularly exposed in marginal production communities and in parts of the developing world where there is little support for production from the state, and not much to be had in the form of grants and endowments. This is precisely the case in Jamaica: a small location where population size does not allow the film to amortize through exhibition to a local audience, success in the marketplace is frequently defined in terms of the film's ability to appeal to the local audience as well as cross over into markets abroad. In such film communities, as Zeinabu Irene Davis points out in reference to black independent film in the United States (considered a minoritarian cinema despite its location in a developed country), questions of style and form are not simply a matter of aesthetic choice but "a matter of extreme hardship – political and economic factors, lack of opportunity and more [that] influence and form aesthetic decisions".[5]

It is precisely for such underdeveloped communities, however, that Fanon identifies a role for culture that eschews the profit motive and is instead concerned with the "struggle for freedom".[6] In a similar vein, in his schema of the stages of the development of Third World films, Teshome

Gabriel draws on Fanon's notion of culture as liberation to describe a final phase of production, the "combative phase", in which film functions as an ideological tool that addresses the lives and struggles of Third World people, and filmmaking has evolved into a public service institution, managed, operated and run for and by the people.[7] Gabriel and Fanon's rhetoric, embraced in earlier decades to speak to culture's potential to support liberation struggles, largely defined within the context of colonialism, now sounds somewhat outdated. In Jamaica, which experienced various ideological shifts after independence and also embarked on a seemingly unending economic crisis in the 1970s, the fiery rhetoric of liberation has been all but abandoned. The imposition of various International Monetary Fund and World Bank–crafted austerity programmes, and decades of structural adjustment that "yielded few benefits for the poor",[8] have left in their wake a society that, for the most part, defines development in socioeconomic rather than humanist terms.

The issue confronting the film sector in Jamaica and other similar locations, then, is defining film's role in contemporary society. In a location where the single most critical issue affecting production is funding, is it still relevant to talk about a cinema of liberation? Is Fanon's assertion that "it is around the peoples' struggles that African-Negro culture takes on substance"[9] passé in an environment where the potential to monetize the cultural and creative industries is now touted as a path to realizing economic growth?

In their discussion of the decline of the Third World paradigm to denote an empowering and "politically inflected cultural practice",[10] Ella Shohat and Robert Stam note that since the late 1980s, "filmmakers have in part discarded the didactic Third Worldist model predominant in the 1960s in favour of a postmodern 'politics of pleasure' incorporating music, humor and sexuality".[11] That didactic Third Worldist model that tended to prioritize ideology over pleasure was never fully operational or dominant in Jamaican cinema, however. The absence of state support for narrative film meant that there has always been pressure in the sector to produce films that would attract a mass audience. Out of necessity, therefore, the notion of pleasure has always been manifest in Jamaican narrative features, whether in the recurring use of humour, the erotic performance of the dancehall, the emphasis on action and dramatic tension, the reliance on the familiar and pleasurable melodies and lyrics of popular music, the referencing of popular genre conventions or the use of realist modes of expression. But these vivid expressions of a politics of pleasure which indicate a mindfulness of the demands of the market have not meant the disavowal of an intention that goes beyond entertainment and profit making and embraces social commentary and larger political concerns. The films discussed in this book may lack the unambiguous ideological perspectives that Gabriel describes, and they certainly do not represent the "cinema of mass participation"[12] that he envisions. As the discussion in preceding chapters has shown, however, even as they strive to appeal to both local and overseas audiences, Jamaican films have consistently expressed a concern with the struggles to which Fanon refers and have consistently addressed the various manifestations of imbalances of power in a society that, as Rex Nettleford states, is yet to be organized in the interests of the majority.[13]

This tension between, on one hand, a concern with social issues that involves challenging imbalances of power and which may require the exploration of alternative aesthetics that allow for more complex and textured representations of place and identity, and on the other, the need to prioritize aesthetics that would maximize profits and facilitate consumption in multiple markets, consistently informs local dialogue on strategies for developing the industry. At a panel discussion on 20 April 2016 at the Edna Manley College for the Visual and Performing Arts in Kingston, titled "Film: A Catalyst for the Creative Economy", Jamaican-Canadian filmmaker Jeremy Whittaker emphasized that in order to survive in the business, Jamaican filmmakers need to make films that appeal to multiple markets. An important condition for doing so, he stated, is the use of Standard English rather than Jamaican Creole in local films. This is not a singular opinion; the recommendation that Jamaican Creole or Jamaican language should be reduced or "toned down" in order to facilitate local films' entry into overseas markets was reiterated at another forum in October 2016 at the National Gallery in Kingston, this time by a respected local producer who has worked in the sector for many years. It might be difficult to imagine a Jamaican film in which Standard English takes precedence over Jamaican Creole, the language that most Jamaicans speak and one of the distinctive elements of Jamaican culture, but Whittaker's film, *Destiny* (2014), a love story set in Canada and Jamaica about wealthy and middle-class characters, was able to keep Jamaican to a minimum and use, for the most part, registers of language that were close to Standard English.

Only time will reveal whether *Destiny* indicates a new trend – long overdue in the view of some – of greater diversity in the types of Jamaican stories reaching the screen, and a shift from social commentary and scenarios that expose the hardships experienced in poor inner-city communities. The proposal, however, that Jamaican films should employ a register of language closer to Standard English in order to satisfy the demands of overseas markets is a critical issue that is pertinent to the question of the role of a national culture and film's role in contemporary Jamaica. I do not mean to say that Jamaican films should not employ the various registers of Jamaican Standard English when appropriate, or even to imply that Jamaican filmmakers should not also explore the lived experiences of the middle class and the elites who may speak a language that is closer to Standard English than Jamaican Creole. A cinema which seeks to explore the diversity of experiences and subjectivities that exist across Jamaican social (and other) spaces is highly desirable.

It is important to note, however, that language remains one of the critical sites at which the struggle for freedom is waged. As a "potent symbol of collective identity",[14] language is "a social battleground", state Shohat and Stam, and "forms the site where political struggles are engaged both collectively and intimately".[15] Brian L. Moore and Michele A. Johnson identify language as a site of struggle in nineteenth and early twentieth century Jamaica, when Jamaican Creole was disparaged and denigrated by cultural elites who felt that English, the language of the colonizer, should be the accepted national language of Jamaica.[16] That denigration continues in contemporary society, with Pauline Christie noting that negative stereotypes and low social status are generally associated with Creole speakers or speakers of what is often referred to as "bad English".[17] If, as George Lamming states, "language may be experienced as a mode of thinking, of receiving and articulating experience",[18] then language must be understood as playing a vital role in what Rex Nettleford refers to as the "unending struggle to define self and society".[19] Nettleford sees this struggle as fundamental to the effort to overcome "the persistent powerlessness of the majority nurtured on self-negation and a false consciousness that leads to identity crises".[20] In the face of cultural domination that produces such powerlessness, the task that Nettleford identifies for the new Caribbean nation is that of fashioning a form of power which enables people to make their own definitions about themselves and act on those definitions.[21] A film sector which privileges the needs and demands of an external market cannot be reasonably expected to participate in this process of cultural empowerment.

Despite the often commercially inflected tone of much of the discussion that takes place locally on the development of film in Jamaica, however, I remain optimistic about the future of the sector and the ability of local filmmakers to use film to meet and address a variety of social and cultural needs: for entertainment, for empowering storytelling, for nation building, for social commentary and critique, and even the need to explore new aesthetics and re-energize more familiar forms.

At (yet) another forum, this one in May 2017, two researchers conducting a study of the film and music sectors asked practitioners to identify the drivers of their success; the researchers wanted to know how practitioners were successfully negotiating challenges as well as how government policy and private sector assistance might be directed and harnessed to help create even more success stories.[22] Although the practitioners were minded to give full vent to their grievances before identifying their successes, it was clear that filmmakers are not sitting and waiting for the proverbial manna to fall from heaven or even from overextended government coffers. Indeed, I came away from that discussion with a great deal of respect for persons in the sector who, despite the paucity of government funding and the reluctance of private investors to support projects, continue to seek new and creative ways of fulfilling a passion for making films. Veteran cinematographer Franklyn St Juste deserves special mention here. Chappie, as he is universally known, started his career at the JFU working alongside the founding director Martin Rennalls. Several decades later, he continues to make films as well as give freely of his time and knowledge in the mentoring of "youngsters". Indeed, there is a vibrant and active community of younger filmmakers who, although clear-sighted about the difficulties, nevertheless proceed with hope, conviction and passion. It is in this spirit of resilience and optimism that Michelle Serieux and Storm Saulter formed a collective that made *Ring Di Alarm!* (2012), an anthology of seven short films.[23] The idea behind the collective was simple but powerful. Each of the six members created scripts for shorts that could be shot during the course of a day, and each person gave time and skills to the making of each film. The result was *Ring Di Alarm!*, which debuted at the British Film Institute and then went on to show to sell-out audiences in Jamaica. States Serieux, "Your creative spirit is going to die if you sit around waiting for someone to give you money. You just need to be innovative and use what you have."[24]

The younger generation is also driving a re-energized and revamped practitioners' association. Under the leadership of Gabrielle Blackwood, the Jamaica Association of Film and Television Producers launched the Propella! initiative in 2015. Funded primarily by the Chase Fund, this project stages a competition that supports the production of five short films annually. Support is also provided by the Jamaican Film Commission which, with film commissioner Renee Robinson, at the helm, has become much more supportive and involved in nurturing local talent and production by providing training and development opportunities. In 2016, Propella! produced five films: *Origins, Sugar, Shoot the Girl, Silent Hearts* and *Shock Value*. As part of its annual film event, "March Is Movie Month at Mona", the Department of Literatures in English at the University of the West Indies, Mona, screened the films. Accustomed to moderate responses to film screenings, the department was overwhelmed by the numbers that turned up and which exceeded the capacity of the 250-seat lecture theatre where the films were shown. Refused entry to the packed room, many people lingered outside hoping to squeeze in. While this was just a single event, the large turnout confirmed a desire on the part of Jamaican audiences to see images of themselves on the screen. In addition, the enthusiastic response to the films also suggested an openness to narrative and stylistic innovation.

The Propella! films told stories from a variety of perspectives, from downtown as well as uptown, and about a variety of subjects. Two of the more exciting films in the collection were *Sugar*, written by Sharon Leach and Michelle Serieux and directed by Serieux, and *Origins*, written and directed by Kurt Wright. In the question and answer session that followed the screening, Serieux explained that she made the difficult (and costly) choice to use continuous takes and keep editing to an absolute minimum in *Sugar* in order to convey the unrelenting pressure that the protagonist experiences as she negotiates the overwhelming demands and difficult obstacles that frustrate her attempt to further her education. Kurt Wright blends magical realism and science fiction in *Origins* to bring figures from Jamaican folklore and history to the screen in a story that uses time travel to suggest the relevance of earlier struggles to contemporary life. Both the Propella! initiative and *Ring Di Alarm!* confirm that Jamaican filmmakers are "tekking hand and mekking fashion", that is, while lack of funding may frustrate the production of full-length features, short films are proving to be a creative and worthwhile response to the challenges and restrictions of limited resources. At the time of writing, the Propella! initiative is in its third edition and continues to play an important role in giving emerging filmmakers the opportunity to develop their craft.

Another important development is the growth of the film festival culture in the Caribbean. Film festivals provide an alternative distribution and exhibition route, especially for short films, documentaries and non-traditional films. They also frequently provide training in the form of workshops, help put filmmakers in touch with investors and producers, and help them develop scripts for production. Some of the more important festivals in terms of their contribution to the growth and development of indigenous cinema in Jamaica and the wider region are the annual Trinidad and Tobago Film Festival held in Port of Spain, Trinidad, Caribbean Tales held in Toronto, Third Horizon Film Festival in Miami and the Timehri Film Festival in Guyana. These festivals provide important opportunities for Caribbean films to be seen and put Caribbean filmmakers in touch with their audiences as well as investors, producers and other key players in the industry. The Greater August Town Film Festival in Jamaica also provides training and exhibition opportunities for local and regional filmmakers. Since its inception in 2013, it has premiered four documentaries and a number of local short films. This festival grew out of the University of the West Indies Community Film Project which, since its inception in 2012, has sought to impart rudimentary filmmaking skills to young people in marginal communities. In 2017, the festival premiered *Children of the Incursion*, a documentary that was conceived by one of the graduates of the film project, Alan Powell, and which shows the impact of the state security forces' incursion into the Tivoli Gardens community in 2010 to apprehend Christopher "Dudus" Coke. Although unsophisticated and "imperfect", *Children of the Incursion*, which stages interviews with a number of young people who were caught up in the events of May 2010, suggests the potential of film to bring diverse voices and perspectives into the public domain.

The cumulative effect of the various developments referred to above, along with the availability of new, more accessible technology, is that filmmaking in Jamaica is slowly becoming more participatory. This is by no means a cinema of mass participation; neither is it, nor does it strive to be, what Martin Rennalls advocated in the days of the JFU, that is, a cinema for "Jamaicans, by Jamaicans".[25] Jamaican cinema is emerging and still developing; in many ways, it has displayed an admirable resilience, but it continues to be fragile in many respects. Jamaican films speak with power and urgency to viewers, those "a yaad" as well as those abroad. They continue to address difficult and complex questions of Jamaican identity in ways that reaffirm, delight, question, trouble and disturb our sense of who we are.

NOTES

INTRODUCTION

1. Tom Rice, *"Favourite for the Jamaica Cup"*, Colonial Film: Moving Images of the British Empire (http://www.colonialfilm.org.uk/node/4450), identifies the proposed film as *Lieutenant Daring and the Labour Riots*, which was released a few months after the company shot the scenes in Jamaica. British and Colonial Kinematograph produced thirteen Lieutenant Daring films between 1912 and 1914.
2. *Daily Gleaner*, 29 January 1913, 4. A total of six letters protesting the film appeared in the *Daily Gleaner*, two of which were written by Price. Price would later go on to help establish Calabar High School, now a prominent boys' school in Kingston. Myrtle Bank Hotel was an elite hotel that looked out onto the Kingston waterfront.
3. *Daily Gleaner*, 31 January 1913, 4.
4. *Daily Gleaner*, 1 February 1913, 3.
5. *Daily Gleaner*, 29 January, 1913, 4.
6. Ibid.
7. This reassurance was false as it appears that the scenes were not excluded. Mr Aspinall of the West India Committee Circular, who was invited to view the films on their release in the United Kingdom, reported that the controversial scenes were inoffensive. The film was also exhibited in Jamaica in February 1914. Rice, *"Favourite"*.
8. *Daily Gleaner*, 1 February 1913, 3.
9. Mybe B. Cham, "Introduction: Shape and Shaping of Caribbean Cinema", in *Ex-Iles: Essays on Caribbean Cinema*, ed. Mybe B. Cham (Trenton, NJ: Africa World Press, 1992), 6.
10. Bruce King, "New Centres of Consciousness", in *New National and Post-Colonial Literatures: An Introduction*, ed. Bruce King (Oxford: Clarendon Press, 2002), 7.

11. Edward S. Casey, "How to Get from Space to Place in a Fairly Short Stretch of Time: Phenomenological Prolegomena", in *Senses of Place*, ed. Steven Feld and Keith H. Basso (Santa Fe, NM: School of American Research Press, 1996), 19.
12. Robert Stam and Louise Spence, "Colonialism, Racism and Representation", in *Film Theory and Criticism: Introductory Readings*, ed. Leo Braudy and Marshall Cohen (New York: Oxford University Press, 1999), 240. Stam and Spence refer here more broadly to Third World filmmakers.
13. I use the word "filmmakers" here in its truly plural sense to reflect the collaborative nature of the film project and to recognize the creative input and aspirations of all those involved in creating the film, not merely the director.
14. Cham, "Introduction", 2.
15. Jean Antoine-Dunne, "Sound and Vision in the Caribbean Imaginary", *Journal of West Indian Literature* 18, no. 2 (2010): 94.
16. Ibid., 95.
17. Diaram Ramjeesingh, "The Jamaican Film Industry: Quo Vadis?" *Ideaz* 9 (2011): 7–8. See table 1, "Jamaican Films Produced Between 1972 and 2012", 8.
18. Paul Willemen, "The National Revisited", in *Theorising National Cinema*, ed. Valentina Vitali and Paul Willemen (London: British Film Institute, 2006), 35.
19. Stephen Crofts, "Reconceptualising National Cinema/s", in *Theorising National Cinema*, ed. Valentina Vitali and Paul Willemen (London: British Film Institute, 2006), 49.
20. Ramjeesingh, "Quo Vadis?", 15.
21. Andrew Higson, *Waving the Flag: Constructing a National Cinema in Britain* (Oxford: Clarendon Press, 1995), 4.
22. The location in *Towards Independence* shifts from Jamaica to London in order to provide coverage of the Jamaica Independence Conference, an event of huge significance to Jamaicans and the crafting of the final stages of independence.
23. Mette Hjort, "Themes of Nation", in *Cinema and Nation*, ed. Mette Hjort and Scott MacKenzie (London: Routledge, 2000), 108. Hjort differentiates between a film's concern with the *theme* of nation and its national qualities. She argues that the intense use of a national setting may be used to determine "aboutness" (of a particular nation), but this alone does not necessarily constitute the *theme* of nation. I have drawn on some of the criteria she offers for determining a particular national quality.
24. Willemen, "National Revisited", 36.
25. Casey, "How to Get from Space to Place", 26–27.

26. Attie de Lange, Gail Fincham, Jeremy Hawthorne and Jakob Lothe, introduction, *Literary Landscapes: From Modernism to Postcolonialism*, ed. Attie de Lange et al. (Basingstoke, Hampshire: Palgrave Macmillan, 2008), xiv.
27. Henri Lefebvre, *The Production of Space*, trans. Donald Nicholson-Smith (Malden, MA: Blackwell, 1984), 26.
28. Doreen Massey, *Space, Place, and Gender* (Minneapolis: University of Minnesota Press, 1994), 2.
29. Ibid., 168.
30. Simon During, *Cultural Studies: A Critical Introduction* (London: Routledge, 2005), 82.
31. Massey, *Space, Place, and Gender*, 169.
32. Ibid.
33. de Lange et al., introduction, xiv.
34. Bill Ashcroft, Gareth Griffiths and Helen Tiffin, *The Empire Writes Back: Theory and Practice in Post-Colonial Literatures* (London: Routledge, 1989), 9.
35. Ibid.
36. Edouard Glissant, introduction, *Caribbean Discourses: Selected Essays*, trans. J. Michael Dash (Charlottesville: University Press of Virginia, 1989), 11.
37. Elizabeth DeLoughrey, "Ecocriticism: The Politics of Place", in *The Routledge Companion to Anglophone Caribbean Literature*, ed. Michael A. Bucknor and Alison Donnell (London: Routledge, 2011), 265.
38. Massey, *Space, Place, and Gender*, 265.
39. Bill Ashcroft, Gareth Griffiths and Helen Tiffin, eds., *The Post-Colonial Studies Reader*. (London: Routledge, 2001), 391.
40. Chris Tiffin and Alan Lawson, "Introduction: The Textuality of Empire", in *De-Scribing Empire: Colonialism and Textuality*, ed. Chris Tiffin and Alan Lawson (London: Routledge, 1994), 3.
41. de Lange, et al., introduction, xiii.
42. André Bazin, *What Is Cinema?*, vol. 1, trans. Hugh Gray (Berkeley: University of California Press, 2005), 14.
43. Elena Gorfinkel and John David Rhodes, "Introduction: The Matter of Places", in *Taking Place: Location and the Moving Image*, ed. John David Rhodes and Elena Gorfinkel (Minneapolis: University of Minnesota Press, 2011), x.
44. Cham, "Introduction", 2.
45. Jane Bryce, "'That Is Not for Beke': Global Versus Local in Two Versions of *Sargasso*", in *Globalisation, Diaspora and Caribbean Popular Culture*, ed. Christine G.T. Ho and Keith Nurse (Kingston: Ian Randle, 2005), 259.

46. Brian Meeks, "The Political Moment in Jamaica: The Dimensions of Hegemonic Dissolution", in *Caribbean Political Thought: Theories of the Post-Colonial State*, ed. Aaron Kamugisha (Kingston: Ian Randle, 2013), 85.
47. Walter Rodney, "Contemporary Political Trends in the English-Speaking Caribbean", in *Caribbean Political Thought: Theories of the Post-Colonial State*, ed. Aaron Kamugisha (Kingston: Ian Randle, 2013), 2.
48. George Lamming, "Colonialism and the Caribbean Novel", in *Postcolonial Discourses: An Anthology*, ed. Gregory Castle (Oxford: Blackwell, 2001), 273.
49. Ibid.
50. Ibid.
51. Meeks, "Political Moment", 85.
52. Stuart Hall, "Cultural Identity and Cinematic Representation", in *Ex-Iles: Essays on Caribbean Cinema*, ed. Mybe B. Cham (Trenton, NJ: Africa World Press, 1992), 236.
53. Willemen, "National Revisited", 30.
54. This also occurred with the early West Indian novelists who, according to George Lamming, were criticized for the absence of novels about the middle class. See *The Pleasures of Exile* (London: Allison and Bubsy, 1960), 38.
55. Douglas Graham, interview with the author, 5 April 2017.
56. A notable exception to the male dominated field of film production in Jamaica is Esther Figueroa, a documentarist who describes herself as an independent activist filmmaker. Mary Wells also wrote and directed *Kingston Paradise* (2013), which was shown in Jamaican cinemas in 2017. Michelle Serieux, a St Lucian resident based in Jamaica, Gabrielle Blackwood, a cinematographer, and Rae-Ann Smith, a Trinidadian national based in Jamaica, have all made short films and are three female talents with great promise.
57. Manthia Diawara, "Black Spectatorship: Problems of Identification and Resistance", in *Black American Cinema*, ed. Manthia Diawara (New York: Routledge, 1993).
58. V.S. Naipaul, *The Middle Passage: Impressions of Five Societies – British, French and Dutch – in the West Indies and South America.* (London: Andre Deutsch, 1963), 58–59.
59. Isaac Julien and Kobena Mercer, "De Margin and De Centre", in *Stuart Hall: Critical Dialogues in Cultural Studies*, ed. David Morley and Kuan-Hsing Chen (London: Routledge, 1996), 453.

CHAPTER 1

1. Siegfried Kracauer, *Theory of Film: The Redemption of Physical Reality* (New York: Oxford University Press, 1960), quoted in Gorfinkel and Rhodes, "Introduction", vii.
2. Gorfinkel and Rhodes, "Introduction", vii.
3. M.M. Bakhtin, *The Dialogic Imagination: Four Essays*, ed. Michael Holquist, trans. Caryl Emerson and Michael Holquist (Austin: University of Texas Press, 1981), 276.
4. Higson, *Waving the Flag*, 7.
5. Willemen, "National Revisited", 30.
6. Ibid.
7. Benedict Anderson, *Imagined Communities: Reflections on the Origin and Spread of Nationalism* (London: Verso, 1994), 12.
8. Homi K. Bhabha, "Introduction: Narrating the Nation", in *Nation and Narration*, ed. Homi K. Bhabha (London: Routledge, 2004), 306.
9. Higson, *Waving the Flag*, 4.
10. See Cham, "Introduction", and Keith Q. Warner, *On Location: Cinema and Film in the Anglophone Caribbean* (London: Macmillan Education, 2000), whose accounts of anglophone Caribbean film make no reference to the earlier documentary production.
11. For a detailed account of the establishment of the JFU, see Terri Francis, "Sounding the Nation: Martin Rennalls and the Jamaica Film Unit, 1951–1961", *Film History* 23 (2011): 110–28; also Rachel Moseley-Wood, "Ambivalence in the Image: The Jamaica Film Unit and the Narrative of the Emerging Nation", *Jamaican Historical Review* 16 (2013): 47–66, an earlier version of this chapter.
12. Executive Council Submission, Jamaica Film Unit, 12 January 1956, prepared by I.S. Lloyd, minister of education and social welfare, 1B/31/48-1956, Jamaica Archives, Spanish Town.
13. Francis, "Sounding the Nation", 116.
14. Government of Jamaica, Public Relations Department, Kingston, "Jamaica Film Unit Catalogue of Films", 1959 ed. The catalogue also provides evidence of the circulation of West Indian films in the region, identifying in the holdings of the JFU library films made by other West Indian colonial units.
15. Minutes of the meeting of the Advisory Committee of the Film Unit, 22 November 1956, Jamaica Archives, Spanish Town.
16. Martin Rennalls, "Development of the Documentary Film in Jamaica"

(master's thesis, School of Public Communication, Division of Broadcasting and Film, Boston University, 1967), 36.
17. Tom Rice, "From the Inside: The Colonial Film Unit and the Beginning of the End", in *Film and the End of Empire*, ed. Lee Grieveson and Colin MacCabe (London: British Film Institute and Palgrave Macmillan, 2011), 135.
18. K.W. Blackburne, "Financial Problems and Future Policy in British Colonies", *The Film in Colonial Development: A Report of A Conference* (London: British Film Institute, 1948), 35.
19. Ibid., 33.
20. Executive Council Submission, "Contribution by Government of Jamaica to the Colonial Film Unit", 23 July 1953, 1B/31/395-1953, Jamaica Archives, Spanish Town.
21. The participants were: I. Carmichael (Barbados); W. Lee (Trinidad and Tobago); R.L. Young (British Guiana); and M. Weller, T. Welsh and M.A. Rennalls (Jamaica).
22. CFU, "Colonial Film Unit Training School in the West Indies", *Colonial Cinema* 2, no. 9 (1951): 40.
23. *Development and Welfare in the West Indies, 1950: Report by the Comptroller for the Year 1950* (London: HMSO, 1951), 53.
24. "Colonial Film Unit Training School", *Colonial Cinema* 9, no. 2 (June 1951), 43.
25. Rennalls, "Development of the Documentary Film", 59–60.
26. Tom Rice, "*Farmer Brown Learns Good Dairying*", Colonial Film, Moving Images of the British Empire, http://www.colonialfilm.org.uk/node/1196 (accessed 1 March 2013).
27. A submission to the Executive Council gives the precise date for the establishment of the JFU as 1 October 1951. Executive Council Submission, Jamaica Film Unit, 1959, Jamaica Archives, Spanish Town.
28. Francis, "Sounding the Nation", 116.
29. Rennalls, "Development of the Documentary Film", 70.
30. Francis, "Sounding the Nation", 115.
31. Ibid., 124–25.
32. Rennalls, "Development of the Documentary Film", 63.
33. Minutes of the meeting of the Advisory Committee of the Film Unit, 14 June 1956 and 22 November 1956, Jamaica Archives, Spanish Town.
34. Rennalls, "Development of the Documentary Film", 63.
35. See Rice, "From the Inside".
36. Executive Council Submission, "Transfer of Responsibility for Beach Control,

the Government Film Unit and Broadcasting to the Chief Minister as Minister of Development", 1B/31/1449-1956, Jamaica Archives, Spanish Town.
37. Rennalls, "Development of the Documentary Film", 99.
38. Ibid., 101.
39. Ibid., 103
40. Ibid., 102.
41. Ibid., 115.
42. Francis, "Sounding the Nation", 123
43. Ibid., 124.
44. Rennalls, "Development of the Documentary Film", 119.
45. Ibid., 123. Unfortunately, Rennalls does not identify these programmes by name.
46. Ella Shohat and Robert Stam, *Unthinking Eurocentrism: Multiculturalism and the Media* (London: Routledge, 2001), 102.
47. Willemen, "National Revisited", 30.
48. Ibid.
49. See "Visual Education in Jamaica", *Colonial Cinema* 8, no. 1 (March 1950): 34–35.
50. In an interview with the author (10 June 2009), Franklyn "Chappy" St Juste, one of the early members of the JFU, also confirms *Towards Independence* as one of the unit's films.
51. Rennalls, "Development of the Documentary Film", 168.
52. Ibid., 170.
53. Ibid.
54. Ibid., 168.
55. Ibid., 169.
56. Rennalls, "Visual Education", 17.
57. Ibid., 16.
58. Higson, *Waving the Flag*, 6.
59. When the JLP announced in 1960 a permanent policy in favour of Jamaican secession from the West Indies Federation in opposition to the government's continuing support for that arrangement, a referendum was called in 1961; the majority voted to opt out of the federation.
60. "West Indian Students Abuse Manley", *Daily Gleaner*, 3 May 1962, 1.
61. "Independence: Premier Hints Aug 1", *Daily Gleaner*, 29 January 1962, 1.
62. *Daily Gleaner*, 2 February 1962, 1. Prior to 1961, 24 May (Queen Victoria's birthday) was celebrated in Jamaica and other British colonies as Empire Day.

63. Simeon C.R. McIntosh, *Caribbean Constitutional Reform: Rethinking the West Indian Polity* (Kingston: Caribbean Law Publishing, 2002), 51.
64. See James B. Kelly, "The Jamaican Independence Constitution of 1962", *Caribbean Studies* 3, no. 1 (1963): 18–83; Trevor Munroe, *The Politics of Constitutional Decolonization, Jamaica 1944–62* (Kingston: Institute of Social and Economic Research, University of the West Indies, 1983); and McIntosh, *Caribbean Constitutional Reform*. These authors comment on the haste with which drafting, debate and consultation took place; the conducting of the drafting sessions in secret, that is, outside public scrutiny; and the inadequate public consultation.
65. McIntosh, *Caribbean Constitutional Reform*.
66. Munroe, *Politics of Constitutional Decolonization*, 149.
67. Tom Rice, "Churchill Visits Jamaica", Colonial Film: Moving Images of the British Empire, http://www.colonialfilm.org.uk/node/1543 (accessed 31 October 2013).
68. Included in this sequence is a brief scene of a flag-raising ceremony where a long bamboo stick functions as a flagpole. The image gives a sense of inclusiveness: poorer rural schools also participated in the ritual and were recognized in the film.
69. The junkanoo scene, however, is awkwardly staged and constructed in the sequence. Whereas the other performances take place on a stage and are watched by large audiences, the junkanoo performance takes place on what appears to be an empty field and no spectators are visible. This gives the sense of the folk performance taking place both literally and metaphorically on the periphery of other sites of performance and participation.
70. Anderson, *Imagined Communities*.

CHAPTER 2

1. Louise Bennett, "Dead Man". This poem was first published in *Public Opinion*, 16 October 1948. Reprinted in *Louise Bennett: Selected Poems* (Kingston: Sangster's Book Stores, 1982), 55–57.
2. A Jamaican word also spelled *rygin* and pronounced *raigin* (with a hard *g*, as in begin). Defined in the *Dictionary of Jamaican English* as angry, heated, severe; vigorous, lively, spirited; very able, top-notch.
3. Alternately referred to as the *Express* and the *Gleaner* respectively.
4. Catherine Roach, "Getting a Good Man to Love: Popular Romance Fiction and the Problem of Patriarchy", *Journal of Romance Studies* 1, no. 1 (2010): 3,

http://jprstudies.org/wp-content/uploads/2010/08/JPRS1.1_Roach_Getting GoodMantoLove.pdf.
5. Carolyn Cooper, *Sound Clash: Jamaican Dancehall Culture at Large* (New York: Palgrave Macmillan, 2004), 146–47.
6. Ibid., 147.
7. Obika Gray, *Demeaned but Empowered: The Social Power of the Urban Poor in Jamaica* (Kingston: University of the West Indies Press, 2004), 129.
8. Ibid., 123.
9. Carolyn Cooper, *Noises in the Blood: Orality, Gender and the Vulgar Body of Jamaican Popular Culture* (London: Macmillan Caribbean, 1994), 110.
10. Bennett, "Dead Man".
11. Michael Thelwell, "*The Harder They Come:* From Film to Novel", in *Ex-Iles: Essays on Caribbean Cinema*, ed. Mybe B. Cham (Trenton, NJ: Africa World Press, 1992), 182.
12. Lynne Macedo, *Fiction and Film: The Influence of Cinema on Writers from Trinidad and Jamaica* (Chicester: Dido, 2003), 122.
13. *Daily Gleaner*, 3 September 1948.
14. Sheila Nicholson, "An Analysis of Elite Response to Socialism through a Comparison of *Daily Gleaner* Editorials on PNP Socialism for 1952 and 1976", in *Perspectives on Jamaica in the Seventies*, ed. Carl Stone and Aggrey Brown (Kingston: Jamaica Publishing House, 1981), 341. One indication of the *Daily Gleaner*'s dominance in Jamaica is that the word "gleaner" was, in the past, used as a synonym for "newspaper". It is interesting to note, however, that despite its status as the newspaper of record, it was the *Jamaica Daily Express* which broke the news of the initial shootings and Rhygin's death, not the *Daily Gleaner*.
15. The initial shoot-out with the police took place at the Carib Hotel.
16. *Daily Gleaner*, 10 October 1948.
17. Ibid.
18. *Jamaica Times*, 16 October 1948.
19. Anonymous, *Daily Gleaner*, 28 February 1893, in *"Squalid Kingston" 1890–1920: How the Poor Lived, Moved and Had Their Being*, ed. Brian L. Moore and Michele A. Johnson (Kingston: Social History Project, Department of History, University of the West Indies, 2000).
20. One such story is told by Herriot Goldson, who was living in the seaside town of Port Royal when Rhygin was killed. Goldson recalled that a story had circulated in the town that Rhygin had committed suicide to avoid being taken alive or killed at the hands of the police. This scenario seems unlikely in view of the

level of detail sustained in press reports on Rhygin's final hours, including one eyewitness account of the events by a *Daily Gleaner* reporter. The story does reflect, however, a desire to sustain belief in Rhygin's indomitable badness and continued defiance, a desire which the ending of the film draws on. Goldson also recalled that it was well known in the town that a local fisherman, known as "Babes", had taken Rhygin to the cay with the promise to get him to Aruba.

21. Thelwell, "*Harder They Come*", 182.
22. Robert Stam, "Beyond Fidelity: The Dialogics of Adaptation", in *Film Adaptation*, ed. James Naremore (New Brunswick, NJ: Rutgers University Press, 2000), 68.
23. Loretta Collins, "*The Harder They Come*: Rougher Version", *Small Axe* 7, no. 1 (2003): 46–71, makes a persuasive argument for greater recognition of Rhone's input in the film.
24. Perry Henzell, telephone call with author, 2005.
25. Prakash Younger, "Historical Experience in *The Harder They Come*", *Social Text* 23, no. 1 (82) (2005): 48.
26. Ibid., 60.
27. See Julianne Burton, "*The Harder They Come*: Cultural Colonialism and the American Dream", *Jump Cut: A Review of Contemporary Media* 6 (1975): 5–7, https://www.ejumpcut.org/archive/onlinessays/JC06folder/HarderTheyCome .html; Kenneth Harris, "Sex, Race Commodity and Film Fetishism in *The Harder They Come*", in *Ex-Iles: Essays on Caribbean Cinema*, ed. Mybe B. Cham (Trenton, NJ: Africa World Press, 1992), 211–19; Gladstone L. Yearwood, "Myth and Signification in Perry Henzell's *The Harder They Come*", in *The Reordering of Culture: Latin America, the Caribbean and Canada in the Hood*, ed. Alvina Ruprecht and Cecilia Taiana (Ottawa: Carleton University Press, 1995), 437–55; and Ifeona Fulani, "Representations of the Body of the New Nation in *The Harder They Come* and *Rockers*", *Anthurium: A Caribbean Studies Journal* 3, no. 1 (2005): 1–2.
28. Burton, "*Harder They Come*".
29. "Mello-Go-Round", *Daily Gleaner*, 7 June 1972.
30. Gordon Rohlehr, *My Strangled City and Other Essays* (Port of Spain: Longman, 1992), 105.
31. Ibid., 106.
32. Kamau Brathwaite, *History of the Voice: The Development of Nation Language in Anglophone Caribbean Poetry* (London: New Beacon Books, 1984), 41.
33. *Daily Gleaner*, 4 September 1948.
34. Clinton Hutton, "Oh Rudie: Jamaican Popular Music and the Narrative of

Urban Badness in the Making of Postcolonial Society", *Caribbean Quarterly* 56, no. 4 (December 2010): 24.

35. Frantz Fanon, *The Wretched of the Earth*, trans. Constance Farrington (London: Penguin, 2001), 30.
36. Ibid., 31.
37. Younger, "Historical Experience", 49.
38. The fight with this man, Longah, which ends when Ivan viciously slashes him across the face with a knife, is another instance when Ivan refuses to submit to unjust authority. The bicycle also has symbolic importance. Yearwood states that the narrative presents a sophisticated paradigm of social change coded in the form of transportation technology, and the bicycle represents an instance in which Ivan has harnessed and mastered technology. Yearwood, "Myth and Signification", 446.
39. Harris, "Sex", 214.
40. Burton, "*Harder They Come*".
41. Bev Braune, "You Can Get It If You Really Want: Viewing *The Harder They Come* Again and Again after a 1977 Interview with Director Perry Henzell", *Wasafiri* 26 (1997): 34.
42. The writer of "Mello-Go-Round" suggests that the crowd stormed the cinema that night because they were under the impression that after the screening the film was going to be sent out of the island for an overseas run.

CHAPTER 3

1. The film credits list Rhone and Henzell as the authors of the screenplay, but Rhone maintained, in an interview with the author, that his input transformed Henzell's original script.
2. *Milk and Honey*, 1988, directed by Glen Salzman and Rebecca Yates, starring Josette Simon, Lyman Ward and Richard Mills.
3. Mervyn Morris, introduction, *Old Story Time and Smile Orange*, by Trevor Rhone (New York: Longman, 2003), ix.
4. Raymond Williams, *The Country and the Town* (London: Chatto and Windus, 1973), 1.
5. Mimi Sheller, *Consuming the Caribbean: From Arawaks to Zombies* (London: Routledge, 2003), 13.
6. Ibid., 27.
7. Eva Illouz, *Consuming the Romantic Utopia: Love and the Cultural Contradictions of Capitalism* (Berkley: University of California Press, 1997), 97.

8. Ian Gregory Strachan, *Paradise and Plantation: Tourism and Culture in the Anglophone Caribbean* (Charlottesville: University of Virginia Press, 2002), 9.
9. Honor Ford-Smith, "Come to Jamaica and Feel Alright: Tourism, Colonial Discourse and Cultural Resistance", in *The Reordering of Culture: Latin America, the Caribbean and Canada in the Hood*, ed. Alvina Ruprecht and Cecilia Taiana (Ottawa: Carlton University Press, 1995), 380.
10. Ibid., 381.
11. Ibid., 385.
12. Ibid., 389.
13. Ibid., 380.
14. Morris, introduction, ix.
15. Morris, *Old Story Time*, ix.
16. Daryl C. Dance, *Folklore from Contemporary Jamaica* (Knoxville: University of Tennessee Press, 1985), 12.
17. Ibid.
18. Ford-Smith, "Come to Jamaica", 390.
19. Jamaica Kincaid, *A Small Place* (New York: Farrar, Straus and Giroux, 1988), 18–19.
20. Ibid., 55.
21. Jean-Paul Sartre, preface to *The Wretched of the Earth*, by Frantz Fanon, trans. Constance Farrington (London: Penguin, 1963), 7.
22. bell hooks, *Black Looks: Race and Representation* (Toronto: Between the Lines, 1992), 94.
23. Ibid.
24. Polly Patullo, *Last Resorts: The Cost of Tourism in the Caribbean*, 2nd ed. (London: Latin America Bureau, 2005), 113.
25. Frantz Fanon, *Black Skin, White Masks*, trans. Charles Lam Markmann (London: Grove Press, 1986), 177.
26. Illouz, *Consuming the Romantic Utopia*, 97.
27. *From Here to Eternity*, 1953, directed by Fred Zinnemann, starring Burt Lancaster, Montgomery Clift and Deborah Kerr.

CHAPTER 4

1. Warner, *On Location*, 41.
2. Ed Guerrero, "'Jah No Dead': Modes of Resistance in *Rockers* and *Countryman*", in *Ex-Iles: Essays on Caribbean Cinema*, ed. Mybe B. Cham (Trenton, NJ: Africa World Press, 1992), 117.

3. Warner, *On Location*, 91–92.
4. Ibid., 91.
5. Ibid., 92.
6. Ibid., 93.
7. *Countryman* (1980) was directed by Dickie Jobson. The film stars Countryman, who plays himself, an ascetic Rastafarian who uses his magical powers to defeat the forces of evil in the form of a corrupt police force and political system.
8. Guerrero, "Jah No Dead", 108.
9. Ibid., 108.
10. Ibid. Emphasis added.
11. Warner, *On Location*, 92.
12. Manthia Diawara, "Black American Cinema: The New Realism", in *Black American Cinema*, ed. Manthia Diawara (New York: Routledge, 1993), 11.
13. Ibid., 7.
14. See M.G. Smith, R. Augier and R. Nettleford, *The Rastafari Movement in Jamaica* (Kingston: Institute of Social and Economic Research, University of the West Indies, 1960).
15. Rex Nettleford, *Mirror, Mirror: Identity, Race and Protest in Jamaica*, rev. ed. (Kingston: LMH Publishing, 2001), 54–55.
16. Ibid., 47.
17. Nathaniel Samuel Murrell, "Introduction: The Rastafari Phenomenon", in *Chanting Down Babylon: The Rastafari Reader*, ed. Nathaniel Samuel Murrell, William David Spencer and Adrian Anthony McFarlane (Kingston: Ian Randle, 1998), 1.
18. Nettleford, *Mirror, Mirror*, vii.
19. Murrell, "Introduction", 9.
20. The enduring popularity of *Rockers* is indicated by the issue of a special twenty-fifth anniversary DVD in 2005, continued public screenings of the film at venues around the world and the 2014 music video of reggae artist Chronixx's "Rastaman Wheel Out" which references the film. See https://www.youtube.com/watch?v=NxhoO-MLHWE.
21. Bryce, "That Is Not for Beke", 261.
22. Guerrero, "Jah No Dead".
23. Paul Gilroy, *"There Ain't No Black in the Union Jack": The Cultural Politics of Race and Nation* (London: Hutchinson, 1987), 169.
24. Ibid.

25. Warner, *On Location*, 94.
26. Theodorus Bafaloukos, "Director's Interview", *Rockers* 25th anniversary edition DVD (Pottstown, PA: Blue Sun Film Co. Music Video Distributors, 2005).
27. Ibid.
28. See *Bicycle Thieves*, directed by Vittorio DeSica, 1948. In this classic film of Italian neorealism, the protagonist, Antonio, desperately searches the streets of Rome for his stolen bicycle. In contrast to Antonio, who, for the most part, receives no help from fellow citizens, Horsemouth has a network of friends and allies upon whom he can depend.
29. Velma Pollard, *Dread Talk: The Language of Rastafari*, rev. ed. (Kingston: Canoe Press, 2000), 4.
30. Ibid., xiii.
31. Bafaloukos, "Director's Interview".
32. Kiddus I, interview with the author, February 2010, Kingston, Jamaica.
33. Braune, "You Can Get It", 32.
34. Fulani, "Representations", 7.
35. Guerrero, "Jah No Dead", 115.
36. Ibid., 112.
37. Adrian Anthony McFarlane, "The Epistemological Significance of 'I-an-I' as a Response to Quashie and Anancyism in Jamaican Culture", in *Chanting Down Babylon: The Rastafari Reader*, ed. Nathaniel Samuel Murrell, William David Spencer and Adrian Anthony McFarlane (Kingston: Ian Randle, 1998), 109.
38. Guerrero, "Jah No Dead", 113.
39. McFarlane, "Epistemological Significance", 115.
40. Nettleford, *Mirror, Mirror*, 36.

CHAPTER 5

1. Paula Morgan, "'Like Bush Fire in My Arms': Interrogating the World of Caribbean Romance", *Journal of Popular Culture* 36, no. 4 (2003): 804.
2. See Ann duCille, *The Coupling Convention: Sex, Text and Tradition in Black Women's Fiction* (New York: Oxford University Press, 1993), who uses the phrase "coupling convention", in part "to destabilize the customary dyadic relation between love and marriage" (14). I use the word "coupling" as an inclusive, collective term to refer, as duCille does, to relationships (in *Children of Babylon*, specifically) where there is no presumption or expectation of marriage, but also to relationships where marriage is the ultimate goal, in keeping with the Western romantic tradition.

3. Belinda Edmondson, "The Black Romance", *Women's Studies Quarterly* 35, nos. 1–2 (2007): 194.
4. Claudia Tate, *Domestic Allegories of Political Desire: The Black Heroine's Text at the Turn of the Century* (New York: Oxford University Press, 1992), 5.
5. Edmondson, "Black Romance", 194.
6. Ibid.
7. Mediamix Ltd, "Historical Perspective: *Children of Babylon*", http://www.mediamix-palm.com/children_historical_main.htm (accessed 11 July 2017).
8. Glissant, introduction, 11.
9. Horace Campbell, *Sunday Observer*, 21 June 1998, quoted in Warner, *On Location*, 95.
10. Nettleford, *Mirror, Mirror*, 28.
11. George Beckford, *Persistent Poverty: Underdevelopment in Plantation Economies of the Third World* (1972; repr., Kingston: University of the West Indies Press, 1999), 64. Beckford notes that increasing educational opportunities for black people and diversification of the structure of the plantation economies have resulted in some modification of the class structure, but affirms the continued importance of race as a factor in class divisions (68).
12. It is notable that the group at the great house does not reflect the post-emancipation arrival in Jamaica of other ethnic groups from Asia, and later from the Middle East. Instead, Little-White retains a racial composition that speaks to the tension and conflicts that originated in the period of slavery and which remain critical and urgent.
13. Mediamix, "Historical Perspective".
14. Carl Stone, "Decolonisation and the Caribbean State System: The Case of Jamaica", in *Perspectives on Jamaica in the Seventies*, ed. Carl Stone and Aggrey Brown (Kingston: Jamaica Publishing House, 1981), 6.
15. Ibid., 27.
16. Meeks, "Political Moment", 86.
17. Stuart Hall, "New Ethnicities", in *Stuart Hall: Critical Dialogues in Cultural Studies*, ed. David Morley and Kuan-Hsing Chen (London: Routledge, 2003), 443.
18. Ennis B. Edmonds, "Dread 'I' In-a-Babylon: Ideological Resistance and Cultural Revitalization", in *Chanting Down Babylon: The Rastafari Reader*, ed. Nathaniel Samuel Murrell, William David Spencer and Adrian Anthony McFarlane (Kingston: Ian Randle, 1998), 24.
19. Hall, "Cultural Identity", 223.
20. Ibid.

21. Stone, "Decolonisation", 9.
22. See Victoria M. Marshall, "Filmmaking in Jamaica: 'Likkle But Tallawah'", in *Ex-Iles: Essays on Caribbean Cinema*, ed. Mybe B. Cham (Trenton, NJ: Africa World Press, 1992), 105.
23. Bob Marley, "One Love/People Get Ready", *Exodus* (Tuff Gong Records, 422-846 208-2. 1979), track 10.
24. See the Jamaica Tourist Board website (http://www.jtbonline.org/jtb/one-love/) to view the One Love advertisement.
25. Ford-Smith, "Come to Jamaica", 384.
26. Cooper, *Sound Clash*, 179–80.
27. Rex Nettleford dates the emergence of the Rastafari movement as 1930. See Nettleford, *Mirror, Mirror*, 42.
28. Ibid, 46.
29. Rick Elgood, interview with the author, Kingston, Jamaica, 20 May 2008.
30. Sheller, *Consuming the Caribbean*, 13.
31. Barbara Bush, *Slave Women in Caribbean Society 1650–1838* (Kingston: Heinnemann Caribbean, 1990), 17–18.
32. Edmondson, "Black Romance", 195.
33. Roach, "Getting a Good Man".
34. See Samuel Richardson, *Pamela; or, Virtue Rewarded* (London: Penguin, 1980).

CHAPTER 6

1. Sonjah Nadine Stanley-Niaah, *Dancehall: From Slave Ship to Ghetto* (Ottawa: University of Ottawa Press, 2010), 1.
2. Norman C. Stolzoff, *Wake the Town and Tell the People: Dancehall Culture in Kingston* (Durham: Duke University Press, 2000), 1.
3. It is important to note that while the fashion and dance featured in *Dancehall Queen* may, by contemporary standards, look quite tame, when the film was released, these images were considered shocking by many people. For many, the film provided their first glimpse of dancehall culture and performance.
4. Cooper, *Sound Clash*, 125–26.
5. Donna P. Hope, *Inna di Dancehall: Popular Culture and the Politics of Identity in Jamaica* (Kingston: University of the West Indies Press, 2006), 74–75.
6. Bibi Bakare-Yusuf, "Clashing Interpretations in Jamaican Dancehall Culture", *Small Axe*, no. 21 (2006): 161–73.
7. Bibi Bakare-Yusuf, "Fabricating Identities: Survival and the Imagination in Jamaican Dancehall Culture", *Fashion Theory* 10, no. 3 (2006): 12.

8. Michael Reckord, "Dancehall Queen Has Mass Appeal", *Sunday Gleaner*, 17 August 1997.
9. Cooper, *Sound Clash*, 128.
10. Stuart Hall, "Encoding, Decoding", in *The Cultural Studies Reader*, ed. Simon During (London: Routledge, 1994), 102.
11. Christine Gledhill, "Pleasurable Negotiations", in *Imagining Women: Cultural Representations and Gender*, ed. Frances Bonner, Lizbeth Goodman, Richard Allen, Linda James and Catherine King (Cambridge: Polity Press, 1992), 195.
12. Ibid., 194.
13. See Laura Mulvey, "Visual Pleasure and Narrative Cinema", in *Feminisms: An Anthology of Literary Theory and Criticism*, ed. Robyn R. Warhol and Diane Price Herndl (New Brunswick, NJ: Rutgers University Press, 1996).
14. Bakare-Yusuf, "Fabricating Identities", 12.
15. Marita Sturken and Lisa Cartwright, *Practices of Looking: An Introduction to Visual Culture* (Oxford: Oxford University Press), 58.
16. Cooper, *Sound Clash*.
17. Ibid., 131.
18. It is ironic that Priest, the badman and murderer, is the only man whose attraction to Marcia is not dependent on her transformation through dancehall fashion. He, of all the men in the narrative who desire her, has never seen her adorned in dancehall fashion.
19. Bibi Bakare-Yusuf, "Fanon Can't Dance: Antiphonies of the Gaze in *Dancehall Queen*" (paper presented at the Reggae Studies Unit Film Seminar Series, University of the West Indies, Mona, Jamaica, March 1999, Library of the Spoken Word Collection, University Archives, University of the West Indies, Jamaica).
20. Stuart Hall, "The Spectacle of the Other", in *Representation: Cultural Representations and Signifying Practices*, ed. Stuart Hall (London: Sage/Open University, 2003), 274.
21. Bakare-Yusuf, "Fanon Can't Dance".
22. Ibid.
23. Mulvey, "Visual Pleasure".
24. Cooper, *Sound Clash*, 125.

CHAPTER 7

1. Carl Stone, *Democracy and Clientelism in Jamaica* (New Brunswick, NJ: Transaction Books, 1980), 100.
2. Chris Browne, interview with the author, Kingston, Jamaica, 8 June 2009.

3. Ibid.
4. Chris Browne, "A Retrospective" (lecture delivered at the "March Is Movie Month at Mona" series, University of the West Indies, Mona, Jamaica, 9 March 2012).
5. Browne, interview.
6. Andrew Clunis, "JA's Film Industry bright with *Third World Cop*", *Gleaner UK*, 20 October 1999.
7. Garth Rattray, "*Ghett'a Life:* A Social Commentary", *Gleaner*, 25 July 2011.
8. Arjun Appadurai, "Disjuncture and Difference in the Global Cultural Economy", *Theory, Culture and Society* 7 (1990): 299, http://www.arjunappadurai.org/articles/Appadurai_Disjuncture_and_Difference_in_the_Global_Cultural_Economy.pdf.
9. Massey, *Space, Place, and Gender*, 5.
10. Anderson, *Imagined Communities*, 7.
11. Browne, interview.
12. Steve Neale, "Questions of Genre", in *Film Genre Reader III*, ed. Barry Keith Grant (Austin: University of Texas Press, 2007), 178.
13. Robert Stam, *Film Theory: An Introduction* (Malden, MA: Blackwell, 2000), 142.
14. Robert Stam, introduction to part 5, "The Question of Realism", in *Film and Theory: An Anthology*, ed. Robert Stam and Toby Miller (Malden, MA: Blackwell, 2000), 225.
15. bell hooks, "Cultural Criticism and Transformation: Part 1 on Cultural Criticism" (YouTube video), posted by ChallengingMedia, 3 October 2006, https://www.youtube.com/watch?v=zQUuHFKP-9s.
16. Erich Auerbach, *Mimesis: The Representation of Reality in Western Literature*, trans. Willard R. Trask (Princeton: Princeton University Press, 1953), 491.
17. Wahneema Lubiano, "But Compared to What?: Reading Realism, Representation, and Essentialism in *School Daze, Do the Right Thing*, and the Spike Lee Discourse", in *Representing Blackness: Issues in Film and Video*, ed. Valerie Smith (New Brunswick, NJ: Rutgers University Press, 2003), 105.
18. Ibid., 106.
19. Kobena Mercer, "Diaspora Culture and the Dialogic Imagination: The Aesthetics of Black Independent Film in Britain", in *Welcome to the Jungle: New Positions in Black Cultural Studies* (New York: Routledge, 1994), 58.
20. Ibid.
21. Craig A. Smith, "(de)Constructing Patriarchal Masculinities in Cess Silvera's

Shottas", *Journal of West Indian Literature* 21, nos. 1–2 (November 2012–April 2013): 156–57.
22. Neale, "Questions of Genre", 178.
23. Ibid., 163.
24. Browne, interview.
25. Timothy O. Lenz, "Conservatism in American Crime Films", *Journal of Criminal Justice and Popular Culture* 12, no. 2 (Spring 2005): 122.
26. Smith, "(de)Constructing Patriarchal Masculinities", 155.
27. Robert Warshow, "Movie Chronicler: The Westerner", in *Film Theory and Criticism: Introductory Readings*, 5th ed., ed. Leo Braudy and Marshall Cohen (New York: Oxford University Press, 1999), 667.
28. Barry Chevannes, *Learning to Be a Man: Culture, Socialization and Gender Identity in Five Caribbean Communities*. (Kingston: University of the West Indies Press, 2001), 211.
29. See the novels *The Dragon Can't Dance* by Earl Lovelace (London: Andre Deutsch, 1979), *Miguel Street* by V.S. Naipaul (London: Andre Deutsch, 1959), and *The Harder They Come* by Michael Thelwell (New York: Grove, 1987), also Macedo, *Fiction and Film*.
30. Laurie Gunst, *Born fi' Dead: A Journey through the Yardie Underworld* (Edinburgh: Canongate, 1995), xv.
31. Ibid.
32. Portland is a rural parish in Jamaica.
33. See Stone, *Democracy and Clientelism*, and Gray, *Demeaned but Empowered*.
34. Massey, *Space, Place and Gender*, 5.
35. Stone, *Democracy and Clientelism*.
36. Lubiano, "But Compared to What?"
37. Susan Hayward, *Cinema Studies: The Key Concepts* (London: Routledge, 2006), 82.
38. Ibid.
39. Massey, *Space, Place and Gender*, 5.
40. Although neither political party is named, the explicit colour coding of territory in the film corresponds to the use of green and orange by the JLP and PNP respectively.
41. Amanda Sives, *Elections, Violence and the Democratic Process in Jamaica 1944–2007* (Kingston: Ian Randle, 2010).
42. Brian Meeks, *Narratives of Resistance: Jamaica, Trinidad, the Caribbean* (Kingston: University of the West Indies Press, 2000), 12.

43. "Making of *Ghett'a Life*", special feature, *Ghett'a Life*, Jamrock Films, 2011, DVD.
44. According to the *Dictionary of Jamaican English*, ed. F.G. Cassidy and R.B. LePage (Kingston: University of the West Indies Press, 2002), the word "fassy" is a general term for sores or eruptions on the skin. In more contemporary usage it can refer to an undesirable person or element, or someone to be scorned, such as an informer.
45. Hayward, *Cinema Studies*, 83.

CHAPTER 8

1. Teshome H. Gabriel, "Third Cinema as Guardian of Popular Memory: Towards a Third Aesthetics", in *Questions of Third Cinema*, ed. Jim Pines and Paul Willemen (London: British Film Institute, 1988), 54.
2. Ibid.
3. Emiel Martens, "Towards a New Caribbean Cinema? An Interview with Jamaican Filmmaker Storm Saulter", *Imaginations: Journal of Cross Cultural Image Studies* 6, no. 2 (2015), http://dx.doi.org/10.17742/IMAGE.ccn.6-2.
4. Arthur Marwick, *The New Nature of History: Knowledge, Evidence, Language* (Houndmills: Palgrave, 2001), 32.
5. Robert A. Rosenstone, "Reflections on What the Filmmaker Historian Does (to History)", in *Film, History and Memory*, ed. Jennie M. Carlsten and Fearghal McGarry (Houndsmills, Basingstoke: Palgrave Macmillan, 2015), 183.
6. Ibid., 185.
7. Ibid., 195.
8. Ibid., 185.
9. Ibid., 195.
10. Ibid., 194.
11. Gabriel, "Third Cinema", 53.
12. Hayden White, "The Politics of Historical Interpretation: Discipline and De-Sublimation", *Critical Inquiry* 9, no. 11 (1982): 122.
13. Ibid., 123.
14. Gabriel, "Third Cinema", 54.
15. See the classic essays of Third Cinema: Fernando Solanas and Octavio Getino, "Towards a Third Cinema" (http://www.marginalutility.org/wp-content/uploads/2017/03/Towards-a-Third-Cinema-by-Fernando-Solanas-and-Octavio-Getino.pdf) and Julio Garcia Espinosa, "For an Imperfect Cinema" (https://www.ejumpcut.org/archive/onlinessays/JC20folder/ImperfectCinema.html).

16. Gabriel, "Third Cinema", 60.
17. Martens, "Towards a New Caribbean Cinema?"
18. *Daily Gleaner*, 6 January 1978.
19. *Daily Gleaner*, 11 January 1978.
20. On January 21, the *Daily Gleaner* reported that the JLP was calling for a full public enquiry into the incident.
21. *Daily Gleaner*, 26 January 1978, 1.
22. Sives, *Elections*, 105.
23. Edward Seaga, *My Life and Leadership*, vol. 1, *Clash of Ideologies 1930–1980* (Oxford: Macmillan Education, 2009), 290.
24. Ibid.
25. Gray, *Demeaned but Empowered*, 129.
26. Ibid., 123.
27. Ibid., 129–30.
28. Ibid., 122–23.
29. Ibid., 130.
30. Ibid., 129.
31. Sives, *Elections*, xxiii.
32. Ibid., xxiv.
33. Ibid.
34. See *The Water-Babies*, Charles Kingsley's 1863 children's novel, in which the protagonist is transformed into a water-baby after he falls into a river and drowns.
35. Gabriel, "Third Cinema", 59.

EPILOGUE

1. Fanon, *Wretched of the Earth*, 188.
2. Hall, "Cultural Identity", 235.
3. Maryse Condé, "Epilogue: Cinema, Literature and Freedom", trans. Marise La Grenade-Lashley, in *Ex-Iles: Essays on Caribbean Cinema*, ed. Mybe B. Cham (Trenton, NJ: Africa World Press, 1992), 371.
4. Randal Johnson, "In the Belly of the Ogre: Cinema and State in Latin America", in *Mediating Two Worlds: Cinematic Encounters in the Americas*, ed. John King, Ana M. López and Manuel Alvarado (London: British Film Institute, 1993), 210.
5. Zeinabu Irene Davis, "The Future of Black Film: The Debate Continues", in *Cinemas of the Black Diaspora*, ed. Michael T. Martin (Detroit: Wayne State University Press, 1995), 454.

6. Fanon, *Wretched of the Earth*, 188.
7. Teshome H. Gabriel, "Towards a Critical Theory of Third World Films", in *Questions of Third Cinema*, ed. Jum Pines and Paul Willemen (London: British Film Institute, 1989), 33–34.
8. Brian Meeks, "Introduction: On the Bump of a Revival", in *New Caribbean Thought: A Reader*, ed. Brian Meeks and Folke Lindahl (Kingston: University of the West Indies Press, 2001), viii–xx.
9. Fanon, *Wretched of the Earth*, 189.
10. Shohat and Stam, *Unthinking Eurocentrism*, 28.
11. Ibid., 29.
12. Gabriel, "Towards a Critical Theory", 33.
13. Rex Nettleford, *Inward Stretch Outward Reach: A Voice from the Caribbean* (New York: Caribbean Diaspora Press, 1995).
14. Shohat and Stam, *Unthinking Eurocentrism*, 191.
15. Ibid., 193.
16. Brian L. Moore and Michele A. Johnson, *"They Do As They Please": The Jamaican Struggle for Cultural Freedom after Morant Bay* (Kingston: University of the West Indies Press, 2011), 82.
17. Pauline Christie, "General Introduction: Forty Years On", in *Due Respect: Papers on English and English-Related Creoles in the Caribbean in Honour of Professor Robert Le Page*, ed. Pauline Christie (Kingston: University of the West Indies Press, 2001), 5.
18. George Lamming, "Language and the Politics of Ethnicity", in *Beyond Borders: Cross-Culturalism and the Caribbean Canon*, ed. Jennifer Rahim and Barbara Lalla (Kingston: University of the West Indies Press, 2009), 20.
19. Nettleford, *Inward Stretch*, 102.
20. Ibid.
21. Ibid., 103.
22. The meeting was convened by the Creative Industries Unit at JAMPRO and the Ministry of Culture, Gender, Entertainment and Sport. The study is being conducted by the United Nations Economic Commission for Latin America and the Caribbean along with the Institute of Caribbean Studies at the University of the West Indies, Mona.
23. It is important to note that St Juste and Serieux are originally from Trinidad and St Lucia respectively. Their presence and impact on local cinema denote the regional and global currents that contribute to the development of the sector in Jamaica.

24. Jonathan Ali, "Riding the New Wave of Caribbean Cinema", *Caribbean Beat*, September–October 2010.
25. Rennalls, "Visual Education", 17.

SELECTED BIBLIOGRAPHY

Ali, Jonathan. "Riding the New Wave of Caribbean Cinema". *Caribbean Beat*, September–October 2010.

Anderson, Benedict. *Imagined Communities: Reflections on the Origins and Spread of Nationalism*. London: Verso, 1994.

Antoine-Dunne, Jean. "Sound and Vision in the Caribbean Imaginary". *Journal of West Indian Literature* 18, no. 2 (2010): 95–114.

Appadurai, Arjun. "Disjuncture and Difference in the Global Cultural Economy". *Theory, Culture and Society* 7 (1990): 295–310.

Ashcroft, Bill, Gareth Griffiths and Helen Tiffin. *The Empire Writes Back: Theory and Practice in Post-Colonial Literatures*. London: Routledge, 1989.

———, eds. *The Post-Colonial Studies Reader*. London: Routledge, 2001.

Auerbach, Erich. *Mimesis: The Representation of Reality in Western Literature*. Translated by Willard R. Trask. Princeton: Princeton University Press, 1953.

Bafaloukos, Ted, dir. *Rockers*. Rockers Film Corporation, 1978. DVD. MVD Visual, 2005.

Bakare-Yusuf, Bibi. "Clashing Interpretations in Jamaican Dancehall Culture". *Small Axe*, no. 21 (2006): 161–73.

———. "Fabricating Identities: Survival and the Imagination in Jamaican Dancehall Culture". *Fashion Theory* 10, no. 3 (2006): 1–24.

———. "Fanon Can't Dance: Antiphonies of the Gaze in *Dancehall Queen*". Paper presented at the Reggae Studies Unit Film Seminar Series, University of the West Indies, Mona, Jamaica, March 1999, Library of the Spoken Word Collection, University Archives, University of the West Indies, Jamaica

Bakhtin, M.M. *The Dialogic Imagination: Four Essays*. Edited by Michael Holquist; translated by Caryl Emerson and Michael Holquist. Austin: University of Texas Press, 1981.

Bazin, André. *What Is Cinema?* Vol. 1. Translated by Hugh Gray. Berkeley: University of California Press, 2005.

Beckford, George. *Persistent Poverty: Underdevelopment in Plantation Economies of the Third World*. 1972. Reprint, Kingston: University of the West Indies Press, 1999.

Bennett, Louise. *Selected Poems: Louise Bennett*. Edited by Mervyn Morris. Kingston: Sangster's Book Stores, 1982.

Bhabha, Homi K. "Introduction: Narrating the Nation". In *Nation and Narration*, edited by Homi K. Bhabha, 1–7. London: Routledge, 2004.

Black, Stephanie, dir. *Life and Debt*. Tuff Gong Pictures, 2001. DVD. New Yorker. 2003.

Blackburne, K.W. "Financial Problems and Future Policy in British Colonies". In *The Film in Colonial Development: A Report of a Conference*, 33–35. London: British Film Institute, 1948.

Brathwaite, Edward Kamau. *History of the Voice: The Development of Nation Language in Anglophone Caribbean Poetry*. London: New Beacon Books, 1984.

Braune, Bev. "You Can Get It If You Really Want: Viewing *The Harder They Come* Again and Again after a 1977 Interview with Director Perry Henzell". *Wasafiri* 26 (1997): 31–36.

Browne, Chris, dir. *Ghett'a Life*. Jamrock Films, 2011. DVD. Jinga Films, 2013.

———. *Third World Cop*. Hawk's Nest Productions and Palm Pictures, 1999. DVD. Palm Pictures, 2000.

Bryce, Jane. "'That Is Not for Beke': Global Versus Local in Two Versions of Sargasso". In *Globalisation, Diaspora and Caribbean Popular Culture*, edited by Christine G.T. Ho and Keith Nurse, 259–79. Kingston: Ian Randle, 2005.

Bundy, Frank A., dir. *Jamaican Harvest*. Gaumont British International, 1938. http://www.colonialfilm.org.uk/node/33.

Burton, Julianne. "*The Harder They Come:* Cultural Colonialism and the American Dream". *Jump Cut* 6 (1975): 5–7. https://www.ejumpcut.org/archive/onlinessays/JC06folder/HarderTheyCome.html.

Bush, Barbara. *Slave Women in Caribbean Society 1650–1838*. Kingston: Heinemann Caribbean, 1990.

Casey, Edward S. "How to Get from Space to Place in a Fairly Short Stretch of Time: Phenomenological Prolegomena". In *Senses of Place*, edited by Steven Field and Keith H. Basso, 13–52. Santa Fe, NM: School of American Research Press, 1996.

Cham, Mybe B. "Introduction: Shape and Shaping of Caribbean Cinema". In *Ex-Iles: Essays on Caribbean Cinema*, edited by Mybe B. Cham, 1–43. Trenton, NJ: Africa World Press, 1992.

Chapman, James, and Nicholas J. Cull. *Projecting Empire: Imperialism and Popular Cinema*. London: I.B. Tauris, 2009.

Chevannes, Barry. *Learning to Be a Man: Culture, Socialization and Gender Identity in Five Caribbean Communities*. Kingston: University of the West Indies Press, 2011.

Christie, Pauline. "General Introduction: Forty Years On". In *Due Respect: Papers on English and English-Related Creoles in the Caribbean in Honour of Professor Robert Le Page*, edited by Pauline Christie, 1–21. Kingston: University of the West Indies Press, 2001.

Collins, Loretta. "*The Harder They Come:* Rougher Version". *Small Axe* 7, no. 1 (2003): 46–71.

Colonial Film Unit (CFU). "Colonial Film Unit Training School in the West Indies". *Colonial Cinema* 9, no. 2 (1951): 40–44.

Condé, Maryse. "Epilogue: Cinema, Literature and Freedom". Translated by Marise La Grenade-Lashley. In *Ex-Iles: Essays on Caribbean Cinema*, edited by Mybe B. Cham, 370–77. Trenton, NJ: African World Press, 1992.

Cooper, Carolyn. *Noises in the Blood: Orality, Gender and the Vulgar Body of Jamaican Popular Culture*. London: Macmillan Caribbean, 1994.

———. *Sound Clash*. New York: Palgrave Macmillan, 2004.

Crème, Lol, dir. *The Lunatic*. Island Pictures, 1991. DVD. Island World Video, n.d.

Crofts, Stephen. "Reconceptualising Nation Cinema/s". In *Theorising National Cinema*, edited by Valentina Vitali and Paul Willemen, 44–58. London: British Film Institute, 2006.

Dance, Daryl C. *Folklore from Contemporary Jamaica*. Knoxville: University of Tennessee Press, 1985.

Davis, Zeinabu Irene. "The Future of Black Film: The Debate Continues". In *Cinemas of the Black Diaspora*, edited by Michael T. Martin, 449–54. Detroit: Wayne State University, 1995.

de Lange, Attie, Gail Fincham, Jeremy Hawthorne and Jakob Lothe. Introduction. In *Literary Landscapes: From Modernism to Postcolonialism*, edited by Attie De Lange, Gail Fincham, Jeremy Hawthorne and Jakob Lothe, xi–xxv. Basingstoke: Palgrave Macmillan, 2008.

DeLoughrey, Elizabeth. "Ecocriticism: The Politics of Place". In *The Routledge Companion to Anglophone Caribbean Literature*, edited by Michael A. Bucknor and Alison Donnell, 265–75. London: Routledge, 2011.

De Sica, Vittorio, dir. *Bicycle Thieves*. Produzioni De Sica, 1948. DVD. Criterion Collection, 2007.

Diawara, Manthia. "Black American Cinema: The New Realism". In *Black American Cinema*, edited by Manthia Diawara, 3–25. London: Routledge, 1993.

———. "Black Spectatorship: Problems of Identification and Resistance". In *Black American Cinema*, edited by Manthia Diawara, 211–20. London: Routledge, 1993.

duCille, Ann. *The Coupling Convention: Sex, Text and Tradition in Black Women's Fiction*. New York: Oxford University Press, 1993.

During, Simon. *Cultural Studies: A Critical Introduction*. London: Routledge, 2005.

Edmonds, Ennis B. "Dread 'I' In-a-Babylon: Ideological Resistance and Cultural Revitalisation". In *Chanting Down Babylon: The Rastafari Reader*, edited by Nathaniel Samuels Murrell, William David Spencer, Adrian Anthony McFarlane and Clinton Chisolm, 23–25. Kingston: Ian Randle, 1998.

Edmondson, Belinda. "The Black Romance." *Women's Studies Quarterly* 35, nos. 1–2 (2007): 191–211.

Elgood, Rick, and Don Letts, dir. *Dancehall Queen*. Island Films, 1997. DVD. Palm Pictures, 2004.

Elgood, Rick, and Don Letts, dir. *One Love*. One Love Films, 2003. DVD. Tango Entertainment, 2013.

Fanon, Frantz. *Black Skin, White Masks*. Translated by Charles Lam Markmann. London: Grove, 1986.

———. *The Wretched of the Earth*. Translated by Constance Farrington. London: Penguin, 2001.

Ford-Smith, Honor. "Come to Jamaica and Feel Alright: Tourism, Colonial Discourse and Cultural Resistance". In *The Reordering of Culture: Latin America, the Caribbean and Canada in the Hood*, edited by Alvina Ruprecht and Cecilia Taiana, 379–95. Ottawa: Carleton University Press, 1995.

Frampton, Anthony Bernard. *Beyond the Shadows of Caribbean Cinema: Lighting a Regional Film Industry*. Centre for Tourism and Policy Research Papers, no. 3 (2014).

Francis, Terry. "Sounding the Nation: Martin Rennalls and the Jamaica Film Unit, 1951–1961". *Film History* 23 (2011): 100–128.

Fulani, Ifeona. "Representations of the Body of the New Nation in *The Harder They Come* and *Rockers*". *Anthurium: A Caribbean Studies Journal* 3, no. 1 (2005): 1–2.

Gabriel, Teshome H. "Third Cinema as Guardian of Popular Memory: Towards a Third Aesthetics". In *Questions of Third Cinema*, edited by Jim Pines and Paul Willems, 53–64. London: British Film Institute, 1988.

———. "Towards a Critical Theory of Third World Films". In *Questions of Third Cinema*, edited by Jim Pines and Paul Willemen, 33–34. London: British Film Institute, 1989.

Gates, Henry Louis Jr. *The Signifying Monkey: A Theory of African-American Literature*. New York: Oxford University Press, 1988.

Gilroy, Paul. *"There Ain't No Black in the Union Jack": The Culture Politics of Race and Nation*. London: Huchinson, 1987.

Girvan, D.T.M. "The History of the Jamaica Social Welfare Commission, 1937–1962". *The Welfare Reporter*, August 1962.

Gledhill, Christine. "Pleasurable Negotiations". In *Imagine Women: Cultural Representations and Gender*, edited by Frances Bonner, Lizbeth Goodman, Richard Allen, Linda Jones and Catherine King, 193–209. Cambridge: Polity Press, 1992.

Glissant, Edouard. Introduction to *Caribbean Discourse: Selected Essays*. Translated by J. Michael Dash, 1–12. Charlottesville: University Press of Virginia, 1989.

Gorfinkel, Elena, and John David Rhodes. "Introduction: The Matter of Places". In *Taking Place: Location and the Moving Image*, edited by John David Rhodes and Elena Gorfinkel, vii–xxix. Minneapolis: University of Minnesota Press, 2011.

Gray, Obika. *Demeaned but Empowered: The Social Power of the Urban Poor in Jamaica*. Kingston: University of the West Indies Press, 2004.

Guerrero, Ed. "Jah No Dead: Modes of Resistance in *Rockers* and *Countryman*". In *Ex-Iles: Essays on Caribbean Cinema*, edited by Mybe B. Cham, 106–18. Trenton, NJ: African World Press, 1992.

Gumbs, Desmond, dir. *Rude Boy*. Amsell Entertainment, 2003. DVD. Lions Gate, 2004.

Gunst, Laurie. *Born fi' Dead: A Journey through the Yardie Underworld*. Edinburgh: Canongate, 1995.

Hall, Stuart. "Cultural Identity and Cinematic Representation". In *Ex-Iles: Essays on Caribbean Cinema*, edited by Mybe B. Cham, 220–36. Trenton, NJ: Africa World Press, 1992.

———. "Encoding, Decoding". In *The Cultural Studies Reader*, edited by Simon During, 90–102. London: Routledge, 1993.

———. "New Ethnicities". In *Stuart Hall: Critical Dialogues in Cultural Studies*, edited by David Morley and Kuan-Hsing Chen, 441–49. London: Routledge, 2005.

———. "The Spectacle of the Other". In *Representation: Cultural Representations and Signifying Practices*, edited by Stuart Hall, 223–90. London: Sage/Open University, 1997.

Harris, Kenneth. "Sex, Race Commodity and Film Fetishism in *The Harder They Come*". In *Ex-Iles: Essays on Caribbean Cinema*, edited by Mybe B. Cham, 211–19. Trenton, NJ: Africa World Press, 1992.

Hayward, Susan. *Cinema Studies: The Key Concepts*. 3rd ed. London: Routledge, 2006.

Henzell, Perry, dir. *The Harder They Come*. Xenon Pictures and International Films, 1972, DVD. Xenon Pictures, 2006.

Higson, Andrew. *Waving the Flag: Constructing a National Cinema in Britain*. Oxford: Clarendon Press, 1995.

Hjort, Mette. "Themes of Nation". In *Cinema and Nation*, edited by Mette Hjort and Scott MacKenzie, 103–17. London: Routledge, 2000.

Ho, Christine G.T., and Keith Nurse. Introduction to *Globalisation, Diaspora and Caribbean Popular Culture*, edited by Christine G.T. Ho and Keith Nurse, vii–xxiv. Kingston: Ian Randle, 2005.

hooks, bell. *Black Looks: Race and Representation*. Toronto: Between the Lines, 1992.

———. "Cultural Criticism and Transformation". YouTube video, 6:02. Posted by ChallengingMedia. 3 October 2006. https://www.youtube.com/watch?v=zQUuHFKP-9s.

Hope, Donna P. *Inna Di Dancehall: Popular Culture and the Politics of Identity in Jamaica*. Kingston: University of the West Indies Press, 2006.

Illouz, Eva. *Consuming the Romantic Utopia: Love and the Cultural Contradictions of Capitalism*. Berkley: University of California Press, 1997.

Hutton, Clinton. "Oh Rudie: Jamaican Popular Music and the Narrative of Urban Badness in the Making of Postcolonial Society". *Caribbean Quarterly* 56, no. 4 (2010): 22–64.

Jamaica Film Unit (JFU). *Towards Independence*. National Library of Jamaica Digital Archive, 1962.

Johnson, Dickie, dir. *Countryman*. Palm Pictures, 1982. DVD. Lions Gate, 2003.

Johnson, Randal. "In the Belly of the Ogre: Cinema and the State in Latin America". In *Mediating Two Worlds: Cinematic Encounters in the Americas*, edited by John King, Ana M. Lopez and Manuel Alvarado, 204–13. London: British Film Institute, 1993.

Julien, Isaac, and Kobena Mercer. "De Margin and De Centre". In *Stuart Hall: Critical Dialogues in Cultural Studies*, edited by David Morley and Kuan-Hsing Chen, 450–64. London: Routledge, 1996.

Kelly, James B. "The Jamaican Independence Constitution of 1962". *Caribbean Studies* 3, no. 1 (1963): 18–83.

Kincaid, Jamaica. *A Small Place*. New York: Farrar, Straus and Giroux, 1998.

King, Bruce. "New Centres of Consciousness: New Post-Colonial and International English Literature". In *New National and Post-Colonial Literatures: An Introduction*, edited by Bruce King, 3–26. Oxford: Clarendon Press, 2002.

Kracauer, Siegfried. *Theory of Film: The Redemption of Physical Reality*. New York: Oxford University Press, 1960.

Lamming, George. "Colonialism and the Caribbean Novel". In *Postcolonial Discourses: An Anthology*, edited by Gregory Castle, 272–79. Oxford: Blackwell, 2001.

———. "Language and the Politics of Ethnicity". In *Beyond Borders: Cross-Culturalism and the Caribbean Canon*, edited by Jennifer Rahim and Barbra Lalla, 17–33. Kingston: University of the West Indies Press, 2009.

———. *The Pleasures of Exile*. London: Allison and Bubsy, 1960.

Lefebrve, Henri. *The Production of Space*. Translated by Donald Nicholson-Smith. Malden, MA: Blackwell, 1984.

Lenz, Timothy O. "Conservatism in American Crime Films". *Journal of Criminal Justice and Popular Culture* 12, no. 2 (2005): 112–34.

Little-White, Lennie, dir. *Children of Babylon*. Mediamx Productions, 1980. Film Collection, 2007.

Lubiano, Wahneema. "But Compared to What? Reading Realism, Representation and Essentialism in *School Daze, Do the Right Thing* and the Spike Lee Discourse". In *Representing Blackness: Issues in Film and Video*, edited by Valerie Smith, 97–122. New Brunswick, NJ: Rutgers University Press, 2003.

Macedo, Lynne. *Fiction and Film. The Influence of Cinema on Writers from Trinidad and Jamaica*. West Sussex, UK: Dido Press, 2003.

Martens, Emiel, "Towards a New Caribbean Cinema? An Interview with Jamaican Filmmaker Storm Saulter". *Imaginations: Journal of Cross Cultural Image Studies* 6, no. 2 (2015). http://dx.doi.org/10.17742/IMAGE.ccn.6-2 .

Massey, Doreen. *Space, Place, and Gender*. Minneapolis: University of Minnesota Press, 1994.

McFarlane, Adrian Anthony. "The Epistemological Significance of 'I-an-I' as a Response to Quashie and Anancyism in Jamaican Culture". In *Chanting Down Babylon: The Rastafari Reader*, edited by Nathaniel Samuel Murrell, William David Spencer and Adrian Anthony McFarlane, 107–21. Kingston: Ian Randle, 1998.

Marshall, Victoria M. "Filmmaking in Jamaica: 'Likkle But Tallawah'". In *Ex-Iles: Essays on Caribbean Cinema*, edited by Mybe B. Cham, 98–105. Trenton, NJ: Africa World Press, 1992.

Marwick, Arthur. *The New Nature of History: Knowledge, Evidence, Language*. Basingstoke: Palgrave Macmillan, 2001.

McIntosh, Simeon C.R. *Caribbean Constitutional Reform: Rethinking the West Indian Polity*. Kingston: Caribbean Law Publishing, 2002.

Mediamix Ltd. "Historical Perspective: *Children of Babylon*". Accessed 11 July 2017. http://www.mediamix-palm.com/children_historical_main.htm.

Meeks, Brian. "Introduction: On the Bump of a Revival". In *New Caribbean Thought: A Reader*, edited by Brian Meeks and Folke Lindahl, viii–xx. Kingston: University of the West Indies Press, 2001.

———. *Narratives of Resistance: Jamaica, Trinidad, the Caribbean*. Kingston: University of the West Indies Press, 2000.

———. "The Political Moment in Jamaica: The Dimensions of Political Hegemonic Dissolution". In *Caribbean Political Thought: Theories of the Post-Colonial State*, edited by Aaron Kamugisha, 81–98. Kingston: Ian Randle, 2013.

Mercer, Kobena. *Welcome to the Jungle: New Positions in Black Cultural Studies*, 53–66. New York: Routledge, 1994.

Moore, Brian L., and Michele A. Johnson. *'They Do As They Please': The Jamaican Struggle for Cultural Freedom after Morant Bay*. Kingston: University of the West Indies Press, 2011.

———, eds. *"Squalid Kingston" 1890–1920: How the Poor Lived, Moved and Had Their Being*. Kingston: Social History Project, Department of History, University of the West Indies, Mona, 2003.

Morgan, Paula. "'Like Bush Fire in My Arms': Interrogating the World of Caribbean Romance". *Journal of Popular Culture* 36, no. 4 (2003): 804–27.

Morris, Mervyn. Introduction to *Old Story Time and Smile Orange*, by Trevor Rhone, v–xvi. New York: Longman, 2003.

Mulvey, Laura. "Visual Pleasure and Narrative Cinema". In *Feminisms: An Anthology of Literary Theory and Criticism*, edited by Robyn R. Warhol and Diane Price Herndl, 432–42. New Brunswick, NJ: Rutgers University Press, 1997.

Munroe, Trevor. *The Politics of Constitutional Decolonisation, Jamaica 1944–62*. Kingston: Institute of Social and Economic Research, University of the West Indies, 1983.

Murrell, Nathaniel Samuel. "Introduction: The Rastafari Phenomenon". In *Chanting Down Babylon: The Rastafari Reader*, edited by Nathaniel Samuels Murrell, William David Spencer, Adrian Anthony McFarlane and Clinton Chisholm, 1–19. Kingston: Ian Randle, 1998.

Naipaul, V.S. *The Middle Passage: Impressions of Five Societies – British, French and Dutch – in the West Indies and South America*. London: Andre Deutsch, 1963.

Neale, Steve. "Questions of Genre". In *Film Genre Reader III*, edited by Barry Keith Grant, 160–84. Austin: University of Texas Press, 1986.

Nettleford, Rex. *Inward Stretch, Outward Reach: A Voice from the Caribbean*. New York: Caribbean Diaspora Press, 1995.

———. *Mirror, Mirror: Identity, Race and Protest in Jamaica*. Rev. ed. Kingston: LMH Publishing, 2001.

Nicholson, Sheila. "An Analysis of Elite Response to Socialism through a Comparison of Gleaner Editorials on PNP Socialism for 1952 and 1976". In *Perspectives on Jamaica in the Seventies*, edited by Carl Stone and Aggrey Brown, 339–60. Kingston: Jamaica Publishing House, 1981.

Patullo, Polly. *Last Resorts: The Cost of Tourism in the Caribbean*. 2nd ed. London: Latin America Bureau, 2005.

Pollard, Velma. *Dread Talk: The Language of Rastafari*. Rev. ed. Kingston: Canoe Press, 2000.

Ramjeesingh, Diaram. "The Jamaican Film Industry: Quo Vadis?" *Ideaz* 9 (2011): 6–18.
Rennalls, Martin A. "Development of the Documentary Film in Jamaica". Master's thesis, School of Public Communication, Division of Broadcasting and Film, Boston University, 1967.
———. "Visual Education in Jamaica". *Colonial Cinema* 9, no. 1 (March 1953): 15–19.
Rennalls, Martin, M.S. Weller and T.A. Welsh, dir. *Father Brown Learns Good Dairying*. Jamaica Film Unit, 1951. http://www.colonialfilm.org.uk/node/1196.
Rennalls, Martin, and Trevor Welsh, dir. *A Nation Is Born*. Jamaica Film Unit, 1962. The National Library of Jamaica Digital Collection.
Rhone, Trevor. *Old Story Time and Smile Orange*. New York: Longman, 2003.
———, dir. *Smile Orange*. Knuts, 1978. DVD. Island, 2004.
Rice, Tom. "From the Inside: The Colonial Film Unit and the Beginning of the End". In *Film and the End of Empire*, edited by Lee Grieveson and Colin McCabe, 135–53. London: British Film Institute and Palgrave Macmillan, 2011.
———. "Jamaica Film Unit". *Colonial Film: Moving Images of the British Empire*. http://www.colonialfilm.org.uk/production-company/jamaica-film-unit?sort=year.
Roach, Catherine. "Getting a Good Man to Love: Popular Romance Fiction and the Problem of Patriarchy". *Journal of Romance Studies* 1, no. 1 (2010). http://jprstudies.org/wp-content/uploads/2010/08/JPRS1.1_Roach_GettingGoodMantoLove.pdf.
Rodney, Walter. "Contemporary Political Trends in the English-Speaking Caribbean". In *Caribbean Political Thought: Theories of the Post-Colonial State*, 2nd ed., edited by Aaron Kamugisha, 1–8. Kingston: Ian Randle, 2013.
Rohlehr, Gordon. *My Strangled City and Other Essays*. Port of Spain: Longman Trinidad, 1992.
Rosenstone, Robert A. "Reflections on What the Filmmaker Historian Does (to History)". In *Film, History and Memory*, edited by Jennie M. Carlsten and Fearghal McGarry, 183–97. Basingstoke: Palgrave Macmillan, 2015.
Salzman, Glen, and Rebecca Yates, dir. *Milk and Honey*. American Broadcast Company, Cineflics and Zenith Entertainment, 1988. Film.
Sartre, Jean-Paul. Preface to *The Wretched of the Earth*, by Franz Fanon, 7–26. Translated by Constance Farrington. London: Penguin, 1963.
Saulter, Storm, dir. *Better Mus' Come*. Firefly Films and Indigenous Films, 2010.
Seaga, Edward. *My Life and Leadership*. Volume 1, *Clash of Ideologies 1930–1980*. Oxford: Macmillan Education, 2009.
Sheller, Mimi. *Consuming the Caribbean: From Arawaks to Zombies*. London: Routledge, 2003.

———. "Natural Hedonism: The Invention of the Caribbean Islands as Tropical Playgrounds". In *Beyond the Blood, Beach and the Banana: New Perspectives in Caribbean Studies*, edited by Sandra Courtman, 170–85. Kingston: Ian Randle, 2004.

Shohat, Ella, and Robert Stam. *Unthinking Eurocentrism: Multiculturalism and the Media*. London: Routledge, 2001.

Siegel, Don, dir. *Dirty Harry*. Warner Bros. and the Malpaso Company, 1971.

Silvera, Cess, dir. *Shottas*. Access Pictures, 2002. DVD. Sony Pictures Home Entertainment, 2007.

Smith, Craig A. "(de)Constructing Patriarchal Masculinities in Cess Silvera's *Shottas*". *Journal of West Indian Literature* 21, nos. 1–2 (2012): 155–80.

Smith, M.G., R. Augier and Rex Nettleford. *The Rastafari Movement in Jamaica*. Kingston: Institute of Social and Economic Research, University of the West Indies, 1960.

Stam, Robert. "Beyond Fidelity: The Dialogics of Adaptation". In *Film Adaptation*, edited by James Naremore, 54–76. New Brunswick, NJ: Rutgers University Press, 2000.

———. *Film Theory: An Introduction*. Malden, MA: Blackwell, 2000.

Stam, Robert, and Toby Miller, eds. *Film and Theory: An Anthology*. Malden, MA: Blackwell, 2000.

Stam, Robert, and Louise Spence. "Colonialism, Racism and Representation". In *Film Theory and Criticism: Introduction Readings*, edited by Leo Braudy and Marshall Cohen, 235–50. London: Oxford University Press, 1999.

Stanley-Niaah, Sonjah Nadine. *Dancehall: From Slave Ship to Ghetto*. Ottawa: University of Ottawa Press, 2010.

Stolzoff, Norman C. *Wake the Town and Tell the People: Dancehall Culture in Kingston*. Durham: Duke University Press, 2000.

Stone, Carl. "Decolonisation and the Caribbean State System: The Case of Jamaica". In *Perspectives on Jamaica in the Seventies*, edited by Carl Stone and Aggrey Brown, 3–41. Kingston: Jamaica Publishing House, 1981.

———. *Democracy and Clientelism in Jamaica*. New Brunswick, NJ: Transaction Books, 1980.

Strachan, Ian Gregory. *Paradise and Plantation: Tourism and Culture in the Anglophone Caribbean*. Charlottesville: University of Virginia Press, 2002.

Sturken, Marita, and Lisa Cartwright. *Practices of Looking: An Introduction to Visual Culture*. Oxford: Oxford University Press, 2001.

Tate, Claudia. *Domestic Allegories of Political Desire: The Black Heroine's Text at the Turn of the Century*. New York: Oxford University Press, 1992.

Thelwell, Michael. "*The Harder They Come:* From Film to Novel". In *Ex-Iles: Essays on Caribbean Cinema*, edited by Mybe B. Cham, 176–210. Trenton, NJ: Africa World Press, 1992.
Tiffin, Chris and Alan Lawson. "Introduction: The Textuality of Empire". In *De-scribing Empire: Colonialism and Textuality*, edited by Chris Tiffin and Alan Lawson, 1–11. London: Routledge, 1994.
Warner, Keith Q. *On Location: Cinema and Film in the Anglophone Caribbean*. London: Macmillan Education, 2000.
Warshow, Robert. "Movie Chronicle: The Westerner". In *Film Theory and Criticism: Introductory Readings*. 5th ed., edited by Leo Braudy and Marshall Cohen, 654–67. New York: Oxford University Press, 1999.
White, Hayden. "The Politics of Historical Interpretation: Discipline and De-Sublimation". *Critical Inquiry* 9, no. 11 (1982): 113–37.
Willemen, Paul. "The National Revisited". In *Theorising National Cinema*, edited by Valentina Vitali and Paul Willemen, 29–43. London: British Film Institute, 2006.
Williams, Raymond. *The Country and the Town*. London: Chatto and Windus, 1973.
Yearwood, Gladstone L. "Myth and Signification in Perry Henzell's *The Harder They Come*". In *The Reordering of Culture: Latin America, the Caribbean and Canada in the Hood*, edited by Alvina Ruprecht and Cecilia Taiana, 437–55. Ottawa: Carleton University Press, 1995.
Younger, Prakash. "Historical Experience in *The Harder They Come*". *Social Text* 23, no. 1 (82) (2005): 43–63.
Zinnemann, Fred, dir. *From Here to Eternity*. Colombia Pictures, 1953.

INDEX

adaptation, concept of, 52
aesthetics: and authenticity, 13–15, 151–52; self-reflexivity, 13
agency: of actors, 92–93; black agency, negation of, 40; dancehall culture, 133; individual, as mechanism for social change, 162, 168, 169, 171
ambivalence of national identity, 23, 42–43
Anancy, as trickster character, 70–71, 81–82, 100
Anderson, Benedict: ambivalence of nationalism, 23, 42–43; horizontal camaraderie, 45
Anderson, Cherine, 120, 137
Andy, Bob, 109
Antoine-Dunne, Jean, 6
Ashcroft, Bill, 8
audience perceptions: of dancehall queen, 143–44; *Dancehall Queen* (Elgood/Letts), 132; dissonance of meanings, 21; *The Harder They Come* (film), 55–56; of negative associations, 3–4; populist response to Rhygin, 53; race, and spectator identification, 14–15; as resisting spectators, 15; vernacular, appeal to local spectators, 86
authenticity, 151–52; and aesthetics, 13–15, 151–52; audience perceptions of, 15; in conceptions of place/identity, 5, 149–50; and realism, 18, 151; in representation of ghetto life, 18; and verisimilitude, 154–55, 164

Babylon, Rastafari connotation, 98, 99, 112–13, 125
Bacall, Lauren, 15
badman/badmanism: badness, as determination of status and power, 138; and badness-honour, 184–85; as cinematic gunslinger, 54–55, 63–64, 65; as cultural narrative, 16, 47–49; as expression of resistance, 48–49, 53–54; *The Harder They Come* (film), 46–49, 52–54, 61–63; "othering" of the criminal, 51; perspectives of, 52; and political violence, 18–19; profane language, use of, 170; as tragic hero, 53
badness-honour, 48, 56–57
Bafaloukos, Theodorus: collaborative approach of, 92–94; fascination with reggae, 90; visual style, 94–95. *See also* Rockers *(Bafaloukos)*
Bakare-Yusuf, Bibi, 132; carnal power, 139–40, 143–44; male scopic mastery, 134; patriarchal cinematic codes, 145–46; reciprocity, and identity, 143–44
Bakhtin, M.M., 21
Ballentine, Desmond, 155
Barrett, Kelly, 124

Bartley, Janet, 93
Bazin, André, 9
Beckford, D.C., 1–2
Beckford, George: class/colour hierarchies of plantation society, 108, 217nn11–12
Beenie Man, 135–36
Bell, Winston "Bello", 158–59
Bennett, Louise, 45; Anancy stories, 71; "Dead Man", 46, 49
Better Mus' Come (Saulter), 5, 13; badmanism, and political violence, 18–19, 185–86; badness-honour, 184–85; dream as idyllic space, 178; dream metaphor, 176, 177–79; existentialist approach to Green Bay, 183–84, 192; Green Bay Massacre, 180–83; Green Bay, St Catherine, 174, 178–80; horror within, 179; inspired by historical event, 175–76; linkages with *The Harder They Come*, 185–86, 187, 188; motif of mobility, 190–91; poem sequence, 178, 179–80, 187–88; political gunman as figure of repulsion, 185–86; political identity, and loyalty, 187; popular memory as urban folklore, 173; postcolonial hierarchy of political parties, 186–87; quest for a better life, 189–91; Rastafari spirituality, 190–91, 223n34; repetition motif, 179, 191
Bhabha, Homi, ambivalence of nationalism, 23
Bicycle Thieves (DeSica), 91
black agency, negation of in independence documentaries, 40
black literary tradition: black Victorian love stories, 105; parallels with Caribbean film, 11–12; romance, and nationalism, 105
Blackburne, K.W.: decentralization of film production, 26–27
blackness, stereotypes of, 13
Blackwood, Gabrielle, 206n56; Propella! initiative, 199–200
Bradshaw, Carl, 63, 66, 159
Brathwaite, Kamau, on audience response to *The Harder They Come* (film), 56
Braune, Bev, 62, 92–93
British and Colonial Kinematograph Company Limited: *Lieutenant Daring* controversy, 1–4, 203nn1–2, 203n7
Browne, Chris: music videos, 148–49; production budget, 151. See also Ghett'a Life; Third World Cop
Bryce, Jane, 10, 89
Burning Spear, 98
Burton, Julianne, 55, 61
Burton, Kevoy, 166
Bush, Barbara, 124
Bustamante, Sir Alexander: political unity, 38; as prime minister, 32, 39–40, 43

Campbell, Paul, 137
Carib Hotel, 50, 211n15
Caribbean: Euro-American tourism images, 9–10; Eurocentric representations of history, 40; problematic representations of, 153; role of black majority in resistance to colonialism, 39; use of as exotic background, 4, 15
Caribbean Tales film festival, 200
Cartwright, Lisa, 134

Casey, Edward, 5, 7–8
Central Film Organization: and the JFU, 30; reassignment of departments, 32; transfer to Government Public Relations Office, 31
Cham, Mbye, 4
Charlton, Bob, 59–60
Chase Fund, 199
Chevannes, Barry, 157
Children of Babylon (Little-White), 5, 86, 107–20, 129; anti-romance rural environment, 107, 108; characters as children of Sisyphus, 113; class/colour hierarchies, 108–9; eroticism, and community, 105; great house as crossroads, 113–14; interpersonal relationships, 17, 109–10, 115–20; loss of innocence/idealism, 111–12; nationalism, and community of nation, 106–7, 120; patriarchy, and patriarchal attitudes, 115, 116–17, 119; quest for coupling, 104–5, 216n2; Rastafari connotation of Babylon, 112–13; representation of Rastafari, 116–18; social marginalization, 117–18; social stratification, 112; voice-over narration, 114–15
Children of the Incursion (Powell), 200–201
Christie, Pauline, 197
cinema vans, 26
cinéma-vérité: *Rockers* (Bafaloukos), 96, 154
Clarke, O'Daine, 168
Cliff, Jimmy, 53
Club Paradise, 85
Clunis, Andrew, 148

Coke, Christopher "Dudus", 201
Colonial Cinema: on Film Training School (UWI, Mona), 27–28; JFU role in building a "New Jamaica", 36
Colonial Film Unit (CFU), 25–26; decentralization of film production, 26–27; film training schools, 27–29, 208n21; independence of JFU, 29–30; *Jamaican Harvest*, 26; network of production and distribution, 25–26; pre-independence filmmaking, 23–24
colonial rule, British propaganda screenings, 26
colonialism: British dominance, myth of, 42–43; connotations of Third World, 158; legacies of as threat to national unity, 108–9; of parent-child paradigm, 37–38; psychological impact of, 114–15; retention of colonial traditions, 42–44; social/cultural hierarchies, 22, 23
communications technology as tool of persuasion, 23
Condé, Maryse, 194
consumerism and materialism, tension between, 62
Cooper, Carolyn: appropriation of music, 98, 121–22; on dancehall, 131, 133; heroic badness, 48, 49; shape-shifting, 135; un/dress code of dancehall, 146
Countryman (Jobson), 84, 85, 86, 89, 130, 215n7
coupling, and heterosexual bonding: *Children of Babylon*, 104–5, 216n2; *One Love*, 104, 216n2

Creary, Everaldo, 187
Crofts, Stephen, 6
cultural practices, appropriation of, 89–90

Daily Gleaner: cinematic allusions to Rhygin, 51–52, 211–12n20; coverage of Rhygin, 49–51; dominance of, 50, 211n14; Green Bay Massacre coverage, 181–82; "Mello-Go-Round" column, 55, 213n42
Dance, Daryl C., 71
dancehall culture: agency of, 133; autonomy of, 131, 147; as coping mechanism, 137; costumes and fashion of, 131, 132, 139–40, 218n3, 219n18; female as spectacle/spectator, 142–43; and the folktale, 135–36; as shape-shifting, 135; as space of opportunity, 130–31; un/dress code of dancehall, 146; views of, 130–32
Dancehall Queen (Elgood/Letts), 5, 194; carnal power, and dancehall persona, 139–41; convergence of contesting ideologies, 133–35; critiques of, 132, 133; cross-cutting, 142–43, 144; dancehall as coping mechanism, 137; dancehall deejay as storyteller, 135–36; denunciation of gun violence, 136–37; empowerment of women, 17–18, 130, 147; gendered concerns, 130; middle-class sensibility, intrusion of, 146; modes of spectatorship, 142–44; performer/spectator relationship, 133–35; production budget, 151; role switching, 140–41; shot/reverse-shot editing, 144, 145;

struggle against patriarchal control, 137–38; trickster character, 135
Danvers, Mark, 138, 155
Davis, Carl, 137, 166
Davis, Zeinabu Irene, 194
decolonization: and indigenous film production, 16; and the JFU, 24–25; role of film in, 22; shift in imperial film policy, 26–27
deLisser, Elizabeth, 110
dependent expressivity, 153
DeSica, Vittorio, 91
Destiny (Whittaker), 197
diaologism, *The Harder They Come* (film), 54
Diawara, Manthia: mise en scène, and spatial narration, 86–87; race, and spectator identification, 14–15
Dirty Harry, 156, 157
documentaries: *An Agricultural Show in Jamaica*, 25; *Churchill Visits Jamaica*, 43–44; *Coffee Co-operatives*, 25; *Farmer Brown Learns Good Dairying*, 28–29, 33; farmers education programme, 35–36; *4-H Achievement Day Newsreel*, 25; *Government at Work*, 32; *Historic Jamaica*, 25; *Let's Stop Them*, 25, 33; *One Way Out*, 25, 33; public education role, 30; state-sponsored, 25, 207n14; *You Can Help Your Children*, 25. See also independence documentaries
dubbing of dialogue, 29
duCille, Ann, 105
During, Simon, 8

Eastwood, Clint, 156, 157
Edmonds, Ennis B., 112–13

Edmondson, Belinda, 105, 124
Edna Manley College for the Visual and Performing Arts, film forum, 196
Elba, Idris, 126
Elgood, Rick. *See* One Love *(Elgood/ Letts)*
equality and materialism, tension between, 62

Fanon, Frantz: colonial fetishizing of black male body, 77; culture as liberation, 194–95; national culture, 193; violence as tool for liberation, 159; wealth disparity, 58
Farrell, J. O'Neal, 2, 3
Federation of the West Indies, 24; Jamaican withdrawal, 32, 38, 209n59; political mandate of JFU, 31–32
female directors/writers, 14, 206n56
Figueroa, Esther, 14, 206n56
film: identification with the marginalized, 10; as image manipulation, 9; parallels with West Indian novel, 11–12; as social commentary, 10–11, 13
film festival culture, 200–201
Film Training School (UWI, Mona), 27–29, 208n21; Rennall's influence on, 34–36
filmmakers: cinematic appropriation of Jamaican images, 4; female talents, 206n56; judgement of, 2, 3; local film production, emergence of, 4–5; strategies used by, 13; use of local cultural elements, 13
filmmaking: collaborative nature of, 5, 204n13; film festival culture, 200–201; national/regional affiliations, 6; participatory nature of, 201; pre-independence, 23–24; production financing, 194, 195; as public service institution, 195; strategies for industry development, 196–97, 198–99, 224n22
First Cinema, 176–77
folk tradition, 13; Jack Mandora, 82
folklore, oral historiography as popular memory, 172–73
Forbes, Leonie, 109
Ford-Smith, Honor: resistance, and survival, 71–72; tourism marketing, and cultural racism, 68–69, 121
Francis, Terri: on categories of production, 25; JFU as propaganda vehicle, 32; on Rennall's influence, 34–35; "Sounding the Nation", 23; transatlantic post-production process, 29
Freud, Sigmund, 176
Fulani, Ifeona, 97
funding: decentralization of film production, role in, 27; global marketplace, 194; origin of as marker of nationality, 6; short films, 200; state support for production, 6–7

Gabriel, Teshome: cinema of mass participation, 196; oral historiography as popular memory, 172–73, 175, 176–77, 192; Third Cinema, 177, 195
garrison constituencies: dons as community protectors, 165–66, 167, 170–71; as geographical power domain, 163–64; Green Bay

garrison constituencies (*continued*)
Massacre, 180–83; isolation of, 162–64; and nationalism, 165–66, 167; political partisanship, 148, 164–65
Gaumont-British Instructional Limited, *Jamaican Harvest*, 26
Genie Awards, *Milk and Honey* (Rhone/Salzman), 66
Getino, Octavio, 177
Ghett'a Life (Browne), 5, 148; as coming-of-age story, 166; dons as community protectors, 165–66, 167, 170–71; as film of hope, 149; garrison community, isolation of, 162–64; history as ahistorical, 164–65, 167; individual agency, as mechanism for social change, 162, 168, 169, 171; as mainstream realism, 18, 151–52; as personal project, 151; political partisanship, 164–65; political violence of garrison constituency, 148, 165–66, 167, 221n40; quest motif, 168; religious metaphor, 169–70; review of, 149–50
ghetto. *See* inner-city space
Gilroy, Paul, 89–90
Gledhill, Christine, 133–34
Glissant, Edouard, 8
global marketplace: impact on local values, 84–85; influence of, 194; and local film production, 84–85; production financing, 194; Standard English vs Jamaican Creole, 197
Goldson, Herriot, 210n20
Gorfinkel, Elena, 9, 20
Graham, Douglas, 13

Grason, Anika, 142
Gray, Obika: badness-honour, 48, 184–85; on garrison constituencies, 163
Greater August Town Film Festival, 200
Green Bay Massacre, 180–83
Grey, Sky Nicole, 178
Grierson, John, 28
Griffiths, Gareth, 8
Grove Publishers, 47
Guerrero, Ed, 89; "Jah No Dead", 84–85, 98
Gunst, Laurie, 157

Hall, Richard, 94
Hall, Stuart, 12, 112, 143, 193; negotiation, concept of, 133–34
The Harder They Come (film, Rhone/Henzell), 5, 66, 86, 108, 174, 213n1; audience response, 55–56, 65, 213n42; badman as gunslinger, 54–55, 63–64, 65; badman/badmanism, 185–86; badmanism, 46–49, 52–54, 61–63; bicycle, importance of, 59, 213n38; as cautionary tale, 54; critical reception, 55–56; levels of artifice, 63; linkages with *Better Mus' Come*, 185–86, 187, 188; loss of manhood, 59–60; mise en scène, 154; music, 62; as narrative of resistance, 56–57, 60–62; place, and identity, 16, 58; quest motif, 58–59; sound, 64; treatment of police, 57; treatment of Rhygin story, 52–53; tropes of exclusion, 58–59
The Harder They Come (novel, Thelwell), 52

Harris, Kenneth, 59
Harris, Warren, 142
Harrison, Patrice, 139
Hayward, Susan, 164, 170
Henzell, Perry, 92–93. *See also* The Harder They Come *(film, Rhone/Henzell)*
From Here to Eternity, 78
heroic badness, 48
Higson, Andrew, 22
history: as ahistorical, 164; and community identity, 173, 175; engagement with, 13; popular memory as urban folklore, 172–73
history films, role in understanding the past, 173–74
Hjort, Mette, 7, 204n23
Hollywood films: as First Cinema, 176–77; gunslinger ethos of, 157–58; mimicry of, 153, 157; as reel life, 154; representations of black people, 87; tropes of gun films, 154
homogeneity, myth of, 14
homophobia, 14
hooks, bell: phallocentrism, 75–76; on realism in film, 151
Hope, Donna P., 131–32
Hotel Training School (Antigua), 72
Hulsey, Patrick, *Rockers*, 83
Hutton, Clinton, lumpenproletariat creation, 57–58

I, Kiddus, 92, 98, 99
identity: authenticity in conceptions of, 5; cinematic appropriation of, 1–4; of the collective "we", 4; misrepresentation of, 2–3; and place, 7–9, 16, 58, 149–50; as "placeling", 5; and reciprocity, 143–44; and sense of nationalism, 22–23
Illouz, Eva, 68, 77
improvisation, and body language, 92
Independence Day date conflict, 39–40
independence documentaries: and Jamaica Film Unit (JFU), 23–25, 207n10; and myth of nationalism, 12–13; *A Nation Is Born*, 5, 15–16, 20–21, 33, 35, 36–37, 42–45; selective rendering of history, 39; silencing of dissenting voices, 38–39; state-sponsored, 4, 15–16, 22, 25, 207n14; *Towards Independence*, 5, 15–16, 33, 35, 36–37, 40–42; travel motif, 41–42; use of male narrators, 36–37
Inner Circle, 99
inner-city space: absence of middle class in filmic portrayals, 13, 159, 206n54; Arnett Gardens, 148–49; authenticity in representation of, 18; Browne's representations of, 148–50; cinematic codes of, 153–54; cohesiveness of community, 96–97; "ghetto" as metonym for "criminal", 159; of Kingston, 148–49, 153; media representations of, 153; reggae as expression of resistance, 16–17; in *Rockers*, 83–84; and social mobility, 103; stereotypes of, 13; stigmatization of black urban dweller, 11–12; as Third World, 158; violence as facet of, 153
International Monetary Fund, 195
interpersonal relationships: *Children of Babylon*, 17, 109–10, 115–20
Isaacs, Gregory, 90, 93, 98

Isaacs, Sandra, 139
Island Records, 89–90

Jackson, Samuel, 156
Jamaica: cinematic appropriation of images, 4; constitutional change, 31, 41, 210n64; democratic socialism, introduction of, 110–11; Empire Day, 39–40, 209n62; Euro-American tourism images, 9–10; Federation of the West Indies, 24, 32, 38, 209n59; independence, as parent-child colonial paradigm, 37–38; independence conference, 21–22, 40–42, 204n22; Independence Day date conflict, 39–40; introduction of television, 33; local film production, emergence of, 4–5; 1955 election, 31; 1980 election, 111, 172; postcolonial patriarchal oppression, 118–19; post-independence decolonization period, 110–11; self-government, 24; socioeconomic disparity within, 10; state support for production, 6–7; state-sponsored film production, 4, 5
Jamaica Association of Film and Television Producers: Propella! initiative, 199–200
Jamaica Defence Force, role in Green Bay Massacre, 181–83
Jamaica Film Unit (JFU): advisory committee, 30; autonomous local administrative structure, 29–30; catalogue, 25, 207n14; *Churchill Visits Jamaica*, 43–44; early productions, 24–25; *Farmer Brown Learns Good Dairying*, 28–29, 33; formation of, 16, 23–25, 207n10, 208n27; *Government at Work*, 32; as government information service, 31–32; influence of CFU on, 29, 208n27; processing facilities, 32–33; as propaganda vehicle, 32; subject selection process, 30; television productions, 33; transatlantic post-production process, 29. *See also* A Nation Is Born *(documentary)*; Towards Independence *(documentary)*
Jamaica Information Service, and Central Film Organization, 32
Jamaica Labour Party (JLP): Bustamante as prime minister, 32, 39–40; and Green Bay Massacre, 182–83
Jamaica Tourist Board campaign, 121–22
Jamaican audience, *and Lieutenant Daring* controversy, 1–4, 203nn1–2, 203n7
Jamaican Creole: translation process, *Rockers*, 85, 86, 91; viewer familiarity with, 7
Jamaican Film Commission, Propella! initiative, 199
Jamaican Motion Picture Industry (Encouragement) Act (1948, 1991), 6
Jobson, Dickie, *Countryman*, 84, 85, 86, 89, 130, 215n7
Johnson, Lyndon B., 44
Johnson, Michele A., 197
Johnson, Randal, 194
judicial system, colonial legacy of, 59
Julien, Isaac, 15

Kerr, Deborah, 78
Kincaid, Jamaica, 72
Kingsley, Charles, 192, 223n34
Kracauer, Siegfried, 20

Lamming, George, 197, 206n54; *In the Castle of My Skin*, 11, 12
Lancaster, Burt, 78
language: as cultural empowerment, 197–98; Jamaican Creole, 7, 85, 86, 91; as mode of thinking, 197; negative stereotypes of Creole speakers, 197; profane language, badman use of, 170; Rastaspeak, 84, 86, 91–92; Standard English vs Jamaican Creole, 73–74, 196–97; as symbol of collective identity, 197–98; translation process, *Rockers*, 91–92; use of in subversion of authority, 73–74
Lawson, Alan, 9
Leach, Sharon, *Sugar*, 199–200
Lee, Spike, 152
Lefebvre, Henri, 8
Lenz, Timothy O., 156
Letts, Don. *See* One Love *(Elgood/Letts)*
Lewis, Lennox, 168
Lieutenant Daring controversy, 1–4, 203nn1–2, 203n7
Little-White, Lennie: Jamaican stigma of rude boys, 107–8. *See also* Children of Babylon *(Little-White)*
local cultural elements, 13
Lubiano, Wahneema, 152, 164
lumpenproletariat creation, 57–58

Macedo, Lynn, 50
Manley, Michael, 65, 110; Green Bay Massacre, 182, 183

Manley, Norman: 1955 election, 31; independence conference, 41–42; political unity, 38; on racial harmony, 37
Mansong, Jack (Three-Fingered-Jack), 52
Margaret, Princess, 21, 43; mento song, 44
marginalization: filmmakers identification with, 10; of urban poor, 161
Marley, Bob, 98; "One Love", 121–22
Marley, Ky-Mani, 120
Martens, Emiel, 173
Martin, Ivanhoe "Rhygin". *See* Rhygin (Ivanhoe "Rhygin" Martin)
Marwick, Arthur, 173
masculinity: black virility, myth of, 77; cocksman, as phallocentric model of, 75–76; and dominance, 155–56, 157; mimicry of American films, 153, 157; patriarchy, and patriarchal attitudes, 116–17, 119; playboy trickster character, 16; stereotypes of, 13; threatened masculinity, 75
Massey, Doreen, 8, 150, 165
Maudling, Reginald, 37, 41
McFarlane, Anthony, 98, 100
McFarlane, Chris, 165
Meeks, Brian, 10, 11, 111, 167
Mercer, Kobena, 15, 152, 153
middle class, absence of in filmic portrayals, 13, 206n54
The Mighty Quinn, 85
Milk and Honey (Rhone/Salzman), 66
Miller, Albert, 35

mise en scène, 13; *The Harder They Come* (film, Rhone/Henzell), 154; *Rockers* (Bafaloukos), 96–97; and spatial narration, 86–87
Moore, Brian L., 197
Morgan, Paula, 104
Morris, Mervyn, on *Smile Orange* (play, Rhone), 69, 70–71
multinational production, economics of, 6
Mulvey, Laura, 133, 144
Munroe, Trevor, 43
Murrell, Nathaniel Samuel, 88
music, 13; role in commercial viability of film, 130. *See also* reggae
Myrie, Pauline Stone, 140
Myrtle Bank Hotel, 1, 203n2

Naipaul, V.S., *The Middle Passage*, 15
narrative films: emergence of, 4; female directors/writers, involvement with, 14, 206n56; socioeconomic disparities, and myth of nationalism, 12–13
nation, and national qualities, 7, 204n23
A Nation Is Born (documentary), 5, 15–16, 35; authority of "truth", 36–37; and national self-consciousness, 33; national stadium celebration, 20–21; racial harmony, and national unity, 37–38; retention of colonial traditions, 42–45; tension between formality and celebration, 44–45, 210nn68–69
nationalism: ambivalence of, 42–43; dominance of power blocs, 34; and garrison politics, 165–66, 167; homogeneity, myth of, 14; horizontal camaraderie, 45; myth of unified society, 57–58; national culture, 45, 210n69; pairing with romance, 105; and political partisanship, 192; as process of becoming, 23; role in identification with Western life, 22–23; screen expressions of national culture, 193–94; and sense of identity, 22–23; and socioeconomic disparities, 12–13; unifying myths of, 4–5, 43–45; use of film in myth-making, 33
Neale, Steve: authenticity, and verisimilitude, 154–55
negotiation, in cultural production, 133–35
Nettleford, Rex, 196; class/colour hierarchies of plantation society, 108, 113; language, and cultural empowerment, 197–98; Rastafarian study, 87–88, 103, 122
newsreels: Colonial Film Unit (CFU), 25–26; state-sponsored, 4, 15–16, 24–25; *Towards Independence* (documentary), 21–22
Nicholson, Sheila, 50

Ogden, David. *See Smile Orange* (Rhone/Ogden)
One Love (Elgood/Letts), 120–29; chastity, and sexuality, 124–25, 127–28; community conflict resolution, 120, 129; connection between romance and nation, 120, 121; critique of formal religion, 125–26; funding, and production, 123; marriage ending, 128–29; music competition, 123, 128–29; religious difference, tolerance

of, 126, 129; as romantic fantasy, 123–24; rural landscape as symbol of harmony, 107, 120; screenplay by Rhone, 5, 66; sense of place, 123–24; sexuality of the black female, 105; transformational potential of romantic love, 105–6; as utopian romance, 17, 104, 120
"One Love" (Marley), 121–22
Origins (Wright), 199–200
"othering" of the criminal, 51

Pacino, Al, 157
Palace Amusement, 7, 13
Parchment, Don, 109
patriarchy, and patriarchal attitudes: carnal power, and dancehall persona, 139–41; cinematic codes of, 145–46; erotic performance as resistance to, 130–31; Eurocentric models of, 115; of fundamentalist Christianity, 122–23; negotiation of, 135; passive role of women, 133; in performace of masculinity, 119; Rastafari lifestyle, 100–102, 115, 116–17; reduced status of feminized response, 138; struggle against, 137–38; subordination to male authority, 125
Patullo, Polly, 76
Peckinpah, Sam, 158
People's National Party (PNP): 1955 election, 31; democratic socialism, introduction of, 110–11; election slogan (1972), 188–89; and Green Bay Massacre, 182–83
Phillips, Tobi, 109
place: authenticity in conceptions of, 5; concepts of, 7–9; in construct of nation, 5; dimensions of, 8; as element of identity, 1–4; and identity, 16; internal/external perspectives, 2–4; post-colonial context, 8
political partisanship: divisiveness of, 164–65, 192, 221n40; garrison constituencies, 163–64; Green Bay Massacre, 180–83; loyalty to party, 169–70, 222n44; and national unity, 174; 1980 election, 172; status of political identity, 186–87; violence of, 18–19, 148
politics of subversion, 71–72, 73–74
Pollard, Velma, 91
popular memory as urban folklore, 172–73, 175, 176–77
post-colonial contexts of place and identity, 7–9
poverty: external factors of urban poverty, 161; and partisan identity, 186–87; and post-emancipation elites, 57–58; stereotypes of, 13
Powell, Alan, *Children of the Incursion*, 200–201
power relations: colonial hierarchies, as social control, 35; of hotel sex trade, 76–77; imbalances of, 196; of intimidation, 48; marginalization of ghetto residents, 161; of nationalism and national identity, 33–34; of poor urban communities vs state authority, 194; social pyramid of plantation society, 113–14; societal imbalances, 14
Price, Ernest, 1, 203n2
production: commercial nature of, 13; economics of, 6; local film production, emergence of,

production (continued)
national funding for film production, 84; state support for, 6–7
Propella! initiative, 199–200

quest motif: *Ghett'a Life* (Browne), 168; *The Harder They Come* (film), 58–59; national unity, 104–5; *Rockers* (Bafaloukos), 91, 216n28; romance, and coupling, 104–5, 216n2

race: as factor in class divisions, 108–9, 217nn11–12; and spectator identification, 14–15
racial violence in controlling of sexuality, 76–77
Ramjeesingh, Diaram, 6
Rastafari: acceptance in society, 87–89; Babylon, connotation of, 98, 99, 112–13, 125; commercialization of, 121–22; intersection with Christian theology, 98–99, 122–23; Lion of Judah, 100; as network of "brethren", 17; patriarchy, and patriarchal attitudes, 100–102, 115, 116–17; Rastaspeak, 84, 86, 91–92; and reggae, 93, 95, 96–97, 121–22; *Rockers*, 83–84, 95; spirit of collaboration, 97; stereotypes of, 85, 86, 87
Rattray, Garth, 149–50
realism, 18; as aesthetic commodity, 151–52; in Caribbean film, 152, 153; fallacy of "truth", 152, 164; history as ahistorical, 164; uncritical acceptance of, 152
Reckord, Michael, 132
reel life, 154, 156; the American dream, 168–69; truth of realism, 164
reggae: commercialization of, 88, 121–22; corporate selling of, 89–90; economic importance of, 86, 95; as expression of resistance, 16–17, 86, 97–98; international popularity of, 85; *Rockers*, 83–84, 93, 95
Reid, Audrey, 130, 159
Rennalls, Martin, 201; as director of JFU, 23, 25–26, 198; and Film Training School (UWI, Mona), 34–36; informational reportage of JFU, 32; MA thesis, 35–36; as production director Central Film Organization, 30; on training methods, 28
Rhodes, John David, 9, 20
Rhone, Trevor. *See* Smile Orange (Rhone/Ogden); The Harder They Come (film, Rhone/Henzell): One Love
Rhygin (Ivanhoe "Rhygin" Martin), 16; animal imagery, 51; as iconic badman, 46, 210n2; public fascination/fear of, 49–51; as urban gunslinger, 50, 211n15, 211–12n20
Rice, Tom, 26, 43; narrative structure of British colonial instructional film, 28–29
Richardson, Samuel, *Pamela*, 127
Ring Di Alarm! collective, 199, 200
Roach, Catherine, romance as "cultural narrative", 47, 126–27
Robinson, Renee, 199
Rockers (Bafaloukos), 5; anti-establishment tone, 85; assumption of local audience, 89; cinéma-vérité, 96, 154; collaborative

approach of, 92–94; construction of gender politics, 100–102; dialogue, translation process, 91–92; direct address to camera, 86, 94–95, 99; establishing shot, 94–95, 96; as historical artefact of Jamaican music, 83; musical performances, 93, 95, 98–99; network of interactions and relationships, 97; popularity of, 88, 215n20; quest motif, 91, 216n28; reggae as expression of resistance, 16–17, 97–98; self-reflexivity, 154; unsophisticated look of, 84–85; viewer as bystander, 94; visual motifs, 99–100; visual style, 94–95

Rohlehr, Gordon, 55

role play, and cultural conventions, 93–94

romance: as "cultural narrative", 47, 126–27; and eroticism, 127–28; heterosexual bonding, and coupling convention, 104, 216n2; *One Love*, 17; *Smile Orange* (Rhone/Ogden), 78–79; Western romantic tradition, 104, 216n2

Rosenstone, Robert A., 173–74

Rude Boy, 86

Salmon, Lenford, 159, 165

Salzman, Glen, *Milk and Honey*, 66

Sangster, Donald, 40

Sartre, Jean-Paul, 73

Saulter, Storm: dream metaphor, 176, 177–79; Green Bay Massacre story, 180; history, and community identity, 173, 175; *Ring Di Alarm!* collective, 199. See also *Better Mus' Come (Saulter)*

Scarface, 157

Scott, Dennis, 66

Seaga, Edward: on Green Bay Massacre, 183; pro-American administration, 111

Second Cinema, 177

self-reflexivity, 154

Serieux, Michelle, 206n56; *Ring Di Alarm!* collective, 199, 224n23; *Sugar*, 199–200

sexuality: of the black female, 79, 105, 124–25; black sexuality, representations of, 105; black Victorian love stories, 105; carnal power, 139–40; and chastity, 124–25, 127–28; church's attempts to police, 125–26; cocksman, as phallocentric model of masculinity, 75–76; colonial stereotypes of black sexuality, 124–25; dancehall culture, 17–18, 130–33; erotic performance as resistance to patriarchy, 130–31; eroticism, and community, 105; gendered language of tourism marketing, 68–69; *The Harder They Come* (film), 59; heterosexual bonding, and coupling convention, 104, 216n2; historical taboo of plantation society, 76; homophobia, 14; hotel sex trade, 75–76; objectification of female erotic performance, 133–35; woman as sexual commodity, 138, 139

Sheller, Mimi, 124; *Consuming the Caribbean*, 67–68

Shepherd, Sheldon, 174

Shock Value, 199

Shohat, Ella, 33, 197; politics of pleasure, 195–96

Shoot the Girl, 199
short films, funding, 200
Shottas, 86, 156
Silent Hearts, 199
Sives, Amanda, 167, 183, 186–87
"Slave Master" (song), 90
slavery: abolition of, 39; hotel/plantation comparison, 16, 67, 68; strategies of survival, 71
Smile Orange (play, Rhone), 66, 69, 70, 71–72
Smile Orange (Rhone/Ogden), 5, 66, 108, 194; hotel sex trade, 75–76; hotel/plantation comparison, 16, 67, 68, 72–73, 74–75, 77–78, 79; politics of subversion, 71–72, 73–74; psychological bondage of plantation politics, 81–82; racial divisions within hotel staff, 72–74; romance montage, 78–79; subversion of authority, 73–74; tourism fantasy of Caribbean, 67–69; trickster as hero, 80–81; trickster character, 16, 66–67, 81–82
Smith, Craig A., 153, 156
Smith, Rae-Ann, 206n56
Smith, Roger Guenveur, 188–89
social alienation: of black urban dweller, 11–12
social hierarchy: of class and colour politics, 60, 116–17, 167; class/colour hierarchies of plantation society, 108–9, 217nn11–12; engineered poverty, and post-emancipation elites, 57–58; gender-based, 116–17; in independence celebrations, 44–45, 210n68; politics of subordination, 68–69; racial divisions within hotel staff, 72–74; and social stratification, 112; tropes of exclusion, 58–59
Solanas, Fernando, 177
sound: dialogue dubbing, 29; in post-production process, 29; voice-over narration, 29, 36–37, 42
St Juste, Franklyn "Chappie", 198, 224n23
Stam, Robert, 33, 197; adaptation, concept of, 52; politics of pleasure, 195–96; on realism, 151
Stanley-Niaah, Sonjah, 131
stereotypes: colonial stereotypes of black sexuality, 124–25; criminality of inner city residents, 51, 154; genre codes, 154; of Rastafari, 85, 86, 87; reproduction of, 13; tropes of exclusion, 58–59
Stolzoff, Norman C., 131
Stona, Winston, 120
Stone, Carl: geographical power domain, 163–64; post-independence decolonization period, 110–11; power relations of plantation society, 114
Strachan, Ian Gregory, 68
Sturken, Marita, 134
Sugar (Leach/Serieux), 199–200

Tarantino, Quentin, *Pulp Fiction*, 156
Tate, Claudia, 105
Thelwell, Michael: coverage of Rhygin, 49–50; *The Harder They Come* (novel), 47
Third Cinema, 195; and popular memory, 176–77
Third Horizon Film Festival, 200
Third World Cop (Browne), 5, 86, 148; alienation from ghetto, 160; cameo

appearances, 167, 168; as a Clint Eastwood movie, 156; excessive police force, 156–57, 158–59; external factors of urban poverty, 161; "ghetto" as metonym for "criminal", 159; gunslinger ethos, 157–58; as mainstream realism, 18, 148; masculinity, and dominance, 155–56, 157; production budget, 151; review of, 148

Third World, derogatory connotations of, 158

Thompson, Donald, 138

Thompson, Dudley, 183, 184

Three-Fingered-Jack (Jack Mansong), 52

Tiffin, Chris, 9

Tiffin, Helen, 8

Timehri Film Festival, 200

Tosh, Peter, 98

tourism industry: Caribbean images, 9–10; gendered language of, 68–69; *Historic Jamaica*, 25; hotel as contact zone, 67; hotel/plantation comparison, 16, 67, 68, 72–73, 74–75, 77–78, 79; iconic fantasy of Caribbean, 67–68; local perception of white tourists, 72; marketing, and cultural racism, 68–69; "One Love" (Marley) advertising campaign, 121–22; politics of subordination, 68–69; psychological bondage of plantation politics, 81–82; racial divisions within hotel staff, 72–74; service jobs as units of production, 72

Towards Independence (documentary), 5, 15–16, 35; authority of "truth", 36–37; independence conference, 21–22; location, 7, 204n22; and national self-consciousness, 33; negation of black agency, 40; problematic representation of history, 40–42

Toyloy, Neville, 181–82

trickster character: as " a good nobody", 74; Anancy, 70–71, 81–82, 100; *Dancehall Queen* (Elgood/Letts), 135; as hero, 80–81; politics of subversion, 71–72, 73–74; as sexual commodity, 72, 76–78; *Smile Orange* (Rhone/Ogden), 16, 66–67, 69–71; strategies of survival, 71

Trinidad and Tobago Film Festival, 200

United States, relations with Manley government, 111

University of the West Indies, Mona: Community Film Project, 200; film forum (2012), 14; film screenings, 199

urban poor: criminal stereotypes of, 51; everyday life of in *Rockers*, 91

verisimilitude, and authenticity, 154–55, 164

Victoria, Queen, 40, 209n62

violence: and badmanism, 48; badmanism, and political violence, 18–19, 185–86; badness, as determination of status and power, 138; and code of silence, 153; denunciation of, 136–37; and excessive police force, 156; as facet of ghetto life, 153; as form of resistance, 188; 1980 election, 172; political violence of garrisons, 165–

violence (*continued*)
  66, 167, 186–88, 221n40; Rastafari stereotypes, 86; and sexual performance, 155–56; stereotypes of, 13
voice-over narration, 29, 36–37, 42, 114–15

Wallace, Leroy, 83–84, 92
Warner, Keith, on *Rockers*, 84–85, 90
Warshow, Robert, 157
Wells, Mary, 206n56
Welsh, Trevor, 35
Western gunslinger ethos, 157–58
White, Hayden, 175
Whittaker, Jeremy, 196; *Destiny*, 197

Wide Sargasso Sea, 89
Wild Bunch (Peckinpah), 158
Willemen, Paul, 6, 7; on representation of nationalism, 12, 22–23
Williams, Raymond, 67
women: dancehall as space of autonomy, 131; dancehall culture, 17–18, 130–31; empowerment of, 17–18, 130, 141–42; filmmakers, 206n56; as sexual objects, 131–32, 138, 139–40
Wright, Kurt, *Origins*, 199–200

Younger, Prakash, 54

www.ingramcontent.com/pod-product-compliance
Lightning Source LLC
Chambersburg PA
CBHW030040240426
43667CB00035B/179